Hotel in Flight

First published in September Mcmxxxix
by Faber and Faber Limited
24 Russell Square London W.C.1
Printed in Great Britain
at the Bowering Press Plymouth
All Rights Reserved

Contents

Contents

I

Running Gun-Runners

It was hard to believe that there was a war on. We often said this to ourselves as we sat in the sunshine on our terrace, gazing over the peaceful curve of blue sea, the grey walls of the old town reflected in the clear water, the new town clustered white and shining round the beach, the smoke lazily wreathing into the still air.

We looked straight down on to the little café on the front. The leaves were off the plane trees and we had a clear view of the crowded tables in the sun. From that distance it was not possible to see that all the occupants were in carabineros' uniforms. They might have been the usual group of winter visitors in peace-time. We stretched ourselves comfortably in our long chairs. We could hear our guests getting up. The fact that we had four people staying in the hotel made the whole Spanish War seem even more fantastic. There was Francisca working again in the kitchen—we could hear her singing as she did the washing up—Leon was coming over the bridge from the village with his shopping basket just as usual. The only difference would be the backstairs way he did the shopping. Buying food in war-time very much depended on one's friends. Leon had lots of friends.

Beetle, my black pekinese, was taking her morning sun-bath. She lay flat on her back on the terrace, warming her stomach in the glow of the morning sun. Soon it would be too hot for her and she would retire to the shade outside the kitchen door, where she would sleep entirely regardless of the fact that every one had to step over her.

The Spanish War had been going on for six months. After our guests had been whisked away by excited British warships, Archie and I and our young partner Leon had shut down our hotel and continued to live there as private individuals. At first, in spite of, or perhaps because of, the war, we thoroughly enjoyed ourselves. We were appreciating the advantages our guests had had; for the first time since we opened the hotel we were enjoying our own sun terraces and, although we worked hard enough, doing all the housework, cooking, laundry, gardening and writing a book, we had leisure to enjoy the Spanish War.

I realize that one should never enjoy anything so horrible as war, but somehow the Spanish brand then seemed different, only a feeble attempt at a rebellion by some disgruntled generals. We all believed that it would soon be put down, and if in the putting down it were possible to set up a better régime in Spain, the few thousand dead would not have died in vain.

Although we had no trouble of any sort in or around Tossa, we knew that plenty had happened in Barcelona only fifty miles away, but somehow hot-blooded killings and street battles do not seem so appalling in Spain. One accepts them in the same way that one accepts the scorching sun. The same happenings in London would fill one with horror, the same sun would cause many deaths.

We met, and were meeting every day, many of the anarchists and revolutionaries who had fought through the Barcelona streets, who attacked and burned Barcelona churches, many of which were being used as fortresses by the rebels. We knew that probably these same charming young men who sat peacefully in the café or who came up to pay polite calls on us in order to see these unique foreigners who had not flown the 'red terror' had killed perfectly innocent people in the excitement of the moment; that, although they scrupulously obeyed the rules of etiquette that insisted on all weapons being piled on the table when one was drinking with a friend, they were ready to snatch and use these same weapons lying among the glasses should the occasion demand it.

But mixed up with all the fighting and killing was a fascinating, if mad, chivalry. In the Barcelona street fighting, care was taken by both sides to avoid any clashes between the hours of eight and ten in the morning and again between six and seven in the evening; man must eat and women must do the shopping. A party of fighters were holding out in a provision shop that had no drinks. They were shooting at another party in a wine shop that had no food. It was by mutual consent that hostilities were stopped while both parties stocked up from each other's strongholds. When one exclaims with surprise at stories like these, the Spaniards concerned do not understand. Fighting is a regrettable necessity and human life is relatively unimportant, but why fight in more discomfort than necessary?

In all their savagery, women and children are sacred to the Spaniard. Whole battles are stopped because a child strays in the street. Women have stopped the fighting altogether by refusing to clear out of the way for the battle to recommence. On the Aragon front both sides played football together between rifle shots. If a village near the lines had a fiesta, men from both sides came to it. In between they fought savagely and ruthlessly, but during the lulls they would exchange tobacco and cigarette papers.

There was something fascinating about this kind of warfare. There was fascination in its very idiocy. One got a glimpse of the Middle Ages when unnecessary slaughter before breakfast was so much admired. The trouble was that modern weapons, even the 'modern' weapons used by the Loyalists, were so much more destructive than the good old mediaeval battle-axe. But the Loyalists might as well have been armed with bows and arrows when foreign intervention began on a big scale. It was then we ceased to get the slightest amusement out of the Spanish War. A few thousand 'reds' careering down Barcelona streets could not do an eighth of the damage done by one Italian bomb.

C-rack! Boom-boom-boom! Beetle tried to get from the flat of her back on to her four short legs in one movement. It was a complete failure. She rolled over twice and ended up among the marigolds. She crept out, her tail trailing on the ground, her eyes bulging. Was it thunder?

'It's all right, Beetle,' I said reassuringly. 'It's only a bombardment.'

She was not convinced and made for my bedroom. She always felt safe on my bed during thunderstorms.

The firing went on continuously. Donald appeared sleepily on his terrace. Elizabeth peered out of her window. Marianne and Ulrich took no interest. They were both on leave from Madrid.

Archie rushed up to the top of the hill. He waved to us to follow.

A merchant ship was being attacked by the *Baleares*, the *Canarias*, and the *Cervantes*. Some smaller rebel warships were standing by while the cruisers fired their guns, presumably not at her, because the shells were falling wide all round. Suddenly we saw a little ketch running like mad before the wind. It seemed to shave past the *Canarias* and made for Tossa Bay like a frightened hare. The guns followed her, the shells splashing up the water on all sides, but she kept on her course and the big ships let her go. She came into the bay with a rush and took shelter behind the island, her sails flapping quietly. Presently a boat put off and rowed for the shore.

We lost all interest in the ketch. A French cruiser suddenly appeared and sailed majestically up to the rebel warships. There was a long pause with all the ships stationary, looking as if some one ought to put in another sixpence and the naval battle would begin again. I decided it would be more amusing to go down to the shore to speak to the crew of the ketch. I ran happily down the side of the cliff, completely forgetting the new fortifications. But I only forgot them for a moment. The next instant I was lying flat on my back at the bottom of a trench filled with carabineros. They stood over me with fixed bayonets, looking more businesslike than I believed the Tossa carabineros could look. I hastily explained my mistake. They reluctantly helped me up, but

15

warned me that no one was allowed within a fortified area.

'How is one to know?' I asked, as they brushed the sand off my back. 'You camouflage your fortifications so beautifully no one can see them, and there are new ones every day. You ought to mark them with a stick or something.'

Leon came down to the café with me, and we asked the crew up to lunch. Even over a delicious mushroom omelette they refused to be drawn. They were no ordinary ketch crew. They were six in all and they looked the very best type of merchant-service officer. The captain ought to have been on the bridge of an Atlantic liner. They said they came from Marseilles, but they spoke beautiful French without a trace of an accent. They said they had gone down to Valencia in ballast to fetch oranges. We suggested it was poor business to come down without a cargo. They smiled and said they never touched anything except oranges. They had been chivvied all round the coast by rebel ships. The mate had a handkerchief round his hand where he had burnt it letting the sheet slip through too fast on their dash into the bay. We had to give up hope of getting a story about gun-running.

After lunch we saw that some one had provided the sixpence. The rebel ships were sailing away and the French ship was escorting the cargo boat towards France. The crew of the ketch decided to run into Port Vendres while the going was good. Tossencs were very relieved when they left. They did not approve of ships making dashes to Tossa for safety; it was not at all safe for Tossencs. Why! who could forget the day when three French cargo boats came right into our Marmenuda Bay to escape a bombardment up the coast and the whole village had fled into the hills thinking they were rebel warships?

Our four guests decided to pay a visit to the famous Tossa refuge. Tossencs were very proud of their refuge which was probably the best constructed one in Catalunya. It consisted of a series of tunnels hollowed out of a big hill behind the village. The tunnels opened at intervals into chambers lined with seats. The largest cavern had a small cupboard in one of its walls containing brandy and a first-aid outfit. There were two excellent lavatories, a ladies' and a gent's, side by side, carefully screened from each other by a wall. Unfortunately some one forgot the doors, so the occupants would be in full view of the rest of the people in the cavern— except for one thing. The refuge had electric lighting, but the current was turned off at the power station at the first whisper of a bombardment anywhere along the Catalan coast, so the refuge was plunged into darkness.

There were one or two other drawbacks to this excellent refuge. One was the distance from the village. Acting on the principle that the further a refuge is from the scene of a bombardment the safer it becomes, the constructors had built it well outside the village. It was a good ten to fifteen minutes' walk from most of the houses. But the greatest snag of all was that the long, dark, exciting tunnels were too long, dark, and exciting for the good morals of the village. It was all the fault of the refuge that Consuelo lost her reputation, Federico went before the judge, and I lost a cherished illusion.

Consuelo was a young lady of independent ideas. She was fifteen, and had been brought up by an elder sister who was not particularly interested in her. Consuelo enjoyed life and did pretty much as she chose. The village mothers wagged their tongues nearly out by the roots, but young Consuelo laughed, and if she felt like sitting at the café in the evenings with the Tossa boys, she did so, much to the envy of the pure Tossa maidens who could only walk arm in arm with one another, throwing wistful glances at the open-air dance floor. There was a certain Federico, aged about sixteen, who danced more often than was seemly with Consuelo and who had even been seen walking alone with her up the street towards her house. Federico's mother did not approve of Consuelo and considered she was leading her son astray.

I approved wholeheartedly of Consuelo. Here at last was some one with the courage to defy the ridiculous traditions of Tossa, and she seemed to be no worse for it. But that was before the refuge was built and the militiamen came to Tossa.

Militiamen were stationed all along the coast ready for the famous Italian landing that was advertized for the beginning of February. They were to be rushed to the strategic point at a moment's notice. What good they would have done when they got there, no one knows. They spent their days loafing in the café, playing dominoes and billiards, and they never even went for a walk. However, they were charming young men, and one of them discovered the refuge and Consuelo. The result was twofold: Consuelo accused Federico of having given her a baby, and the five doors of the refuge were locked.

The village was shocked to the core. In the last forty years there *had* been another case of an illegitimate baby, but the mother and child luckily removed to another village. There had also been a narrow escape only the year before, the hasty, almost shot-gun marriage of the Tossa electrician, which gave rise among the Tossa men to many remarks about insulation and other electrical terms.

Federico's mother rose to do battle. She took the matter to the Tossa judge. The judge referred the matter to a higher judge than he—to the courts at Santa Coloma. Consuelo, Federico, his mother and, oddly enough, the ex-Tossa priest, who seemed to have a mistaken idea of claiming parenthood himself, all appeared before the Santa Coloma judge. The priest was persuaded to abandon his claim, and Federico was triumphantly acquitted. Poor Consuelo went back to her sister to have the militiaman's baby by herself. The militiaman by this time was far away, stationed somewhere else. The refuge was firmly locked, all five doors.

When our four guests and I got to the refuge there were crowds of people shouting and milling outside. It took some time to understand what was the trouble. It took even longer to persuade the excited women that any danger from foreign warships was, for the moment, past. They were all screaming at the tops of their voices, more in anger than in fear. The five doors were locked and the man with the key was in Blanes.

As we slowly climbed our hill towards tea (Elizabeth had brought us some from Barcelona) I saw something unusual on the cliff near the fortifications. It was a long stick, painted red and white, the sort of stick used by surveyors. The carabineros in the fortifications had taken me at my word and had kindly marked the trenches for me.

2

Taming a Commissar

From the moment we decided to take visitors again, we had two or three always in the house. There was food, but because of the difficulties of getting it, we felt it was only fair to limit our guests to people doing some sort of war work. We could have filled the place with rich Barcelonese wanting to escape air-raids, but somehow the idea did not attract us. A number of our friends in England suggested coming to us to write their books, but although we knew that they would not mind slight discomforts like cold water and the risk of bombs, we felt it was not fair on the kind Tossa friends who let us buy food without waiting hours in queues.

Nikolaus was the only guest who was not involved in some kind of work. He and the Marks, the bar-keeper architect who designed our house and his wife, were the only survivors of the Tossa foreign colony except ourselves and a German mother and daughter who worked with the fishermen. The Marks still ran their tiny bar for the benefit of the carabineros, militiamen and the FAI. Nikolaus came up to live with us shortly after the war started, and he remained serenely in Room 2 with its sun terrace and did nothing more efficiently than anyone I know. He sat for hours on his terrace, a huge, fat man with a profile straight out of the Old Testament, and vaguely occupied himself with making childlike sketches of the view; or he started the first chapter of a novel (autobiographical) or made notes for a series of volumes on the Jewish invasion of Spain. When he was doing none of these things, he spent interminable hours rearranging stamps and sticking them in penny exercise books. Sometimes he played a sort of two-handed ludo; occasionally he played patience. But whatever he did, he amused himself magnificently. I have never met anyone who was so absolutely made for a life of ease.

We had a battle with our Francisca. It was over wages. I told her that we would pay one peseta an hour instead of the pre-war rate of half a peseta. She refused to take it. Fifty centimos was her price and fifty centimos she would have.

'But what about food prices?' I said. 'Everything is at least double.'

'Well,' she said. 'If you have to pay double for your food, why should you pay double for my wages?'

I said if she did not accept my wages she could not work for me. So she said she was very, very sorry, but if that were the case, then she could not work for me.

At last I hit on a formula. I explained that we charged the guests extra to cover her rise in wages. This worked wonders. She said she would accept gladly, prices being what they were; but on no account would she take extra money from us when we had so little. She made another condition. If there were suddenly no guests she would come up just the same and work for nothing. At the current rate of exchange she was getting about tuppence halfpenny an hour.

Taming a Commissar

I had no difficulty with Quimeta. In the old peace days little Quimeta from the Casa Blanca used to fascinate our men guests by bringing up their breakfasts with the air of a small duchess conferring a favour. She began to do dressmaking after the war started, and with that and her work on the farm she was busy. But she was interested to hear that we were taking guests again and promised to come over if Francisca needed help. We had her over once or twice when Francisca wanted to go to Gerona for shopping. I paid her the increased amount but there was no comment. I mentioned it to her to see what her reactions would be.

'Twice as much?' she exclaimed. 'Why, I never counted it!'

Later Francisca came up our hill on a rising tide of indignation.

'The idea!' she spluttered. 'That woman I do washing for—she still wants to pay me fifty centimos an hour. *I* told her, "And what about food prices?" I said. "Everything gone up double, wages ought to go up too!"'

Francisca's rise in wages was justified on another ground. The Jellineks were staying with us.

The Jellineks have a gift of living in one room. Wherever they go they take all their possessions in a few suitcases. But it is simply amazing what can come out of those few suitcases. Any ordinary room would be swamped, and the Jellineks have a tendency to chose small rooms with enormous beds. I have seen many Jellinek rooms in many hotels in many towns and I have often wondered if the Jellineks ever use their beds for anything excepting putting things down on. I suppose it might be possible to creep between the sheets under a top-heavy mass of newspapers, manuscripts, paint tubes, easels, pieces of material, unfinished frocks which caused the pieces of material, books, shoes, and invariably a large shapeless piece of knitting. This knitting only varies from bedroom to bedroom in colour. It is always the same size and always abandoned.

In our house at least they had a big room, but it was surprising what they could do. When one remembered that there was yet another room in a Barcelona hotel which bore the brunt of the Jellinek attack, it was astounding. Our room did have the disadvantage of containing, besides the litter, the Jellineks themselves. Frank took up very little space. He hunched in a corner over his typewriter, clutching it with one hand while he poked the keys with the forefinger of the other. Margueritte spread herself whether she was dressmaking, painting in oils, drawing in charcoal, or merely wandering about the room making observations on life in general. She loved to follow me about the kitchen when I was cooking. I was so fond of Margueritte that I endured her in the kitchen, only making the stipulation that she must sit on a chair in one spot. She is a very efficient cook herself, although her remarks have a childlike *naïveté* which is surprising. She was watching me cooking potatoes one day. She said: 'You know, when Frank and I were in our little house in Altea, I used to cook all the potatoes for a week at one go. Then there were always potatoes ready when we wanted them. Why don't you do that?'

I said I would just as soon do them every day. I found peeling a few every day less work than sitting down to do an enormous quantity at once.

Margueritte nodded her curly head. 'Oh, yes, I suppose it is about the same really. I never worked it out you know. You see, I only had a very big pot.'

Margueritte was being rather a problem. Frank was busy with a book, but she had nothing to do. She had no urge to paint; she had made herself enough of the voluminous skirts and fluffy blouses that she had adopted as her own style; there were no interesting young men among the guests. Fat Nikolaus would have been delighted to have amused Margueritte, but she did not care for Nikolaus and spurned his obvious adoration. Marianne and Ulrich were completely absorbed in each other in the first leave they had had together since the war started. Margueritte flapped aimlessly around the terraces.

Archie found the solution. He suggested that Margueritte should make a path up through the woods behind the house. She was enchanted. Every day she set forth armed with a billhook, a hacker, a hatchet, wearing a bathing suit and a pair of gauntlet gloves. She made an excellent path which she named Passeig Goig, or Joy Passage.

Marianne and Ulrich were enjoying themselves. Ulrich looked like the very best type of Aryan. Blonde, very good-looking, he was the tall, thin German type who manages to escape being stolid, but who looks as if he ought to be in uniform. Ulrich would have been a charming Prussian officer, if there could be such a thing. Marianne told me that she had always feared the soldier in Ulrich. He was an instinctive soldier, but as instinctively hated everything to do with Prussian officers. He had worked for years for the Communist Party in Germany until he had been hunted out. Then he came to Barcelona with Marianne, whom he met while he was fleeing through Hungary. Funny little dark Jewish Marianne, with her marvellous eyes and beautiful legs, she followed Ulrich to Barcelona, and for a year they had lived in peaceful bliss. Ulrich had a job with a film company; Marianne gave up translating other people's books for a living and settled down to enjoy life. She became beautiful in Spain. Her heartshaped little face filled out and browned in the Spanish sunshine; she was tanned a rich chestnut all over. Her dark hair produced unexpected lights, deep red, purplish brown like a copper beech, shading to the colour of burnt mahogany, where it fell in a thick fringe over her high forehead. Marianne's fringe was fascinating. It was cut slanting up at each side, so that it fell in a peak in the middle of her curving eyebrows. She told me that it was entirely an accident. Ulrich had cut it for her and had clipped it too far up at one side. There was nothing for it but to cut the other side to match. The effect was so startling that she decided to adopt the new style as her own.

The Spanish War appalled Marianne. Ulrich adored it. He loved the first days in Barcelona, fighting behind the barricades; he joined the International Brigade and helped to save Madrid. He became a captain and assisted in the rout of the Italians at Guadalajara. Marianne went to Madrid as interpreter and to work on the radio. She saw Ulrich whenever he could snatch a few days' leave. He was the complete soldier in his perfectly fitting uniform, picked up second hand from an English political commissar. Marianne knew that she had lost him, temporarily. His whole energies, his keen brain were fixed on the war. Marianne tried to concentrate on her wireless talks in Hungarian and German; on her translations of French, Polish, and Russian. In Tossa she had him again. He might grow eloquent describing battles for our benefit, but Marianne knew she had him. The army officer was sent packing by the eager little boy determined to enjoy his holiday at the seaside. She would lose him again in Madrid, but she was prepared to lend him to the cause of the Spanish people. She could get him back at the end of the war, if he were not killed.

It was because we liked Marianne and Ulrich so much that we agreed to have Max and Gretel to stay. Ulrich was warm in his praises of Max. He had met him once or twice in Spain, but he knew him well in Russia several years before. Max was charming, brilliant. He had been sent by the Communist Party to Spain as foreign political commissar for Barcelona. That meant that all foreigners, especially Germans and those whose countries recognized the Rebels, would be under his control. They were both certain we would like Max. We gathered that Gretel was a sort of echo of the great man; neither Marianne nor Ulrich had much to say about her.

Frank Jellinek suddenly decided to go to Barcelona. Marianne and Ulrich had to leave the day Max and Gretel were to arrive. That left only Nikolaus, Margueritte and ourselves to deal with the Barcelona foreign commissar.

We controlled ourselves for a few days. For one thing we were all fond of Marianne and Ulrich and wished to give friends of theirs every chance. We clung pathetically to the idea that they might 'settle down'. Then we faced up to facts. Max was simply frightful.

He was all the things that ideal Communism lays down as being *ausgeschlossen*. He was grossly self-indulgent, selfish, ill-mannered, dogmatic. He started throwing his commissar weight about the moment he arrived, ordering this and demanding that and behaving to us as I hope no one does behave to servants. We soon stopped that. Quite nicely and gently, but we stopped it. I never realized how useful my two years in Germany were going to prove. First I was able to hold my own with Mark, the architect, and now I could tell Max just what I thought of him in his own language.

If it had only been a question of his attitude to us we should not have disliked Max so much as we did. His manners changed towards us after my little chat, and if he had contented himself with being rude and aggressive to poor little down-trodden Gretel, we would have left it at that. At first I was sorry for Gretel, then I realized that Max's bullying was meat and drink to her. She adored it. She was like a spaniel that raised adoring eyes every time it was kicked. Not that Max kicked her; it might have strained his heart. Yes, Max had a bad heart. So many fat, flabby people have. Our hill was a great trial to him, but it was surprising the way he could take it when it was meal time.

I think it was Max's behaviour at meals that first made us realize that something had to be done about him.

There was still food to be got, thanks to Leon's winning ways with his old women, but there was not what one might call food in abundance. The most that can be said is that no one was hungry. Usually people coming out from Barcelona found our meals too luxurious; we still had two courses and managed a fairly adequate hors-d'œuvres. Bread was rationed, but there was enough for two good slices per head for each meal. Before Max came, we served the food on one dish, handing it round for everyone to help themselves. We left the bread on a plate on the table. Max's coming altered all that.

He snatched the dish first, unless some one beat him to it—and we were not accustomed to having to battle for our rations—and took about a quarter of the contents. We were seven people altogether. No one ever got their second slice of bread, until I noticed the practical Leon taking two slices at once. We began to feel hungry for the first time. So I simply had to help everyone myself, feeling like a seaside landlady and, like the landlady, I played favourites, or rather un-favourites. Now it was Max who began to feel hungry. But only for a little while. He soon saw that the good old days of private enterprise at table were gone for ever, so he started eating Gretel's food as well. That rather stymied me. I was forced to give them both their full ration. Then if Gretel liked to be so silly, she could starve. My conscience was clear.

We all realized that Max must go. To make things more unpleasant, Max suffered from spy-mania. He was always seeing submarines and enemy ships; every Catalan was a spy; all foreigners were suspect. He could not do very much about us because, being British, we did not come under his control, but he fell on poor Nikolaus with a whoop of joy. Nikolaus must be a spy. Otherwise he would not be idling in Tossa when he ought to be at the front. Nikolaus was either a spy or he must join the International Brigade.

The persecution of Nikolaus reached the most absurd proportions. Max got to the stage of doing agent-provocateur work. It was Nikolaus who drew my attention to a bundle of papers which were always left lying about the sitting room. It was a bundle which I remembered vaguely Max had been carrying about mysteriously for some days. Nikolaus explained that it was left there for his benefit. He had stalked past it for several days, but he felt he would have to look at it if I didn't do something about it. I chose an evening when Nikolaus, Margueritte, and Leon were in the room. Max and Gretel were sitting side by side reading pocket editions of Lenin's works. I picked up the bundle and carefully turned over the pages. They were covered with incomprehensible diagrams. I saw that the two *agents* had spotted me and were watching breathlessly over their Lenins. I flipped the papers with my fingers and walked to the fire.

'I'm sick of seeing these lying about,' I said.

Max leaped to his feet. 'My God!' he cried, and snatched the papers from me.

There was a shriek of laughter from Margueritte,and in a few moments everyone except Max and Gretel were weakly mopping their eyes. Max clutched his precious papers to his bosom and stalked out, followed by Gretel, who was delayed because he slammed the door in her face.

Three things brought matters finally to a head. Frank Jellinek came back from Barcelona; May Day was celebrated in the PSUC hospital in the village and the POUM came to stay.

3

May Day in the Fifth Form

Barcelona seethed with odd short syllables denoting the various political parties. PSU was the Partido Socialista Unificado, in Catalunya it was the PSUC, the united socialist party of Catalunya. It embraced all the Left parties, including the communists, but the anarchists had their own FAI, Federación Anarquista Iberica, and the revolution-for-revolution's-sake leftists belonged to the POUM, Partido Obrero Unificado Marxista, the united Marxist workers' party. The unfortunate use of the word Marxista misled a great many enthusiastic young foreigner volunteers who later found themselves accused of being Trotskyists. Max was attached to the PSUC, although he gave the impression the PSUC was attached to him.

We tried to enliven the tedium of having Max in the house by playing little games on him. None of us could go for a walk along the cliffs without seeing something sinister like an enemy submarine or an obvious spy which we carefully reported to Max. Nikolaus was out of this game because he was suspect already. We were so tired of Nikolaus being suspect that we tried to find

30

another victim. We finally chose Frank Jellinek who was still in Barcelona.

Frank spends a lot of time carefully circulating the most extraordinary rumours about himself. He hotly denies this, but Frank will deny anything if he thinks any secret of his is discovered. If one meets him going to the beach carrying a towel and if one is indiscreet enough to say, 'Hello, Frank, going bathing?' he will reply, 'Certainly not,' and will go to the café for a drink instead.

Max had heard of Frank. Who hadn't? He thought it was a good opportunity to find out more about him in his absence. Unfortunately for Max we were all ready to talk. But we all said different things. Frank's politics remain a mystery to many. One reviewer of his Paris Commune book said brightly that 'quite frankly I have no idea of Mr. Jellinek's political opinions'. Unfortunately it was too dangerous to make up many facts about Frank without his consent, so we waited hopefully for his return, dropping careless hints about the dark horse here and there. Max rather pathetically tried to get me to tell him the truth about Frank. For some reason he had a touching faith in my political integrity. Perhaps from the way I bullied him he thought I was a political commissar in disguise. I had to bully Max or life would have been unbearable. Oddly enough he liked it. But Gretel loathed me. She watched me browbeating Max in the same way as he browbeat Nikolaus, and she curled up in corners and oozed hate. If she had not been a modern young communist she would certainly have made a wax image of me and have stuck pins into it, instead of glaring at me round the back of Lenin's works. It surprised me how anyone could read

Lenin and still think Max was a good communist.

At last Frank returned. Margueritte had added fuel to Max's suspicions by becoming very friendly with a gentle anarchist who was one of the FAI sent to convert Tossencs. Just about the time Frank got back Max had decided he must be an anarchist.

Margueritte did not help matters. She sent poor Max nosing off on odd scents. She would say loudly at mealtimes, 'Do you remember, Frank, when you were with Bela Kun in Budapest', and afterwards Max would ask me seriously if I knew just what Herr Jellinek had been doing in Budapest. Or Margueritte would remind Frank of the time some one tried to shoot him in the Polish Corridor—'so difficult to dodge the bullets there, you know'—Max would be obviously itching to get at his card index. Sometimes Max would dedicate the evening to Frank and would pin him in a corner questioning him closely. Frank would mumble his fluent but hardly audible German and Gretel would stand by to catch anything that Max missed.

Then one day everything was ruined. Max was playing with the radio—it was apparently his duty to listen in to all the rebel stations—and he got Moscow by mistake. Gretel was dragged from her bed to interpret, Max being one of those lordly souls that never learn the language of any country but their own. After the statement was finished there was a pause and the Moscow announcer said something which made Gretel turn pale. She told us in a hushed voice that the announcer had said he would now read an article in the series 'Where is Europe heading?' by their honoured collaborator Frank Jellinek.

What was good enough for Moscow was all right by

Max. He could not make enough of Frank after this. Frank was horrified and grew more and more secretive. He only left his room when he knew Max was out. He finally told us either he or Max must leave.

We never discovered if it was the May Day fiasco or the POUM, the Unified Marxist Workers' Party, that upset Max most.

The POUM arrived first. When I rashly said that anyone in Barcelona who needed a rest should come to the Casa Johnstone, I had not reckoned with so many political entanglements. I should have remembered the old days when we built the hotel and had to keep rival carpenters and rival tile-layers segregated in order to keep the peace.

The POUM arrived four strong. I knew one of them before the war, a German girl called Magda who used to stay in Tossa. She joined the POUM at the beginning of the war and, like so many people with no notion of politics, became a violent convert. Her friends were a rather tiresome Austrian woman called Kaete, a beautiful old man called Rossini, and a little monkey of a creature called Klaus Heber. The last was the most interesting of the four. He never spoke, but just smiled gently to himself and always I expected to find he had soft brown eyes and each time I got a shock to find that they were a cold grey. Rossini and Kaete talked Italian all the time, she obviously sitting at the feet of the master. I understood when they did not speak too fast. She was bitter against the PSUC party, which incorporated the communists. Rossini murmured gently from time to time, his old eyes fixed on the distant view, 'La Rivoluzione!' but seemed to have nothing more constructive to say. In fact, the POUM quartet were all completely destructive in their viewpoints, except perhaps Klaus Heber. One felt that he knew what he was doing far better than they did.

Max nearly exploded under the strain. I let him understand that if he did not care for the people staying in the house there was an obvious remedy. Max did not want to leave. He could not go back to Barcelona because of his weak heart and there was nowhere else to stay in Tossa. Nowhere, that is, except the PSUC hospital. When I suggested this he nearly collapsed. The noise would kill him. In his weak state he had to be very careful. It seemed to be a toss-up between a noisy hospital on Party lines or the Trotskyist Casa Johnstone. Finally comfort won, and Max resigned himself to seeing Poumist literature lying about the room and what was worse, the Poumists themselves lying about the terrace.

It was entirely owing to Max's attitude to the POUM that we became temporarily its champions. Magda was busy trying to convert us, and we were interested to hear the POUM point of view, but our native common sense told us that now was not the moment to try to revive the revolution. We were concerned with getting on with the war. The Poumites staying with us were as rabid against the PSUC and communists as Max was against the POUM. For a purely slanging match it was about equal. But we liked Magda and we heartily disliked Max, so temporarily we became POUM supporters. That is to say, we left the POUM bulletin lying about where Max must see it: we took *Batalla*, the POUM paper, as well as *Treball*, *Humanitat*, and the *Vanguardia*. Even the gloomy Kaete began to take an interest in us. She thought we were beginning to see light. Little Klaus Heber was not deceived. He made no comment but he had a twinkle in his round face which never reached his cold eyes. He said nothing and he missed nothing.

Magda was the only one who tried conclusions with Max, and we rallied to her aid. Archie was always firm and lucid and while seeming impartial, his arguments were in reality always against the POUM. Margueritte and I baited Max and found ourselves hotly supporting even assertions that the war was secondary to the revolution, and if the revolution had indeed failed why go on with the war? Frank, with his usual caution, refused to take any part in these discussions and thoroughly disapproved of our baiting Max. Max, he kept reminding us, was a very important man. He could easily get anyone, even holders of British passports, thrown out of Spain. I agreed that Max was important, but I went on the principle that the more one attacks bullies the less they bully. Max certainly was less rude to me than to anyone else in the house. I was held back from actually throwing him out of the house because of Nikolaus and Leon. Both of them were directly under Max's control, and he could make things very unpleasant for them.

We heard about the great preparations for May Day from some German boys at the PSUC hospital. They were friendly with Nikolaus and asked him if he was coming down to celebrate with them. There was to be a great meeting in the market square; Max was to address the crowd; red bunting was to be everywhere; Frau Mark was busy painting lifelike posters of Stalin and Lenin. The Marks had been taken under the wing of the Barcelona foreign commissar. They trotted round after him like faithful dogs. They no longer spoke to Nikolaus, who was in disgrace, and they were cold to us. They did not approve of our attitude to the great man, and, what was more important, the great man was far more useful to them than we were.

May Day was not mentioned in the Casa Johnstone. We were by now all tarred with the POUM brush because we allowed the Poumists to stay in the house. The atmosphere became more and more like that of the fifth form. Max and Gretel whispered in corners; the Poumists muttered Italian; Frank became so secretive he hardly appeared at all; Nikolaus went about with a leer because he knew what Max and Gretel were whispering about him. Only Leon and Archie kept their imperturbability. Archie was busy scaping the garden— i.e. standing for hours with his head on one side gazing at the hillside—and nothing in the way of politics could possibly affect Leon. He did not care for Max, but he treated him with the same icy charm that he reserved for hotel guests who tried to make love to him. May Days and red bunting meant nothing in his young life.

On April 30th Frank disappeared. Margueritte said blithely that he must have gone to Barcelona because he had hotly denied any intention of going there. Max appeared unaccountably gloomy, and the Poumists strangely animated. Then we heard that all demonstrations for May Day had been forbidden by the Government. So Max could not speak in the market place and Frau Mark had expended all her remaining black ink on Stalin's moustache in vain. The Poumists were delighted because it solved their immediate problem about the demonstration, which had been roughly, should the PSUC be allowed to get away with it unmolested? After all, May day was not a monopoly of the Communist Party.

However Max still had something up his fifth-form sleeve. No one could stop the PSUC hospital from having its own fiesta.

There were a fair number of convalescent Germans in the hospital, but the majority of the soldiers were Spaniards. Max had the Germans in his pocket—as good party members they had no choice—but the Spaniards disliked him heartily. Spanish soldiers were tired anyway of foreigners who would not let them alone to run their own war on their own lines, and when it came to foreigners trying to tell them how to run fiestas it was too much. A German May Day just about finished Max with the Spanish soldiers. They approved of Frau Mark's posters of Stalin and Lenin, but they wanted some of Miaja, Aguirre, and Companys. Most of all they wanted to be left alone.

Max made his biggest mistake when he invited the Marks to dinner at the hospital. More Germans were the last straw. The place was in an uproar. The Spaniards demanded the room to be cleared of foreigners. They started throwing bread about, then got going with the plates. They broke up chairs and pulled off the table cloths. The Spaniard running the hospital, who was terrified of Max, tried to control the situation, but he was swamped under showers of wine and soup. Finally the Marks were hurriedly rushed out and Max managed to rush himself out at the same time. Gretel was abandoned but managed to crawl out by herself.

The Spaniards decided that supper might proceed now that the disruptive element had left. They tolerated the wounded Germans, who, after all, *had* been fighting.

Max stayed in bed the next day, and the director of the hospital tried to punish the naughty wounded by forbidding them to go out and by stopping their wine for meals. He succeeded in keeping them indoors for one morning; he did not succeed in stopping their wine for one meal. At lunch time there was an absence of the usual bottles on the long tables. The Spaniards banged their knives on the tables and shouted *'Vino!'* It was brought immediately. In the afternoon everyone went out as usual. The First of May was over.

The Poumists hurriedly packed up and went to Barcelona. Without them in the house, Max turned his attention to Nikolaus.

I still do not know just what was in Max's mind, but he was determined that Nikolaus should join the International Brigade. I doubt that it was the Party line to force unwilling foreigners into the Brigade, so I can only suppose it was a foible of this particular commissar. There were several reasons why Nikolaus should not join the Brigade. He was entirely disinterested in politics; he hated fighting; he came to Spain for a quiet life and saw no reason why he should not have it in spite of the war; he was much too fat. The only really strong reason for joining the Brigade seemed to be that he would be arrested as a spy if he did not. At least Max made it quite clear in a roundabout way that he would not give much for Nikolaus's chances unless he joined the Brigade.

Max had been working on the Marks for some time, but he still had not driven Mark into the International Brigade. The poor old man was toying with the idea, egged on by his wife, who was tired of running a bar for anarchists. They were such young anarchists. Tossa was a home for boys of seventeen who called themselves FAI. They had been sent to convert the Tossencs to a better life. Tossencs responded by boycotting them. No one would speak to them, drink with them or dance with them, so they took refuge in Mark's bar. It was by far the most effective method of dealing with the FAI that had been tried in Catalunya.

Because old Mark still hesitated, Max was determined to capture Nikolaus. He grew less restrained in his methods. At last I had to intervene. Whether it was dangerous to cross a political commissar or not, things had gone too far. I told Max to pack up and leave.

He was amazed. He simply could not believe that I was really asking—no, telling—him to leave the house. When he did grasp it he became very German and stiff and marched upstairs to break the news to Gretel. I do not know what he told Gretel, but she never spoke another word to me. They both marched off grimly down to the PSUC hospital. The director told them with tears in his eyes that he dared not have them there. They left Tossa by the afternoon bus.

The next day Archie and I went to Barcelona. Archie had received an odd telegram from Frank telling him to come in at once, but Margueritte was to stay in Tossa. Archie decided to go. I went with him to match some wool.

4

War within War

I could not match the wool. Only food shops were open in Barcelona, and these only between eight and nine in the morning and six and seven at night. The rest of the time the streets were a rattle of machine-gun fire with a field gun whooping at intervals down the Paralelo.

Frank was slightly perturbed when he saw me with Archie. He could not believe that we had not known all about the POUM and anarchist rising. He was indignant when we suggested he might have made it a little clearer to us. He practically declared that he had kept us informed of all the plans of all parties.

'Well! As you are here you'd better come along and see the fun, but for goodness sake don't get hit. There is such a fuss when a foreigner gets hit.'

Archie's reputation as peace-bringer held good even in the middle of a rising. Whenever I was with him we walked up and down streets and nothing happened. We stepped over deserted barricades and listened to the racket from the battle raging in the next street. When I was on my own or with anyone else we always seemed to get in the middle of things. Machine-guns started up from unexpected places; we took refuge in doorways to find them full of militiamen, who pressed revolvers into our backs and told us to go away. We never knew which side was which. Most of the fighters themselves were vague about this. I decided that Archie was the person to stick to. I had long ago made up my mind to run a mile if I met Frank. Frank seemed to attract trouble.

I was alone when I met Marianne. She was running down the street and there was something odd about her. Then I saw she had no shoes on. We drew into a doorway. She started to tell me some of her adventures in the radio station. I was surprised to see her in Barcelona, but she told me she had a temporary job on the radio there. Ulrich was back on the Madrid front. We laughed so much over a silly story about getting down the stairs at the radio station that we forgot the shooting in the street. The story had nothing whatever to do with the present troubles, but it was nearly as dangerous for Marianne. It appeared that the militiaman on guard at the top of the stairs of the radio building had taken an instant dislike to her. He could not read, and when Marianne held out her permit to enter the broadcasting room he refused to let her in. She got in by pointing over the curling bannisters and saying 'Look!' He looked and she slipped past him into the building. She did not give the matter another thought and, her work finished, went down the stairs as usual with some other workers. Suddenly one of them looked up. With a cry of horror he pulled Marianne out of the way. The militia guard was carefully aiming his rifle through the bannisters at her. Everyone shouted for the superintendent of the building, who appeared down in the hall and told the militiaman to control himself. A few steps lower, Marianne looked up, and there was the man again, drawing a careful bead on her. Everyone shouted again, and this time Marianne skipped down the rest of the stairs while the superintendent argued with the guard. Presently everyone gathered round the superintendent in the hall, protesting about this odd behaviour of the radio guard. Suddenly, the superintendent gave a yell and dragged everyone into his office. There was a dull report as the militiaman missed Marianne and hit the tiled floor.

She was just telling me how she had been shut up in the building for forty-eight hours and this was her first chance to get out when a bunch of young anarchists took refuge in our doorway.

'You must go away', they told us.

'Where to?' we retorted. There was a barricade at each end of the street and rival factions were firing at each other.

The anarchists did not know. But they did not want us in their doorway.

'Please go away,' they said.

'Tell your friends to stop firing and we'll go with pleasure,' we suggested.

This seemed reasonable. One of the boys, they were all under twenty, nipped out into the street and made his perilous way from doorway to doorway until he reached one of the barricades. Presently the machine-guns from this barricade stopped firing. Almost immediately the other end of the street was quiet. It seemed some sort of prearranged signal. We saw the boy standing up by the barricade shouting to us to come on. The anarchists in the doorway almost pushed us into the street.

'Run!' they said.

War within War

We ran. I managed one look back at the group in the doorway. They were mounting a sub-machine gun. Even as we sped down the now strangely silent street I found time to wonder if they were going to shoot impartially at both barricades.

We were helped behind the barricade, where we stood and panted. It was the first time I had been behind an occupied barricade. It seemed very safe. It was made of paving stones and sandbags of concrete. It was quite a permanent affair. There were no dead or dying lying about, just a group of rather dirty but extremely cheerful young men. They grinned at us.

'Ola! guapas,' they said.

We would have stayed and talked to them, but we had a feeling we were interrupting something.

'Thank you very much,' we said. 'Good-bye! Salud!'

We had an awful feeling that we should not have said 'Salud', then we remembered that both sides in this private war would be saying that.

As we hurried down a side street we heard the rattle of machine-guns break out again. The truce was over.

Marianne had to rush back to her hotel to keep an appointment. It was not until I rejoined Archie at the Loret Hotel that I realized I had completely forgotten to ask Marianne what she had done with her shoes.

Archie had been paying a visit to the Telefonica building. The Government asalto guards were in on the ground floor, and the anarchists and POUM were in the upper stories. In between, the telephonists were presumably getting on with their work. At least the telephone worked normally throughout the rising. Archie could not get in from the street, so he visited the top floor. He entered by the Hotel Bristol roof by which convenient way the besieged were getting provisions. He was as angry as it is possible for him to be when he heard of my adventures. He thought I had been needlessly exposing myself to danger.

'And you?' I retorted. 'What were you doing in a building that is being taken by assault?'

We decided that we were both foolish to have left our peaceful haven of Tossa.

I had never been anywhere near machine-gun fire before, and I was surprised at my reactions. I had thought I would be scared stiff, but oddly enough I could not connect the machine-gun bullets with myself. I came to the conclusion that it was because all this fighting had nothing to do with me that I remained remote from the danger. Also I was entirely concerned with fears of an air raid. I had never been in a raid and I was terrified that I should be terrified. I wandered about the streets of Barcelona during the days of May 5th, 6th, and 7th, in far greater danger from stray bullets than I should have been from bombs, but I was mostly concerned that there should not be a raid. I need not have worried. The fascists were far too clever to stop the rising by presenting a common danger to both sides.

We went back to Tossa admitting that Max had been right about the POUM. Not that we believed that all the members of the POUM were double-dyed villains, but they did seem to be either villains or fools. The kindest thing one could say about the POUM was that they were useful instruments for the fascists. The saddest thing about the POUM was that many of the fighters who had been ordered back from the Aragon front to fight in the streets of Barcelona were genuine anti-fascists who were only interested in fighting fascists. They had joined up in the POUM because its offices were in one of the first buildings one saw coming from the docks or the station, in the old Hotel Falcon. It had the word Marxist in its name and that was good enough for them.

We helped a few of the young POUM militia boys to escape during the big round-up which followed the May rising. They arrived at Tossa hungry and disillusioned, having tramped from Barcelona over the hills to avoid the guards. We let them spend the night with us and then gave them enough food and money to take them to the frontier. We felt no disloyalty to the Spanish Government about this. We would have cheerfully handed over some of the POUM leaders to the police.

One of the POUM boys told us that Rossini was dead. He had wandered across a line of machine-gun bullets while pondering on the Rivoluzione. He had died in the Plaça Catalunya, the scene of so many battles for the revolution.

Frank stayed on in Barcelona to see 'if any more balloons were going up'. Luckily some one had arrived to amuse Margueritte. He was a young man called Stevens.

Archie had met him in the early days in Barcelona. He had come to Spain to fight for the Right and/or write for the Press. He decided that writing for the Press was easier, but it seemed he was not popular among his colleagues. He had some kind of tie-up with a news agency and 'milked' the Barcelona papers for it, although he knew hardly any Spanish. Archie showed him a story in the *Vanguardia* about some Barcelona celebrity who had died from appendicitis ('*victima de un atac apendicular*') and told him, 'That's a real flowery Spanish way of describing some one getting a direct hit from a bomb. Rather absurd when you think that bombs never drop perpendicularly.'

Stevens cabled the story. At least he handed it in and paid for the cable, but the censors stopped it.

In Tossa, Stevens gave Margueritte one look and was lost. She adored adoration and wore all her wildest dresses. She was upset because her hair was not at its best. Usually Margueritte's hair is a rich blonde with a slight tinge of ginger. Unfortunately she had washed it with a new Spanish soap.

'It should have been all right,' she said, looking at the mass of pale pink curls rioting in the glass. 'They told me it was guaranteed to take oil stains out of mechanics' overalls.'

Not that the hair mattered at all. Margueritte was unique. I have tried to take her in hand; to brush her hair so that it lay in waves close to her head instead of curling madly in all directions; to dress her in a shirt and a well-cut skirt instead of the mass of frills and weird Edwardian braided effects she so loved. She would be delighted with the restrained effect for a few days and poor Frank would find all his shirts half-dirtied and his hair cream used up. Then she would have a violent reaction and appear in cerise velvet with bunchy sleeves and a trailing skirt. But Margueritte could get away with anything.

We stopped thinking about Stevens when Edna arrived.

Edna was a nurse from Madrid. One can only use the word magnificent in connection with Edna. She had

46

red hair—really red hair—a dead white skin and a great many curves. Voluptuous ought to be another word to use about Edna, but she was far too innocent. She prattled on about the doctors and the soldiers and how she loved all the dear boys, but they did get rather out of hand at times, and should she dye her hair black because red hair is so conspicuous and really the things that went on in hospitals we wouldn't believe, and she was looked on as really rather peculiar because she wouldn't have affairs with the doctors, as if there wasn't enough to do, and she always seemed to be on night duty because the other girls were always having trouble one way and another.

We loved Edna. Nikolaus, who was rather disgruntled because Margueritte ignored him so completely, made great friends with her, but he admitted to me afterwards that he was quite unable to convey to her what he really had in his mind. The Tossa lads, the carabineros, the FAI boys who somehow had not yet been rounded up, all clustered in their dozens to watch Edna bathing. Watching Edna they were very silent and absorbed.

But Edna, whom I thought could never cause me a moment of anxiety, had something up her sleeve. Or rather, that was just what she had not. It was my two-piece bathing suits that started the trouble.

I always make my own bathing suits and, for the convenience of both knitting and swimming, I make a pair of pants and a small brassière. I consider I can just get away with it. I am no sylph, but I am sunburnt all over and muscular. Although a good hearty young woman, I have no rolls of fat. The first day Edna saw

me in a rust-colour two-piece suit she declared that was
what she had been wanting all her life.

I did my best. I explained that there was no wool in
Tossa; she said she would send to Barcelona. I said I
had no time to make it for her; she said she would try
herself and I could help her. Mercifully, it really was
difficult to get anything sent from Barcelona, and I was
unhelpful about it. At last I thought she had forgotten
the two-piece suit. She seemed quite contented in her
very attractive pale green one which was ample and
suited her beautifully. It was moulded so that it kept
her large proportions tidily together, and the colour
suited her white skin.

Then Edna came down to breakfast wearing her
bathing wrap. She confided to me: 'You know, I think
there must be something not quite right. It doesn't
look a bit like yours. Do be a dear and help me.'

She had cut her green bathing suit in two. She had
tried to shape a top—she had cut away lots and lots of
material, but somehow it wasn't right—and she looked
like a lewd drawing in a French magazine. It was
astounding what an expanse of white skin there was,
white skin over soft rolls of flesh bulged oddly round,
over and under strips of green wool.

Something had to be done. I went up to her room
and saw that we were saved. She had not used the skirt
of the suit. I snatched it up and folded it round her
bosom. After an hour's hard work and many pins all
was well. It could never look so tidy as the original suit,
and there was one roll between the top and the pants
which nothing could control, but at least I felt I had
done something to protect Nikolaus and the carabineros.

5

Lhude Sing Cuccu

Edna left us to go back to her work in Madrid. She was still not defeated about the two-piece suit and declared she was going to knit herself one to play tennis in at her base hospital. She sent us a line from Barcelona. She was machine-gunned just outside Mataró. The train was stopped because a raid was in progress and the planes swooped down on their way back and sprayed the train and the surrounding fields. In some miraculous way few people were killed or injured, although the only cover was rows of beans. Edna was annoyed about it. She said she expected to be attacked when she was in an ambulance or any vehicle with a red cross but not in an ordinary train.

The usual effect on Tossa of war's approach in the form of raids on nearby villages, or when a few Tossencs were in a machine-gunned train, was to confirm their belief that all war was silly and useless, but that this war was especially so. Tossencs were not so politically unconscious as the English, but they were war-unconscious. They liked their politics served up in a mass of words and even a revolver shot or two, but an organized war seemed to serve no purpose whatever. Food was short and getting shorter; more and more young men were being called up. The Tossencs objected to their young men being sent to defend Madrid. Madrid was not a Catalan town. Catalans had driven fascism out of Catalunya and that should be sufficient. All these foreigners were just making a lot of trouble for peaceful people. It was quite impossible to explain the difference between a Nazi and a German Jewish refugee. Tossa had had both. Both had run away at the first signs of danger and neither had paid their debts. Now they were trying to blow each other up and were killing a lot of Catalans and destroying valuable property. To hell with all foreigners, said Catalunya.

To the anti-foreign feeling was added the spy mania. Every one thought everyone else a spy and all foreigners automatically became suspect. When the *ayuntamiento* rang us up and asked us as a special favour to allow a friend of the mayor's to stay with us, we said at once the man must be a police spy. We thought this quite amusing until the little man arrived and Francisca decided right away that he *was* a police spy. We told her not to be absurd and not to spread rumours round the village because it was dangerous.

Although we called the little man Puñetas, that word being his favourite expression and meaning, roughly, 'Nonsense!' or 'Curse it!', we still talked of him as 'the Spy'. He was an addition to our party. Luckily we were able to eat outside because he liked picking up bones in his fingers and flinging them over his shoulder. Beetle liked this too. He also spat when he thought about it, and we had no spittoons; but Leon, who never had failed us yet, did remember to put toothpicks on the table. Unfortunately Margueritte decided that she could bait Puñetas.

We were very fond of the Jellineks, but they had peculiar habits. They persisted in talking in English if there was some one there who understood no word of English. Both Margueritte and Frank were good linguists, but on these occasions there was nothing to be done except to answer in whatever language was the appropriate one. That gave the foreigner a vague, if one-sided, idea of the conversation. It usually ended by no one knowing what the conversation was about, except, perhaps, the Jellineks, who were talking at the same time and therefore had two separate versions.

We battled bravely to keep the conversation at meals in Spanish for the sake of Puñetas. Margueritte could not keep her chatter off a spotted tie that he always wore. He had a method with this tie. He wore it as far as the beach. Then he took it off and put it carefully under a stone, while he removed his shirt and trousers, under which he wore a brown bathing suit. A bathing suit for a man was unusual in Tossa, where all the men wore bathing shorts, but Puñetas was even more original. He wore it back to front so that it had a high neck at the back and a low front with two crossed straps over his hairy chest. He would then walk gingerly into the water. 'Ouch! *Puñetas!*' was his daily chorus.

When he came up to lunch he was wearing his tie. He sat down and took it off and hung it carefully over the back of his chair. Then he undid the front of his shirt and rolled the collar and lapels carefully inside exposing a chest very pink beneath the hair, with two white intersecting lines across it. Then he tucked his table napkin into the low V of the shirt and started on his food.

Margueritte kept on about this tie. She referred to it every few minutes in English. Puñetas ignored her. He told some very vulgar and very funny stories in Catalan with his mouth full. Presently Margueritte became so wild that he stopped eating to look at her. She was babbling away about his tie, shrieking with laughter and, like a child, repeating phrases until some one answered her. Frank disclaimed any responsibility. He always did this with Margueritte. Puñetas suddenly got up and deliberately unrolled his shirt collar and put on his tie. He then walked slowly into the house. We were rather shaken. Frank told Margueritte she would be responsible if we were all sent to prison, and she had better follow him and apologize.

Puñetas came back again, still wearing his tie but carrying something in his hand. It was another tie, identically spotted. He sat down again to his unfinished food. He smiled. He stretched out his hand with the tie to Margueritte and turned to us.

'Tell the lady to go and hang herself with this,' he said, and went on with his food.

We were sorry when Puñetas left. He was a dear little man, and he liked Archie and me. But when we saw our next visitors we were thankful. Etta and Ilse would have been too much for him altogether.

Etta and Ilse had been several times to Tossa before the war, but they had not stayed with us. They were Germans, and seemed to be companions to various tired German business men from Barcelona. Now the business men had run away but Etta and Ilse remained. They were doing war work. We never inquired the exact nature of the work, but they both declared they had come to Tossa for a rest. Etta was exactly like a

Picasso drawing, large face, tiny shoulders and bust, colossal thighs. She was extremely good-natured, too good-natured. Ilse was better looking but not so fascinating. She was plump and wore tight silk shirts always slightly torn under the arms.

The Jellineks suddenly decided to go to Mexico, and to have a baby. So they went to London. That left us with the faithful Nikolaus, Ilse and Etta and a few workers from Government offices. The only other foreigners in Tossa were the Marks, and the Reifenbergs. The Reifenbergs hardly counted as foreigners. They had become completely native and lived independently in the village. We saw them occasionally because we liked them and found them interesting and we would have willingly seen more of them but they were busy people. At five-thirty a.m. they were on the beach hauling in the big seine net. Then one or both would go off into the hills to get wood and to pick wild strawberries, wild asparagus, mushrooms, whatever was in season. They eked out their earnings by helping in the gardens and getting an occasional vegetable. They were popular in the village except among the old women. Tossa's old women do not like anyone. They disapproved of Lo, the daughter, because she was good at arithmetic. This meant that she always worked out the exact amount of money due to the people hauling in the nets. The net owner left all calculations to her. The old women were convinced she did not reckon enough for their share. Luckily the old women were themselves so frightened of policemen that they could not denounce the Reifenbergs when the great round up came, and they were left in peace.

We first realized that sinister things were about to

happen when we saw the secret policeman in the café. The police system in Spain was always a mystery even in peace-time. Then it seemed that it was part of the Civil Guard's work to take a vague interest in any situation calling for a village constable's attention. I tried hard to discover what they did in a case of petty theft, but the trouble was that Catalans do not steal. After much thought a kind man in the village who knew I was anxious to find out about the police system because I was writing a book about Tossa, discovered that some one had once stolen a bicycle. I asked him eagerly what had happened. Had the Civil Guard clattered off on their horses in pursuit? 'No,' he said. 'The man brought the bicycle back.'

'Did the owner prosecute him?' I wanted to know how one set about prosecuting anyone.

'But the man brought back the bicycle,' said my friend in a shocked voice.

The war altered the police system in Catalunya. The old Guardias disappeared. At least they still remained in Tossa in civilian jackets and guardia trousers. They got army pay, but could not serve in the army because the Guardia Civil were not considered trustworthy. They also got seven pesetas a day extra because they were guardias. They spent their time between the beach and the café.

Instead of the picturesque guardias we had a number of mysterious people who appeared and disappeared suddenly. They sometimes arrived in large cars with POLICIA written neatly on them: then we knew they were not being secret police that day. But when the same men arrived casually by bus, one knew they were on business and it was tactless to greet them as old friends. There did not seem to be any particular uniform even for unsecret policemen, but anyone could buy himself a policeman's set consisting of a Sam Browne belt and an imitation leather peaked cap. An expensive set also had an american-cloth coat. Revolvers were not included in the sets because everyone had them.

A secret policeman was instantly recognizable because he invariably wore a very Barcelona suit with a black trilby pulled well over one eye. It was the Barcelona suit that distinguished him from an English journalist. Most of the people dressed up in policemen's sets had nothing to do with the police. They were people who had not been called up by the army, boys on leave or heavily disguised spies of both sides.

The policeman who attracted our attention at the café was noticeable because he was unpleasant-looking. Most of the Spanish officials who visited us from time to time were charming. This man looked sinister. He had a strange glint in his eye. He sat by himself and took a great interest in our party. Later we saw him again in Marks' bar. He stared so hard that I smiled politely and said, 'Good evening'. He looked very surprised and meekly said, 'Good evening', too. The next day he arrested Etta and Ilse.

Nikolaus heard the news in the village and rushed to the beach to tell us. The two girls were shut up in the house that used to be the old Revolutionary Committee's headquarters. Nikolaus wanted to go at once to see what he could do for them. We begged him not to. We knew nothing about the girls, and while it was improbable that they were spies (the fact that they had been arrested almost proved their innocence), Nikolaus was the last person who should get mixed up with the police. We decided we had better see if we could do anything. As we had British passports there was always the assumption that the British Consul would have to do something if we were arrested. We forbade Leon to go near the 'prison', and advised Nikolaus to keep right out of the whole affair.

We found a very angry carabinero on guard at the door, who let us in at once. He told us that it was ridiculous. The girls were very nice girls; he knew them both personally. He was not so sure about the others, but the girls were all right. He told us to go right in. The policeman was away for the afternoon.

We went in, and found the Marks there as well.

The carabinero was charming. He said we could come whenever we liked and bring food and clothes for the prisoners, but we must chose our moments. He told us that the policeman was the son of a nobody, *M' cag'n Dios*, he was.

Nikolaus would not listen to us, and insisted on trying to ring up Barcelona. He had some idea that Max might be able to do something to help. The fact that it was strictly forbidden to telephone to Barcelona, except through the police headquarters, and that Max did not like him, did not seem to strike him. He did not get through to Barcelona. In an hour or so the policeman came back and arrested Nikolaus.

The day after the arrests the policeman came up to the Casa Johnstone to search the suspects' rooms. We had already taken the precaution of doing this, but we had found nothing incriminating. Or so we thought. The policeman knew what was incriminating better than we did. He pounced on a childish sketch of the lighthouse. He swooped on an electric torch and switched it on and off. It did not work, but that proved how much it had been used. Nikolaus's drawing illustrating the migration of the Jews was the policeman's real triumph. Nikolaus had coloured the sails of the shaky little boats red and yellow, the monarchist colours. That and a book with a photograph of Hitler was enough for the policeman. He turned to us as we stood silently by. 'Before I *suspected*. Now I *know*!' he said simply. There seemed to be nothing to say.

He was reticent about what he found in the girls' room. He even seemed slightly embarrassed. But he was determined that they were better under lock and key.

The next day I was down at the prison early. All five prisoners had slept on mattresses on the floor. They were not allowed to use the other rooms in the house. I expected to find the sensitive Mark in a state of collapse. For years he had slept only with difficulty and had to have a room to himself far away from all disturbances. He assured me he had slept beautifully. Every one was in the highest spirits. The two carabineros on guard, although all the jokes were in German, appreciated the fact that there *were* jokes and laughed heartily with us. They promised to warn us if the policeman was coming so that I could hide. However, we were all laughing so much that he was upon us before we knew. He ignored us all completely and stalked across the room to the double doors on the far side. Above the doors hung a cuckoo clock. He pushed it until the cuckoo cuckooed, then, with a sigh of content, he went through to his office beyond.

I decided to stay. In a few minutes Nikolaus was summoned for questioning.

The prisoners had discovered that it was possible to hear if one stayed near the doors. We all pressed our heads together to listen to Nikolaus. At first the policeman talked rapidly and inaudibly, but when he realized that Nikolaus had only a skimpy knowledge of Spanish, he shouted. I had a point of vantage by the keyhole. I saw him take up the flashlamp.

'Is this yours?'

'*Si*,' said Nikolaus.

'Ha! You admit it then. It's your lamp, is it?'

'*Si*,' said Nikolaus.

'And I suppose you go for walks sometimes?'

'*Como?*' said Nikolaus.

'I say you go for walks in the woods?'

'*Si! si!*' said Nikolaus.

'I thought so, walking in the woods, eh? *Along the cliffs?*'

'*Si, si,*' said Nikolaus.

'Aha! And I suppose you would like me to believe that you always walk in the daytime, eh?'

'*Si,*' said Nikolaus.

'That is not true. You walked at night, on dark nights, and you had this flashlamp and you signalled with it. Oh! yes, you did. It isn't any good trying to argue with me. I know exactly what you are. A spy. That's what you are. A spy.'

'*Si,*' said Nikolaus.

We managed to control ourselves. The Marks looked scared, but Etta, Ilse and I were hysterical with suppressed laughter. Presently the little man tried something else.

'Do you know Hitler?' he asked suddenly.

Actually he did not say that at all. He meant to say it, but for all Spaniards the word 'Hitler' is impossible. He said, 'Do you know Il'er?'

Nikolaus has a wife in Germany. Her name is Tilla.

'*Si! si!*' said Nikolaus enthusiastically, at last understanding something.

The policeman nearly burst. This was better than anything he had hoped.

'So you know Il'er?' he asked in a strangled voice.

Nikolaus was delighted to be able to help. He summoned all his Spanish.

'*Si! si!* She is my wife,' he brought out triumphantly.

The policeman's roar of fury drowned our shrieks of laughter. He stormed out with a scarlet face and slammed his way through the room. He reached the door and stared unseeingly at the terrified carabineros who had leapt for their rifles. Then he turned and stumped back through the room. He never glanced at us. He reached the doors of his office (we could see the astonished Nikolaus still sitting there), and he stopped under the cuckoo clock. He pushed it. 'Cuckoo! cuckoo,' said the clock. The policeman sighed; his ill-humour vanished, and he stepped round the mattresses carefully. Just as he reached the door he saw me, sitting on the floor. He stared at me with what, on another face, might have been a smile.

'*Buenos dias!*' he said, and went out.

6

Prison Visiting

The prisoners were one week in Tossa. Their food was brought in every day by Rovira of the Fonda Rovira. Rovira did say once or twice that the policeman had refused to pay anything, but he told the anxious prisoners that he would continue to bring them food even if he never got paid. As a matter of fact, we discovered long afterwards that no one had remembered to pay him. When we offered to make good the damage he was indignant. It was not our affair, he assured us.

Frau Mark was released after a few days. The only incriminating things found in Mark's house were the inevitable torch lamp and a case of geometrical instruments. This proved conclusively that Mark must have spent his time drawing plans of the coast by the light of the lamp. But the policeman was fair-minded. There was nothing to connect Frau Mark with all this, except that a wife should be expected to aid and abet her husband. Therefore, with some reluctance, she was released. She went at once to Barcelona to see if her friend Max could help them.

We did not worry about the Marks. Obviously the great Max could easily get them set free. The two girls were so unconcerned themselves that we did not feel agitated about them. But poor Nikolaus was in a tough spot. He not only was hated by his own commissar, but his papers were not in order.

This was entirely his own fault. He had never bothered to get his Spanish *cedula*, or identity paper. While we had all rushed to Gerona and waited hours in draughty offices, Nikolaus had stayed peacefully in Tossa, doing nothing. He just could not be bothered. Without his *cedula* he was not able to get any other papers, and getting papers in Spain was like a snowball letter. One also frequently found oneself in the position of having to have a certain paper before another one could be obtained and needing the second paper in order to get the first. We were always applying for important documents. We used to get our five copies of this and that, six photographs, thumb prints, letters of recommendation from the Tossa secretary (these cost far more than the final document), and hand them in hopefully. In a few weeks we would get a formal receipt for all this, saying that the papers had all gone to Madrid and that we would get our document shortly. In the meantime the receipt would count as the document. Long before the document arrived the law would be changed and one started all over again and collected another receipt.

Nikolaus had not bothered about little things like papers. He had not foreseen the civil war. During the first year of the war he decided that papers were not important, although his German passport was useless in Loyalist Spain.

We hoped that Max might arrange a general release of all the prisoners and that Nikolaus would get out with the others. It would be very pointed if he alone were abandoned, but the lack of papers might give Max an excuse. We waited hopefully to see what Frau Mark had achieved.

The weather was heavenly. We persuaded the carabineros to let the prisoners slip down to bathe when the policeman was away. We also had parties in the prison. The carabineros insisted on giving a party for us. They brought their wives and families and many bottles of *anis*, and we all sat on the mattresses on the floor. Nikolaus explored the upper rooms of the house and kept appearing with lampshades on his head and large glass doorknobs like diamond rings on his fingers. We gave an imitation of the policeman with his cuckoo clock. Mark, a changed man, did an impassioned tango with the stout Etta. Archie did his ventriloquist act sitting on the knee of one of the carabineros. Only poor Leon was out of it all. There was the danger of the policeman returning suddenly, and so far he had not noticed Leon. We felt that to thrust another German upon him would be tactless. Leon kept passing along the street where the prison was, and peering in at the window. Most of Tossa collected at one time or another to see the cheerful prisoners. Public opinion rushed from one extreme to another. At first Tossencs condemned the wicked spies; then they saw that Force, as exemplified by the carabineros, and Foreign Opinion, which we represented, were in favour of the prisoners, and Tossencs wavered. Then the policeman was damned out of hand. He arrested a Tossenc.

Puig was the owner of a grimy general shop near the church. It was a dismal shop, run by the sad Puig and his two toothy, grim sisters. They must always have

been miserable, and it seemed as if Fate had decided
that a few buffets would not make much difference to
them. In three years Puig lost his daughter through
tetanus; his wife got religious mania; one of the sisters
had a foot amputated, and the Puig son, a handsome
young man with a merry eye, to make up for his family's
Right opinions, enlisted as a volunteer. It was always
funereal to buy a reel of cotton in the Puig shop, but
after the final blow it became terrifying. The old sisters
invariably started shouting threats against the Spanish
Government for accepting the young man as a volunteer; their teeth gnashed as they fumbled for buttons or
olives; they were like two aged crones shrilly uttering
curses as, with trembling hands, they mechanically
measured off yards of flannel. In the background old
Puig stood leaning against the door into their sitting-
room, his thin black hair plastered down above his
vacant eyes, while his wife huddled in a corner of the
room on a straight-backed chair frantically telling her
beads to the accompaniment of Queipo del Llano's
amusing obscenities from the Seville radio.

The policeman arrested Puig because he searched
his shop and found a store of silver *duros* and a large
quantity of oil. Tossencs not only condemned the
policeman, but started offering, in the most generous
manner, to sell one another oil. Small change suddenly
reappeared in circulation, a great relief after weeks of
waving hundred peseta notes and having to remember
what one owed. Puig was sent direct to Barcelona. We
were relieved because he would have cast a gloom over
our prisoners. But we had not reckoned on the policeman. He took our prisoners to Barcelona as well.

This was serious. We knew that Barcelona prisons

were overcrowded after the big POUM and anarchist round up. We also knew that getting released from a Barcelona prison would be a very different matter from getting out of a Tossa one. While we were wondering what to do Frau Mark came back to Tossa, not knowing the latest developments. Max thought he might be able to release Mark, because Mark wished to join the International Brigade. Max could do nothing for the others.

Archie and I went to Barcelona.

It took us nearly a week to get permission to see the prisoners. We battled our way into *prefecturas*, police barracks, secret police haunts. We waited for hours, we fought our way on to trams, we used all our friends. At last we were allowed to visit the prison.

It was an emergency prison, a pitch dark, underground collection of cellars. A few feeble electric-light bulbs burned. At the foot of some twisting stairs there was a long passage with cells opening into it. At one end were the lavatories; at the other end were the cells of the *incommunicats*. The solitary cells had solid doors and the others were barred. The atmosphere was appalling. Nikolaus and Mark said they liked it; they were semi-conscious nearly all the time. Mark said he was sleeping magnificently.

We were escorted, quite impressively, by a captain, as far as the stairs. He looked at our permits once more, and then handed us over to one of the prison guards. There were several of them standing about, rattling their bunches of keys in an important manner. The moment the captain disappeared, the guards stopped looking important and Nikolaus and Mark rushed out of their cell to greet us. We were introduced to the guards. We had brought Archie's last store of cigarettes intending to bribe them if they were unfriendly. We gave them the cigarettes because they *were* so friendly.

Nikolaus explained that the cell doors were never locked, but the prisoners had to promise to be in their cells with the doors pulled shut if the guards gave warning that some one was coming. While we were talking Etta came strolling down the stairs. She was swinging a bunch of keys on one finger. She was delighted to see us. The guards were delighted to see Etta. It appeared that she and Ilse had the run of the prison. They had the guards in their pockets, so to speak. Etta produced some chocolate. One of the guards had spent his day off searching Barcelona for it.

We were introduced to some of the other prisoners. There was a French boy of about seventeen who had run away from his mother on holiday in Banyuls. He was arrested on the train from Port Bou for having no papers. An Australian, an Irishman and an Englishman, like a not very funny story, had all joined the POUM by mistake. They were chuckling over their first parcel from the British Consulate. They had been in the prison three weeks before anyone could summon up enough Spanish to ask the guards to send a message to the Consulate. The parcel contained chocolate, English cigarettes, tins of sausages, tea, several old copies of *The Times*, and three copies of *Judge*. It was the inclusion of *Judge* that amused them. Was it possible that there was some one with a sense of humour at the Consulate?

We asked Mark if it was true that he wanted to join the International Brigade. He said yes. Nikolaus said he would rather stay in prison. We told Nikolaus we would get him out. We told Etta that we did not know what we could do for them, but we would do our best. Etta told us not to worry. Both she and Ilse were having a swell time.

I went to see Max. I went without Archie for a reason. As a rule I drag Archie with me into desperate situations, and it is usually his calm common sense that saves the situation. But this time I did not want any restraining influence. I had my own methods for dealing with Max. Archie did not approve of them.

I waited some time in the PSUC headquarters. I was glad that I had had nothing to drink. The PSUC headquarters were confusing. To begin with the windows were of different sizes, but that would not have mattered if they were all of the same shape. The big one with the sloping side was reasonable enough, but a little one looked as if it had been poked through the wall from the outside. There was another with the top slanting down and the bottom slanting up which was worrying. I was also wondering if it was a good idea to have a motoring road running up inside one's house. In any case, I decided, it should look as if an engineer had designed it and not some one suffering from alcoholic poisoning. What most annoyed me, waiting for the great man to finish a conference, was the thought that so many beautiful buildings had been destroyed by bombs and the Gaudi house was untouched. Gaudi's unfinished nightmare of a cathedral had also escaped, looking like mould seen under a microscope, while the lovely Barcelona Cathedral had been hit. But Catalunya's original architect had designed exactly the right house for the PSUC headquarters.

Prison Visiting

I will draw a veil over my interview with Max. I am a pacifist in theory, and I still do not approve of borrowing a bully's weapons to fight him with. Max was rude and tough. I was very rude and very tough. What defeated him was my utter contempt for his so-called authority. I sneered at the idea that he *could* get Nikolaus out of prison. Bullies seem to be childish. Max got Nikolaus out of prison.

Nikolaus was sent for by the *jefe* of the prison at three o'clock in the morning. He was asked to look over the objects on the table and identify his property. The *jefe* handed him an envelope with some hundreds of pesetas. 'Please count them,' he said. The *jefe* was very tired. Nikolaus found the money intact. He said that a blue leather letter-case was missing.

The *jefe* turned to the guard. He scarcely raised his voice above a whisper. 'Do you know anything about this?'

The guard shrugged. 'I saw the captain with a leather letter-case under his arm.'

'Where is the captain?'

'At home, in bed.'

The *jefe* rang a bell. Two asalto guards appeared.

'Go to Captain Moreno's house and search for a blue leather letter-case.'

Nikolaus looked through his belongings. 'There was a book of photographs——' he hesitated.

The guard looked uncomfortable. He glanced appealingly at the *jefe*, but his superior's look was blank. He fumbled in the breast pocket of his tunic. He gave the book to Nikolaus.

'It was the pretty *chicas*,' he whispered.

'Please keep it,' said Nikolaus hastily.

67

Prison Visiting

The guardia stole a look at the *jefe*. 'No, no, you had better keep it.' The *jefe* seemed in a trance. The guardia whispered: 'Do you know any of the *chicas* who posed? You might tell me——'

The asaltos returned with the letter-case. 'We did not wake the captain,' they said. 'It was on his desk.'

Nikolaus received it solemnly.

'Am I to be questioned or anything?' he asked.

'You are now at liberty,' said the *jefe*, washing his hands of the whole affair.

The friendly guard escorted him to the door of the prison. He shook hands warmly. Contrasted to the cold inhospitable streets of Barcelona, prison was warm and pleasant. Suddenly Etta appeared. She was bulging out of a dirty cotton kimono, and she looked as if she had that moment risen from someone's bed. She flung her arms round Nikolaus. He almost wept. He loved Etta. He loved the guard. The lights in the hall hurt his eyes, the street outside was inky black. The guard was still babbling about the addresses of the pretty *chicas*. Nikolaus picked up his blanket and his cushion and walked away uncertainly in the darkness. He expected to be rearrested at any moment.

Mark was released the next day. He joined the International Brigade. Frau Mark returned to Tossa, already a war widow. She enjoyed it for a few weeks and then she was bored. She was so bored that she went to bed.

Nikolaus decided to stay in Barcelona. He could pick up some kind of a living, and there was a chance of getting his papers arranged. He thought of volunteering as a stretcher bearer. He did realise that he could not continue to live for ever ignoring the fact that there was a war on.

Before Archie and I went back to Tossa we were sent for by Max. Archie was full of misgivings. Max wished to explain that he had done what he could for Nikolaus. He also had something to show us. First of all he gave us a closely written typewritten sheet to read. It was a detailed report on every one staying in our house. We seemed to have made an excellent impression. The report on Nikolaus was short: 'He seems to have little interest in anything but women.' I tried to read the signature. Archie suddenly started to roar with laughter.

'Don't you know who that is?' he asked. 'It's Puñetas. He *was* a police spy!'

Then I understood why the report on Margueritte simply stated: 'This woman is mentally defective.'

Max had another surprise. He showed us a list of suspected houses where the police thought an enemy radio transmitter might be stationed. The first house on the list was Casa Johnstone, Tossa. Max drew a line through it.

'You won't have any trouble about that,' he said genially. 'I have arranged everything.'

We had one more shock before we left the PSUC building. We met a group of three men coming down one of the crooked passages. The one in the middle was Klaus Heber. His arms were tightly held. We heard later that he was a tremendously important Nazi agent.

We went back to Tossa and Max went to Paris to see a heart specialist, in spite of the fact that I had repeatedly assured him he was suffering from nothing more than over-eating.

7

The Signaller was Learning

We settled down to our usual peaceful routine in
Tossa. The cuckoo policeman was arrested before he
could arrest us. We had been warned by carabinero
friends that he was itching to search our house, which
would have meant arrest. We took the precaution of
burying about a dozen flashlamps, relics of the night
life of our guests, but we soon decided that it was
hopeless to try to guess what that policeman might
think was compromising. So we hoped for the best and
luckily the policeman was discovered by the Tossa
mayor stealing lead piping from an abandoned house.
Tossencs prided themselves on the way they looked
after abandoned property, and the mayor actually summoned up enough courage to protest. The policeman
told him that there was a war on. The mayor retired
feeling snubbed but vindictive. When, later, he found
the policeman filling his pockets with silver from the
'prison', he fetched the police from Lloret. When asked
why he was doing this, our policeman said simply: 'I
have some poor relations in Barcelona who have no
silver.'

The new policeman was young and handsome and

liked to come up to the Casa Johnstone for an apéritif. We felt secure once more.

Leon was busy these days. He taught German and French in the mornings and Catalan and English in the afternoons. There was a group of Catalan children in Tossa whose parents were in despair about their education. They dared not send them to any of the excellent government schools in Barcelona because of the raids. The children were safe enough in Tossa, but they had all passed the highest standard of the village school, and there seemed to be difficulties about a resident tutor or governess. Leon as usual filled the breach.

There was plenty of work for us in the garden. We had Oskar's garden to look after, and we planted every available bit of earth with vegetables for the winter. Tossencs scratched up all the possible land far up into the hills and planted potatoes, maize and turnips. Every one realised that it would be a lean winter. No one had much faith in a rationing system. We were the only people in Tossa who really believed that the Government would evolve some way of distributing and rationing food for the winter. We resolutely refused to hoard sacks of beans and maize. We were lucky about oil because we still continued to receive every month the twenty-gallon container that we had had when we were a peace-time hotel. For some reason the firm had never countermanded the order. Oil was almost unobtainable in Catalunya, and there were heavy penalties for hoarding it, but the Gerona firm filled our container month after month for nearly two years after the war started.

Archie's landscape gardening was beginning to show

results. His rock gardens were full of colour; the main slope was entirely covered with Californian poppies, from deepest flame to palest pink; the oleanders were tall trees, and the eucalyptuses were as high as the house. We were inspired to do great things with the garden. We planned to open up the wild part behind the house and to make a huge rockery. We had enough money to pay for labour and really big rocks. My book was selling well, and our occasional guests were keeping us. We had plenty of leisure and energy. But there was no labour and no materials. We were relatively rich because what little money we had was in pounds sterling; we also had plenty of leisure, but we were helpless without materials, even if we could have done the heavy work ourselves. We were not the only people in this paradoxical position. Every one who had pesetas realized that it would be better value to use the pesetas as quickly as possible, to improve property or buy goods. The fishermen became desperate in their efforts to get rid of their money.

For some strange reason fish prices had not been controlled. Actually all prices were uncontrolled in that it was impossible to buy anything at the controlled prices, but there had been no attempt to cope with the fish situation. Fish prices were fantastic, out of all proportion to the cost of living or supply and demand. It was hard to compare pesetas with any other currency, because there were always at least three rates of exchange: the official Government exchange which bore no relation to the real value of the peseta; the outside exchange which was about double that of the official rate, but which was legal; and the black or illegal exchange which was eight or ten times the official rate and which was nearer the real value of the peseta than the others. The only way to get a relative idea of values was to compare costs and wages with before the war.

One night a boat with a crew of eight sold its catch for 175,000 pesetas. Our total expenditure before the war on buying our land and building the house was around 50,000 pesetas. Even allowing for a substantial rise in the cost of living, it was fantastic that a boat could earn, *night after night* for several weeks on end, three times the value of a hotel. It added to the unreality to think that at least half the night's work consisted of lying down in the boat sleeping. The fishermen amassed pesetas and tried to spend them. They did have the advantage of being able to go to Gerona, Olot or Figueras to search for food. There was still enough food for every one, but only those with piles of pesetas could afford it. The Government complained it could not issue rations because people *would* pay enormous prices for contraband goods, and the people retorted they were forced to buy 'behind the counter' because the Government did not issue rations. The retailers complained they were forced to charge exorbitant prices because fish prices were so high. The fishermen complained when they could not spend their pesetas. They wanted to improve their houses, to buy furniture, to build.

For a few months they could do this; then one thing after another ran out. The fishermen accumulated stores of paper called pesetas. They tried desperately to spend them. They went to Barcelona and had huge meals in the 'Ritz' and the 'Majestic'. They thought nothing of paying the equivalent of two or three pounds for one course. They worked harder trying to spend their money than they worked earning it. They racked their brains to think of new ways to use it up. It never struck any of them to give it to some of the people who needed it. There were plenty of refugees from other parts of Spain who were forced to live in the poor quarters down by the docks, whole families to a room, in the most bombed quarters of the town. There were empty flats in the richer parts of Barcelona, but the refugees could not afford to live there. There were plenty of Barcelonese who could not pay the high contraband prices for food. The fishermen were not concerned. All their lives they had been hard working, poorly paid, and at last they were getting their rights. They were earning lots of pesetas even if they did turn to paper in their pockets.

Fish prices were indirectly responsible for a tragic air raid on San Feliu, a little port five miles by sea from Tossa.

The fascist espionage system in San Feliu was extremely efficient. A ship could hardly be five minutes in the port before the enemy planes appeared. The fascist idea seemed to be to terrorize the town, not to hit the ship, no doubt under the assumption that the infuriated townsfolk might insist on the port being closed. While one ship was unloading in the harbour, planes raided the town twice a day for a week, exactly at seven in the morning and five in the afternoon. Naturally the townsfolk retired to the hills at five minutes to seven and at five minutes to five. We, five miles away, hurried to see that all the windows were open. We invariably forgot one.

This was a little window in my sitting-room. I had had great difficulty with Mark about this window. He declared it spoiled the line of the house; I said I wanted that particular view. In the end I got my window, but during the intense San Feliu bombings I began to see Mark's point of view.

The effect of the raids on our house was strange. In Tossa itself there was a great deal of noise and no concussion; on our hillside, nearer to San Feliu, there was hardly a sound except the violent rattling as every door shook in its frame, and the house rocked. With the windows open the glass rattled a bit, but remained intact; this horrid little window, invariably forgotten, had its glass cracked at seven o'clock and the bits fell out at five o'clock.

The next day the glass-less window merely kicked slightly in its frame. After a few days we found which of our five carpenters had made this window, and he put in a new glass. The next day it was broken again. This time the carpenter was discouraging. He said he could not get any more glass. There was none left in the whole of Government Spain. Archie did a neat job with grease-proof paper. This was alarming until we got used to it. It resounded like a drum at each raid and Beetle thought she had run into a spell of shocking thunderstorms.

After a week the ship sailed away from San Feliu and the raids ceased. The town appeared devastated as we looked down on it from one of the surrounding hills. In the actual streets the damage did not appear so enormous. Shops were open again and people leading normal lives. But from above every gaping roof was visible; one looked into hollow shells of houses. It gave the impression that some malicious giant had ripped off the tiles and scooped out the contents of the houses with his hands. In some places he had just pushed the houses together and tossed the debris into space.

In these fourteen raids ten people were killed and about twenty injured. The destroyed houses were mostly in the poorer parts of the town. In San Feliu the hotels and rich people's dwellings were near the port, which protected it considerably.

A few weeks after the bad raids a single Savoia seaplane came leisurely over Tossa. It was that brief moment of dusk when the sun had just disappeared behind a hard line of hills and everything was suddenly etched sharply and clearly for a breathtaking second before darkness whipped a smoky veil over everything. The old men and women were hauling in the last net and the big plane circled slowly over the toiling lines of black figures. We watched it. We knew from the note of the motor that the bomber was heavily loaded. That meant it probably would not swoop down to machine-gun the tempting target, but it might let loose a couple of bombs. However, it circled the lighthouse and then crossed the village and flew over our house towards San Feliu. We waited. Then it came. Just one terrific crash as all the bombs were released at once.

We were so concerned about the stability of our house that we forgot the people on the beach until we heard their shrieks. The two orderly lines of hauling figures had broken up in confusion. They rushed shrieking in all directions. We could see the two Reifenbergs trying to calm the hysterical women. We ran down to help and presently order was restored. The Reifenbergs thankfully came with us for a drink at the café. They had had their bad few minutes while the plane was overhead. The rest of the people pulling in the nets did not take much interest until they heard the bombs explode. Then they were convinced that their last hour had come. We gave up trying to convince them of the luck of being alive to hear the bombs explode.

San Feliu was not so lucky. We went over there with the friendly policeman on his investigations. The bombs had fallen in the centre of the town. One had struck the *ayuntamiento*, killing the mayor and fourteen councillors. The rest fell in the middle of the *paseo*, which was filled with people taking their evening stroll. There were over a hundred casualties; it took several days to collect all the pieces of human wreckage from the tree branches.

On the way back to Tossa I asked the policeman why no warning had been sent to San Feliu from the Tossa lookout. The Tossa headland commands a perfect view of the headland at San Feliu. The Savoia was visible for ten minutes before it reached Tossa and it circled round the village for another five minutes at least. It was going so slowly that it took five minutes to reach San Feliu. Surely it was possible for the signallers in the Tossa lookout to warn San Feliu the moment an enemy plane was sighted or heard.

The policeman shrugged and said it was all very difficult. He personally had tried to telephone to San Feliu when he saw the plane, but Gerona did not answer.

I was horrified. 'Do you mean to say that to telephone to San Feliu, five miles away, you have to go via a busy exchange like Gerona, twenty-five miles inland?'

'Well,' said the policeman. 'A direct line has been laid three-quarters of the way from Tossa to San Feliu, but San Feliu has never done the last quarter. So I have to ring the Tossa exchange and get through the Gerona and San Feliu exchanges to give a warning.'

I persisted: 'But what was the Tossa signaller doing? Why couldn't he have sent a message direct to San Feliu with his signalling lamp?'

The policeman looked uncomfortable. 'Well,' he said at last. 'The boy wasn't up at the headland at that moment.'

'Why not?'

'He was on the beach pulling in the nets. You see'— very confidentially—'he hasn't had his pay lately and he has to earn some money. And with fish prices as they are——'

'But is there only one signaller? I thought I saw two of them up at the lighthouse.'

The policeman smiled. This was easier. 'Oh yes. But he was educated in a church school. He can't read or write. But he is learning.'

Tossencs were slowly beginning to understand that this war was not directed at them and them alone. At first it was plain that Franco wanted to take Madrid only as a prelude to taking Tossa. Then, as day by day villages all round us got shelled and bombed and Tossa was always missed, the Tossencs came to the conclusion that as long as there was nothing that could be called a war industry (such as a match factory) Tossa was safe. Tossa reckoned without the seaplane and Greta Garbo.

Greta Garbo was the daughter of a shoemaker. She was the most unattractive girl in the village. No one ever danced with her; no one talked with her while waiting for the post to be distributed. Every one called her

The Signaller was Learning

Greta Garbo. The only bright spot in Greta Garbo's life was that she took the name seriously. She thought she was so lovely that strong men quailed before her. She sat out at the dances content that her beauty was such that the boys dared not risk a dance. She was very thin and wore skimpy frocks copied from the latest fashion books, and not all the make-up in the world could disguise the fact that Greta Garbo's face was exactly like a peanut.

The seaplane came down in distress outside Tossa Bay. For a long while the aviator sat in it firing off his machine-gun at regular intervals while most of Tossa went up to the lighthouse to watch. At last it dawned that the man was signalling for help, so a fishing boat went out. The machine was towed into Tossa Bay and anchored just off the beach. The pilot stepped ashore carrying a handful of small bombs and went to see the mayor.

He also saw Greta Garbo.

The seaplane rocked gently on the lisping waves and two carabineros mounted guard on the beach. We watched it during our lunch on the terrace. Francisca came up in the afternoon to say that the Tossa people were nervous that some enemy planes might come over while the plane was there and that would be the end of Tossa. By teatime the carabineros had hauled it out of the water and beached it. Tossa people became still more agitated. We saw that the machine had not left when we had dinner. The next morning it was still there. Tossencs were furious. Where was the pilot?

In the late afternoon of the following day the pilot was seen driving in the police car towards Blanes. At seven in the evening a motor boat came from Blanes and towed the plane away. Tossencs breathed again. So did Greta Garbo.

Three days later a seaplane circled curiously round Tossa, and after some galumping manœuvres, which we realized were 'stunts', it landed in Tossa Bay. The pilot jumped lightly ashore carrying his little bombs, and went to see Greta Garbo.

Tossa was in danger once more. It remained so until the late evening when the pilot flew away. In a few days he was back again. Tossencs discussed lynching Greta Garbo.

By the end of the week the pilot had crashed in the sea further up the coast and that was the end of Tossa's peril and Greta Garbo's romance. Tossencs were sorry about the poor young man, but felt it was a just retribution. Greta Garbo wore deep black and looked even plainer.

8

Poet's Corner

The Spanish War grew daily less comic opera. We tried to explain our personal views to the local people, but it was not possible for them to grasp them. Catalans and Spaniards are neither hypocritical nor cynical. They had complete faith in England. England could not allow such things as the bombing of Gernika. England would protect the Basques who had always been her friends. In spite of one fact after another, all showing clearly that England was favouring the other side, the local people still clung to their belief. Even after the loss of the north, the Catalans pointed out with a pride almost equal to that of England's, that four thousand Basque children had been rescued by the kind British. Even the campaign in England against the children did not damp the firm conviction that because England was a democracy and the English had a reputation for fair dealing, the Spanish people could not be betrayed.

We were cynical. We had no faith left in anything except the Spanish people. We did think at the start of the open invasion that England and France would hinder it as much as possible if only for material reasons. When it became obvious that non-intervention was a farce and that England was unable or unwilling to do anything to interfere with the wishes of the dictators, we simply said to ourselves that it meant killing nearly every man, woman and child in Spain before the dictators could win and, as that would take some time, perhaps some one might come to their senses before it was too late.

One could hardly tell the local people that. We were considered to have much wisdom and knowledge because we were foreigners and sometimes listened to the foreign news on the radio. Progress through the village was interrupted continually by people wanting to know our opinions on the latest situation. Even Tossencs were beginning to get an idea of the immensity of the war. More and more quintas, or levies, were being called up. Nearly every family had some one serving. I hated going through the village. Although men of Archie's age had not yet been called, all the boys of Leon's age were already at the front. Leon was oddly unconcerned about it. The fact was that every one was fond of him and was genuinely glad that he had not to go. I never heard of one word of envy or hate breathed against him, even by mothers of boys his age. Leon sensed the feeling of the village better than we did. He also developed a hard streak in his character which rejoiced me. I had always worried because I thought Leon was a sentimentalist. I changed my mind about him during the Spanish War.

I found that sometimes I could not sleep. I lay awake after the news of some particularly revolting air raid or massacre of refugees, and worried about 'civilization'. Generally, bothering about civilization did not keep me awake, because I had long ago given up any hope of a civilized world, but I could not bear to think that people like the Spanish were being wiped out by people like fascists. Although I knew Catalans far better than Spaniards, I understood a little of the Spanish character, and it seemed to me to be ideal. It is always foolish to generalize about a nation and say the Englishman is phlegmatic, the Frenchman excitable, the Scotsman mean, but I think one can say that the Spaniard is charming. This includes all the states of Spain, even Catalunya. In many ways Catalans disappointed me horribly during the war, but then I realize it had nothing to do with their nationality. It just happened that Catalans had grown soft and rich and consequently grasping and selfish. They were not pulling their weight in the Spanish War. They were magnificent for the first week because they were menaced directly. Then they relaxed and settled down to a fatal Catalan indifference.

The rest of Spain was different. They made mistakes, often vital ones, but they accepted the war as something thrust upon them, and they were magnificent. The Spanish on the home front did as much for the war as the soldiers in the front lines; the Catalan soldiers were splendid, but the Catalan home front was deplorable.

I would lie awake and wonder what could be done to make the village less apathetic. I had visions of myself organizing the village; getting the girls to knit for the soldiers; getting the older men and women to work on the land with some system instead of each frantically scraping away for themselves; encouraging the *ayuntamiento* to force the fishermen to sell a proportion of their fish at reasonable rates for the village. It all sounded so simple in the middle of the night. It was completely impossible by the light of day. It would have been a herculean task for a Catalan to organize Tossa; for a foreigner it was impossible. A foreigner could do anything not directly concerned with the village life, such as run a hospital, a children's colony, organize refugees and other emergency measures. But alter the existing scheme of things by one iota—never. Passive resistance was Tossa's watchword. It defeated the FAI—it would annihilate a foreigner.

I dwell on this lying awake because it was unusual. I slept as a rule nine to ten hours every night. We have never been able to decide what Archie's full ration would be if allowed, but he had to be roused, uttering protests, after ten hours. Leon also managed his nine hours comfortably. I happened to mention that I had been sleeping badly. Archie admitted that even he had wakened once or twice and worried in the night. Leon was amazed. He could not see what there was to worry about.

We had a number of people staying with us. W. H. Auden arrived unexpectedly while we were in Barcelona and we hurried back to meet him. We found him delightful. We gave him rather an exhausting time, eagerly arguing about child education, latest books, the refugee problem, Iceland, and pictures. He got his revenge by cross-questioning us about Catalunya and Tossa in particular, and he prowled for hours about the village, a long looseknit creature with a shock of tow-coloured hair, with the eager clumsiness of a mastiff. He was entranced by the village dance and was sad when I told him he had seen the last one. The village girls had decided that the dances were no fun now that all the boys except the very young ones were away. One of the mothers remarked to me as we stopped in the market square after the dance, 'No more Sunday night dances! Well, this does bring the war home to one.' Then the inevitable question, 'Do you think it can go on much longer? Surely England will stop it soon?'

We were sorry when Auden left. He went off to Barcelona to see if he could do some stretcher-bearing at the front. We felt he had freshened us up. It had been good to listen to some one interested in many different subjects. We had discussed almost everything except modern poetry.

Later we were not so lucky in our young poets. The Spanish War seemed to attract them in droves. They drifted from the bloody battlefields to the Casa Johnstone to recuperate. They sat about the terraces or lounged in *chaises longues* and wrote tiny, tiny poems in large white books with Eversharp pencils. These they read to each other and made suitable comments. Modern poets seem very kind to each other, we thought.

We were mistaken. They occupied their evenings by reading aloud from an anthology of modern poetry, which a modern poet clutches to him through war's alarms in the same way that a political commissar clings to Lenin's works, pocket edition. After each poem there was a chorus of high-pitched criticism.

'How too, *too* fakey!'

'I think it is rather nice in a horrible kind of way.'

'My dear, have you seen this? It really is *too* Isherwood.'

'Have you been anthologized yet? Rather exciting!'

'What do you think of the new Auden?'

'Oh! *Auden.*'

'My dear, the man is completely out of touch with life, don't you think?'

After each batch of poets Archie sat down and wrote a poem on the Spanish War. It was a very short poem and it varied only slightly. It ran:

> *bullets bullets bullets bullets*
> *bullets*
> *bullets bullets*
> *bullets bullets bullets,*

The high point of the poem, according to Archie, was the final comma.

During the summer of 1937 we were never alone in the hotel. There were our 'steadies', people like Elizabeth who worked in the Propaganda bureau, Rosita of the Medical Unit, workers from various foreign relief organizations, a changing stream of nurses on leave, and people on leave from the International Brigade. Miguel was also on the list of regulars.

Miguel was a mystery man. We knew him before the war when he had a house near Tossa. He was a Catalan, but spoke perfect English, and indeed the side that he chose to show was indistinguishable from an unusually intelligent English public-school boy. He disappeared at the start of the rebellion and we wondered if we could have been wrong about him; if after all he was just another of the escaping fascists. But Miguel turned up again, working for the Government, with a perfectly delightful brand-new wife.

Concha was Catalan, with black hair and eyes that put even the Tossa sea to shame. We were delighted when Miguel decided to make his headquarters the

Casa Johnstone and to leave Concha in our charge when he went off on his mysterious errands. Naturally there were plenty of people on peculiar missions coming and going with a certain amount of furtiveness, but Miguel was not at all furtive. On the contrary, he was completely open about his movements. The mystery was what could be this work that always took Miguel where he could have all his comforts; that paid him sufficiently to allow him to live for weeks at his ease in the Barcelona 'Ritz'; sent him on *de luxe* trips to London, Paris and New York and, in between, allowed him to do absolutely nothing for months on end at the Casa Johnstone. Miguel explained it all in his usual disarming way by saying he was a member of the Communist Party.

Elizabeth was nearly as constant a visitor as Miguel, but she was not at all mysterious. We loved her. She helped us to keep our sense of proportion. The very sight of Elizabeth, grey hair beautifully brushed back under a John Frederic hat, luxurious fur coat, her neat American ankles in cobweb silk, marching through the streets of 'red' Barcelona, was reassuring. Her chief job was looking after distinguished foreigners who ventured to come to 'see for themselves'. Elizabeth showed them. One of the sights of Barcelona was Elizabeth conducting a party of British M.P.'s and their wives, all carefully got up to suit the proletarian views of Government Spain, without hats, in aged British tweeds. Elizabeth never wore her American hats on these occasions. She always had one of the very latest Barcelona creations which she perched jauntily on her distinguished forehead. Her fur coat was bought in Barcelona, her shoes, stockings, gloves, handbag also from the Paseo de Gracia. Her frock was by one of Barcelona's expensive dress designers. English visitors were always stunned. Archie called her the Queen of the Popular Front. I used to argue with Elizabeth.

'You do want the poor things to have some impression of Spain to take back with them. They just go away muttering about clothes.'

'I'll teach them to call me a red,' Elizabeth would say fiercely.

Elizabeth was no red. She was brought up in the best Washington society, and she had never really changed her outlook. She was in a dilemma when the civil war broke out. She had lived for fifteen years in Barcelona; she knew Spain as a child knows its nursery; she adored Catalunya and Catalans could do no wrong. Therefore Elizabeth became, in the eyes of the outside world, a red.

Elizabeth was a glorious snob. She had an unquenchable reverence for titles, and royalty made her positively glow. She had not the slightest conception of Marxism or any constructive Left policy. She refused to learn.

'I do not need to read about revolutions,' she would say grandly. 'I am living one.'

She was merciless in her condemnation of anything that upset her personally. An interested visitor would ask:

'Do tell me your opinion about collectivization. You must have seen how it works out in Spain.'

Elizabeth would dismiss collectivization with a wave of a well-shaped hand.

'No use at all! A perfect failure. Since the flats in my block were collectivized the lift hasn't worked.'

One day she asked me rather pathetically: 'Why is

it that people always stop interesting conversations when I come along? I like hearing these communists and people talk. But they always talk about trivialities the moment I join them.'

Perhaps Elizabeth would have enjoyed life more if she had read Marx and if she had been able to hold her own in the interminable arguments and discussions in Barcelona cafés, but she certainly could not have helped the Spanish people's cause any more than she did. She was superb in her own line. She was one of the few foreigners who were interested in the Spanish people as a people. Nearly all foreigners tried to fit Spain and the Spaniards into some pet theory of their own. Elizabeth had a healthy contempt for what she called 'isms' and 'ists'. For her the Spanish plea for the right to live their own lives in freedom was the only creed, provided the Spanish idea of freedom did not clash with that of the Catalan. For Elizabeth the Catalans were the chosen people. Her loyalty to the rest of Spain was badly shaken when the Spanish Government first moved to Barcelona.

Elizabeth could hardly have been more furious if the fascist government had moved in from Burgos. She was especially indignant with the government cars. They sailed round Barcelona flying small republican flags and ignored the one-way street rules. Consequently life was worth even less in Barcelona for the first few weeks of the Government's arrival. The Barcelonese, fatalistic about air raids, were resigned about the cars. Not so Elizabeth. She made a point of shaking her fist after each car that missed her and of expressing her opinion in fluent Catalan of the Central Government. I was with her the day she cursed the French Ambassador.

The poor man had just arrived and was generally treated with extreme honour owing to his bravery in facing the wrath of Mussolini and the bombs. Elizabeth admitted she had been hasty. We walked slowly down the centre of the street discussing the whole burning question of the Central Government's behaviour. I was of the opinion they were wonderfully considerate; Elizabeth was convinced they had simply moved to Barcelona to insult the Catalans. She said suddenly, 'The next time a car comes down the street the wrong way I just shall not move.'

There was a loud clanging behind us. I tried to lead Elizabeth on to the pavement. She walked majestically down the centre of the tram lines. There was much shouting and shrieking of brakes.

'Elizabeth dear,' I entreated, 'I do agree with you about the Central Government. I agree to anything. But I defy you to accuse that tram of having come all the way from Madrid just to insult you.'

9

Talking about Prices

Rosita, the representative of the British Medical Unit in Barcelona, was a fascinating person. Several years ago she decided she wanted to learn languages, lots of languages. So she went to Madrid and managed to scrape a living giving English lessons, and at the end of a year spoke fluent Spanish. Encouraged, she went to Poland, to Russia, Germany, France, Hungary and a few other countries. She moved on whenever she spoke the language fluently. She came to Spain again at the beginning of the war as an interpreter. Then she found herself running a hospital, and later in charge of the medical unit flat first in Valencia and then in Barcelona.

The Barcelona flat was an incredible place. The idea was excellent—that there should be a clearing station for nurses coming from England or passing through on leave. The stores were unloaded there and picked up by the lorries taking them up to the front line hospitals. Rosita had her office in the flat and was supposed to keep an eye on things in general. It all sounded very pleasant and simple.

What really happened was pandemonium. Nurses invariably arrived at the flat and then indulged in a long

postponed collapse. Rosita had to nurse them. Most of
the ones who did not break down had to have their
passports stamped and all their papers arranged for
them to go to England. This meant waiting in offices
for five and six hours at a time for three or four days.
Rosita had to see to that. While the able-bodied inhabitants went to one of the workers' restaurants for
their meals, the sick ones had to be fed at home. Rosita
did the cooking. When lorries arrived at all hours of the
day and night, the stores had to be checked, the drivers
fed and put to bed for a few hours' rest and seen off
later with the right loads for Valencia or Madrid.
Rosita arranged all this. When three hundred tons of
drainpipes were urgently needed for a Valencia hospital
Rosita procured them and shipped them down there.
She kept a check on the nurses and whipped them away
from the hospitals in time to delay their breakdowns
until they got to England, or the flat. She was in constant communication with the London office, demanding supplies of this and that and sending relief lorries
when the others broke down. She was adored by all the
Spanish authorities and the *Sanidad*, the Spanish medical service, ate out of her hand.

When the Central Government was in Valencia,
Rosita was running her flat there. There was a flat also
in Barcelona. It was a perfect example of improvisa-
tion. The girl in charge was charming, but overworked. When some of the drivers complained bitterly
that the beds were never made, she said plaintively:
'But what is the use? As soon as I make them some one
sleeps in them.'

One driver told me that he always left his belongings
in a heap on the floor with a note pinned on with his

name. He invariably found them untouched when he returned after a few weeks in England or Madrid. Except for the little matter of beds, most of the drivers approved of the chaos. They could help themselves to stores of cigarettes and chocolate and no one ever knew. The charming custodian knew very little. When some drivers mentioned they had to get to Madrid as soon as possible she opened her blue eyes wide and said: 'But I thought Madrid had fallen.'

Her prize remark was later, when she was in Valencia and Rosita was ruling the Barcelona flat with a rod of iron. Every one was very depressed because Tortosa had fallen and the road between Valencia and Barcelona was cut. Later there was a slight counter offensive by the Government troops and the kindhearted girl ran brightly through the Valencia flat crying: 'Have you heard? Great news! *We've* cut the road now.'

When Rosita took over the Barcelona flat she made several improvements. One of the drivers complained to me: 'It's sickening. We can't find anything. Everything is locked up.'

Unfortunately Rosita could spare little time to come to Tossa. She took every advantage of the Casa Johnstone when she did get there. She would arrive and go straight to bed. Breakfast in bed, then the whole morning on the terrace in the sunshine, lying flat soaking up the heat. She would come down for lunch, eat plenty of vegetables and retire to her terrace again in the afternoon. By teatime she felt sociable and amused us for the rest of the evening by recounting her latest adventures.

Archie adored Rosita. He was always very critical of my women friends and generally suffered them in the house with resigned Scottish patience, but he loved

Rosita. She filled his requirements as a thoroughly capable person; she was good to look at with her black curly hair and flashing black eyes; she was entertaining and, above all, she got things done. How we loved anyone in Spain who got things done.

The Spanish War had a fatal attraction for well-meaning but incompetent people. The Spaniards were, in their own peculiar way, far more efficient than most of the kindhearted foreigners who flocked to help feed their women and children, nurse their wounded and generally assist on the home front. If only foreign help had taken the form of sending in supplies and leaving it to the Spaniards to deal with them, everything would have been much simpler. But the average foreigner had a firm idea that the Spaniard was incapable of any kind of organization. Judging from what we saw of foreign organization, it did not seem that the Spanish would learn much.

The Spanish Government's attempts to organize Catalunya would have been funny if the situation had not been so serious. On paper everything was wonderful. The Government passed a series of new decrees about food prices, rationing, forbidding transport of food from one district to another. Every one read the decrees and agreed that they were just what was needed. Then every one proceeded to ignore them utterly.

Old Matas, our Quimeta's father, often told us that Spanish laws were only made just to give the people something to break. He ought to know. He and our handyman, Tonet, were the two biggest smugglers in the district. It was Tonet who was concerned with petrol running during the Great War when Juan March was making his huge fortune out of supplying

Talking about Prices

German U-boats, using the coasts of Catalunya and the Baleares as bases. Tonet showed us the bay near Tossa where the submarines came in. It is sandy-bottomed and fathoms deep with a natural harbour of rocks. Matas was heart and soul on the side of France in the war—he was born in France—and would not stoop to petrol running, but he did his bit with tobacco and matches, and the Casa Blanca had many secret storage places that the rest of the family knew nothing about.

I had always imagined tobacco smuggling meant slipping a few packages past the carabineros or maybe a sack or two on dark nights, but old Matas did things on a big scale. He told us that they used to take cartloads over the mountains. In the Casa Blanca there was hidden space for hundredweights of the stuff. Both he and Tonet are small men, tough and wiry and still capable of carrying 250 lbs. of potatoes on their shoulders.

When the Spanish War started the cautious Matas stopped all his smuggling activities. He was not going to be mixed up in anything like that. Tonet was noncommittal for a time and then he too said that things were too dangerous in these times. If Spain was getting contraband arms, it was not through the aid of the Matas and Tonets of small villages in Catalunya. After all, in the old days, one was reasonably sure of the friendly co-operation of the carabineros; during the war no one really knew if all the carabineros were supporting the Government. There had been cases of disloyal carabineros; that would never do in the smuggling trade.

Although the Tossa smugglers gave up their real business during the Spanish War, their experience was useful on a small scale. When it came to bringing a sack or two of potatoes up to the Casa Johnstone after dark, or creeping round the back way with cabbages, both Matas and Tonet were helpful. On a still smaller scale, such as slipping a piece of meat out of the till into Leon's basket in a crowded shop, any of the Tossa shop-keepers were experts. The restrictions were the only compensation of the war. They made life interesting.

We still clung to our belief that the Government would issue regular rations, at any rate for the winter when things would be scarcer. No one else in Tossa had any faith. They hoarded what they could grow them-selves and made long journeys to Gerona in crowded buses and trains to forage for contraband goods. The train journeys were indescribable. There were two trains a day, and the whole of Catalunya seemed to be on the move. Once Archie and I did manage to board a train at Blanes for Barcelona, after waiting six hours for it to arrive. We fought our way on to the steps at the end of a carriage and as the train started we edged our way further into the mass of humanity packed on the outside platform. Archie finally ended up perched on the buffers. It was not so dangerous as it sounds because he was unable to fall off owing to all the other people perched on the buffers. I insinuated myself between two market women laden with packages. One was carrying a duck in her bosom, and its terrified eye glared into my eye as we rocked and swayed without lights towards Barcelona, all hoping there would not be a raid on the way. An old peasant had taken possession of the lavatory. He stood in the doorway and refused to allow the jammed mass to overflow inside. He had several sacks full of chickens lying on the floor; it was his only hope of getting them to Barcelona alive. Every one was

Catalan and merry. No one seemed to mind the discomfort. They all made jokes about how lucky it was that food was short and therefore every one was thinner. '*Conservar la linia*' was good for packing trains. The old peasant in the lavatory pretended to be nervous when we stopped at a station and a frantic ticket collector tried to reach a few people from the platform. 'He'll make me pay extra for room and bath.' I looked at his furrowed old face, the wrinkles thick with filth, and wondered where he had heard of room and bath.

I think Catalans are at their best on crowded trains or trams or in air raids. They never get agitated or lose their tempers; they are resigned, but at the same time find a certain amount of entertainment in their situation. There is inevitably the comic old man, the nervous old woman, the giggling pretty girl and the handsome soldier. Add to that a few sharp-tongued market women, a couple of waggish newly-joined recruits and, however crowded they are, however late the train, there is a flood of good-natured backchat that passes the time pleasantly enough. Unfortunately Archie could not stand crowds; he got claustrophobia at the close proximity of massed humanity, so he preferred the buffers, but I could be propped up between the ample chests of two market women, unable to move hand or foot, with complete equanimity, breathing a mixture of garlic and herb tobacco. I laughed at Elizabeth for her adoration of the Catalans; I cursed them frequently for their selfishness and narrow outlook; but when it came to the point it turned out that I just liked Catalans.

Every one talked about prices. It was the one topic on which every one agreed. Prices were scandalous. It seemed that it was purely the fact of the number of pesetas charged that caused the excitement; no one went into the ethics of the high prices. It was not interesting why prices were high or what might be done to prevent further exploitation. The fact was that now *faro*, or ground maize, cost twelve pesetas a kilo whereas before the war one got a kilo for half a peseta. And so on. On the trains people were just back from foraging expeditions and were eager to discuss prices. The ones who had paid less for eggs were shouting their triumph, while the ones who paid exorbitant prices were equally heroines of the moment. Also there was the glorious excitement that a carabinero might take it into his head to search them at the station. So far the carabineros were being slack, but one never knew when they might get tough. Some of the Tossa women had had their baskets searched in Gerona with horrible results. Their purchases were confiscated and they were repaid only the prices fixed by the Government for each article. Every woman in the crowded trains felt that she was a *contrabandista*, and loved it.

It was not only the Catalans who were concerned with food prices. The mother of a German friend of Leon's came from Barcelona to stay with us. She was very motherly and very Jewish. The Spanish War was a tragedy for her and for her friends who had settled in Barcelona and had started little businesses which were to be worked up into bigger businesses. There was a small Jewish colony of elderly women whose children were trying desperately to make a new life for themselves and their parents. The women clung together; they spoke no Spanish, they took no interest in anything except gossip and news from Germany, which they still considered 'home'. They were horrified by the war and tried to ignore it. They became more and more insular. But the Spanish War was brought rudely home to them by air raids and food prices. I believe that the prices worried them more than the raids. The old ladies would meet in each others' houses and raise their hands and wail.

'I wouldn't like to tell you what I paid for this little packet of noodles. I found it hidden away under all that dreadful omelette powder. Well, Frau Kahn, I will tell you just to show—that tiny packet, it cost five pesetas, it did now. Five pesetas gone just like that.'

'Why, Rosa Silberstein, fancy paying all that just for a packet of noodles. Five pesetas gone in a mouthful as it were. Probably been lying about the shop for months. I wouldn't have bought them, noodles or no noodles. Tho' what are we supposed to live on these days? Why only yesterday I paid——'

'Frau Schwartz told me——'

'Twenty-one pesetas for ever such a little piece. She stewed it nearly all away before it was eatable.'

'Greta Rosenbaum said——'

'What are we to do? Just starve, I suppose.'

'Gerda paid four pesetas for a cabbage——'

'Cauliflowers at five or six each.'

'You surely can't have sardines often. Why, Rosa——'

'Oh! the dried ones. One-fifty each, Frau Weiss told me in the market.'

'I don't know how you manage to keep on with your *pension*, Frau Silberstein. I find it hard enough to manage for ourselves.'

'It is not easy.' Frau Silberstein looked what she was, a good-natured elderly woman harassed by extraordinary conditions almost to a frenzy. 'The Lord knows it isn't easy. The waiting in the queues nearly kills me. Hours and hours it is sometimes and then nothing for it. And sometimes the people aren't nice. They resent a foreigner buying food. But I must say on the whole the people are friendly. Of course I don't understand what they say, but they smile. The worst part is the waiting and waiting and never knowing if you will get anything or not and then if you do, the prices! But I must live. If I shut my *pension* I must starve.'

'How is your business, Frau Kahn? I hear your nephew is doing pretty well, considering.'

'He is indeed, poor fellow. But such a disappointment to him, this war. He had only just come to Barcelona to help me in the shop when it all started. Of course he can't go back now. He is very cheerful, but I often think the poor boy must be hungry.'

'Why yes, it is worse for the young people. And with prices what they are——'

'Terrible. Why only yesterday Frau Goldmann was saying——'

'What each? You must mean per pound!'

'No, I assure you——'

'It is a scandal——'

'And as for sugar——'

'Coffee——'

'Beans——'

'Rice——'

It was Frau Kahn who came to stay with us. She had had influenza and was very run down. We thought a change of air and ideas would do her good. The air was all right, but her mind ran for ever and ever in the same groove. What lovely weather we are having—yes, the lack of rain will make the vegetables even dearer, and do you know what we pay for an aubergine now in Barcelona? The new children's colonies sound so interesting, have you seen any? Indeed, they are wonderful and the children all fed on beans too, extraordinary how they keep so healthy, and beans at twenty pesetas a kilo in Barcelona. We think you are so brave the way you do not seem to mind the air raids—well, they don't come very near us, but the shop where I used to buy my coffee—and that reminds me, the price of coffee is terrible, what do *you* pay?

We took her down to the café after dinner. It was too cold to sit long under the trees, but we went up the cliff road to watch the sardine boats go out. They floodlit the beach with their big petrol lights, showing up the fishermen with their blankets over their shoulders and the smart carabineros on guard with their rifles. The carabineros were supposed to check that each fisherman had his permit to go out. Only trustworthy people were allowed to fish with lights. As there was no way of checking the trustworthiness of a Tossa fisherman they all got permits.

The boats slid into the sea, making pools of grey-green light in the indigo water. We could see the ripples of sand on the sea bottom under each light. The throbbing motor-boats each collected its small boat with the light and slipped through the silky water out to sea. The moving lights threw up the Tossa towers and the dark mass of the island as they passed. The old town was shown up as if in some giant magic lantern. Even Frau Kahn was silent for a few moments. Then she said:

'My dear, sardines! Do you know what they are fetching in the Barcelona market?'

10

Neuroses all the Way

It seems to be the fate of psychologically well-adjusted people to attract neurotics to them. Archie and I seem always to have been surrounded by the clouds of neuroses diffused by our friends. It is an exhausting business; neurotics seem to batten on normal people, but there is always the crusader spirit to make up for it. One feels one is saving some one from something.

As a rule we were fairly successful. Our friends calmed down, and got on with their work as we gradually wilted. Archie was more successful than I. He considered each one objectively as a case. It is one of my ambitions to be impersonal about everything, but I am more interested in people than in facts and abstractions. I try to deny this at times, but it is useless.

Archie and I considered ourselves lucky. We seemed to get so much more out of life than most people. When we lived in London and Archie went to work every night at ten and came home at five in the morning, we still lived better than most other journalists. When any of Archie's colleagues suddenly rang up and said they were broke and please could they come to supper and bring the woman they were living with, we always said yes. We went on saying yes even after one couple, who came to supper, stayed for a year. We never had our flat to ourselves during the three years we lived in it. Our fatal spare room housed everything from dypso-maniacs to abandoned wives. We even had a neurotic American who drugged, but we had to send her into a home.

It wasn't until we told people that we were leaving journalism and building an hotel in Spain that we began to suspect this luck. 'Building an hotel in Spain? Oh, how lucky you are.' It was true that we were lucky to have nearly enough money to build it with, but then I remembered several of the people who envied us had more money than we. A friend of ours had come into the identical amount of money that we had to start our hotel. She had dithered for five years wondering what to do with it, and still kept on working in an office, gradually spending it on nothing. Was she unlucky, or were the Johnstones just intelligent?

This was an idea. Was it perhaps more than luck that Archie was never out of a job and drinking himself to death in a Fleet Street pub? Could it be something else that gave us, on less money than many of our friends, a comfortable flat, well-cooked meals at regular hours, holidays abroad, and opportunities for seeing all the plays and films that we wanted to? No, we were just lucky. The Johnstones have the sweetest little dog, they *are* lucky. Oh dear, I forgot all the restaurants round here shut at ten; I've nothing but an egg in the house. You are lucky to be going home to a nice well-cooked meal. The Johnstones are in France, Spain, Portugal for five weeks. Aren't they lucky? I don't know what we do with our money. Did you really make that lovely jersey? You *are* lucky.

We called it luck and left it at that. We certainly were lucky in the Spanish War. We felt that we should do everything possible for people worked to death in Barcelona. We were willing to be utterly exhausted if some bomb-shocked relief worker could be sent back better mentally and physically. It was easy for us to be normal in Tossa. We had perfect surroundings, perfect climate and comparatively no danger. We owed it to the nurses in the front-line hospitals, to the Barcelona workers, to the people who really were doing something for the Spanish people, to pour out whatever strength we had.

The case of Faith and George was comparatively simple. Faith was furious because she was kept in Barcelona doing nothing while all the other nurses had been sent to the front. She mooned about the Medical Unit flat until at last George told her what was the trouble. George was a peace-loving young man doing relief work.

'The real trouble is that you are too outspoken, Faith. Nobody minds what your private opinions are, but you must keep them to yourself. You may think Mussolini is a great guy, but you simply can't say so here.'

'Oh, so that is it.' Faith's eyes gleamed. 'I thought we weren't supposed to have any political opinions. I thought we were just little Christians who wanted to take care of the wounded. Nobody told me they only wanted communist nurses. I thought trained nurses were wanted in Spain—not a bunch of political commissars.'

'Now, Faith, don't get so excited. Of course we want

trained nurses, and above all trained theatre nurses like you. But you give the impression of *having* political opinions, those of the other side.'

'Of course if you think I am a spy——' said Faith dangerously.

'Don't be an ass. No one thinks you are a spy or even that you are really in sympathy with the fascists. It is just that you have an exaggerated idea of how impartial you must be. No one wants you to join the Communist Party, but——'

'I am sick of being told what I must do by you communists. Why shouldn't I say I think Mussolini is swell? He is a darn sight better than you bullies of communists.'

'You can think what you please, but surely you must see that, to the Spanish people who are getting bombed, you are being, to say the least, tactless. If you made remarks like that at the front the soldiers would probably shoot you, and small blame to them.'

'Was it you who told the committee to keep me here?'

'Faith, please don't get this all wrong. The committee thought you had better stay around here until you settled down. I wanted to tell you. It hadn't anything to do with me. We all felt the same about it. It would be insane to send you to the front.'

'Thank you for telling me. Don't bother to tell the committee anything. I'm leaving. I'm going to work in a Spanish Army hospital. I've had enough of messing about here. And as for you——I suppose all this business of pretending to be in love with me was just some more of your communist beastliness. Don't you dare to follow me. I never want to see you again.'

Faith went to the front. She was put in a mobile

operating theatre. She did her work with savage intensity and seemed tireless. The surgeons swore by her. The mobile theatre was blown up just behind the front lines where it had been dealing with the wounded practically as they were hurt. The two surgeons, the driver and a stretcher bearer were killed. Faith crawled out from the wreckage and found herself after an hour's painful progress in the front lines. She had a wound in her forehead which partly stunned and partly blinded her. When she found her mistake she started back again and was eventually picked up by the hospital ambulance. She recovered in a week and was put in the hospital theatre. She worked magnificently, but implored to be sent back to a mobile theatre. During a big attack she worked single-handed because her assistant was machine-gunned on her way from her quarters to the hospital. The surgeons were lyrical and refused to let her go back to a mobile theatre. Faith went upstairs, pushed a dead man out of her bed, which she had not used for a week, and collapsed. She eventually was brought out to the Casa Johnstone to complete the cure.

It was Archie who really cured Faith. She decided that she could trust him. She told him all her troubles. She was now violently anti-fascist; the shock and disillusion of her experiences of machine-gunned and bombed hospitals were greater than her horror of communists. She told Archie she loved George, but could never forgive him. We sent for George. Perhaps the credit for Faith's recovery had better go to George.

Our biggest psychological failure was Dashiell Whidden. Actually I should take the blame because Archie kept aloof from the whole business. He did not say 'I told you so' because he made no comment whatever.

Dashiell Whidden was an American genius. Otherwise he was a charming young man with a shy stammer and mouse coloured hair that stuck up at the back. He was disarming about his genius, but firm. He was equally firm about his neurosis.

'You know, I'm terribly neurotic,' Dashiell would open all conversations in an apologetic way. He was not apologising. He would remark that he was a genius in the same manner. One instinctively smiled and thought what a nice boy he was. He told us the first time we met him in a Barcelona café that he wanted to write *the* book about the Spanish War.

'Oh yes,' we said politely. We had heard that one.

'Of course it is not easy to write here. I can't seem to get down to it in Barcelona.'

We had heard that one too.

Dashiell called the waiter and ordered another round. He ordered it in Catalan.

'Good God! You speak *Catalan*!'

'Oh yes, I thought it a good idea to learn the language of the country. I am determined to understand every phase of the Spanish situation.'

'Do you speak Spanish?'

'Yes, I lived for a while in Mexico. My Spanish is good and my Catalan good enough. I need to rub up my German while I am here, and I am disappointed that there aren't any Russians. My Russian is bad. But I met a Portuguese yesterday and I've started in on that.'

'Yes,' we said faintly. Then we rallied. 'Let's hear about this book.'

Three hours later we were convinced that Dashiell was a genius. Like all geniuses he had his faults. He was hypercritical. He recognized his own genius and was never satisfied with anything he wrote. He felt that way about most writers. We dismissed one after another the most notable authors of the day and finally came to rest on Mark Twain. Mark Twain seemed to be a real genius. There were no English authors even to be dismissed. Luckily I upheld the honours of the Johnstone family because *Tom Sawyer* is one of my favourite books. I also like Dickens, but after hearing Dashiell's opinion of Dickens I kept this dark.

It seemed to me that the only thing keeping Dashiell from producing his masterpiece was the opportunity to write it. He admitted that he wanted to get away from the Spanish War. He had been in turn a truck driver and superintendent of a hospital. He decided to come to Tossa with us. He thought he could get around to his book at the Casa Johnstone.

A lot of people say to me: 'You have written a book? You are lucky. If only I had the time I could write a wonderful book. It is all here.' They tap their heads. It seems to me that there are two important things about writing a book. One is to sit down and write, and the other is not to tear up everything that is written.

Dashiell sat down and wrote. It took a lot of arranging. He liked to work at night and our sitting-room, with its grey beams and white walls, suited him. He drew inspiration from Oskar's blue horses. We were not so inspired by the sound of his typewriter all night, but we felt genius must not be thwarted. I took a proprietary interest in Dashiell's book. After my success with Frank Jellinek, I was beginning to fancy myself as a book-finisher-offer. To make Dashiell produce a work of art would be an achievement.

There was no doubt that the boy was right when he repeated how neurotic he was. I was puzzled because he took such pleasure in his neurosis that it seemed a shame to attempt to cure it. It was his most cherished possession. He would carry it with him everywhere and take it out and stroke it whenever he wished.

Dashiell admitted frankly that he was bored reading or talking about anything that was not intellectually stimulating. Leon relapsed into utter silence; I occasionally got stung into an argument about the pronunciation of an English word. Out of a community of one American, one Scotsman, one German and one Irishwoman, I, the Irishwoman, had at least been to school in England. Archie was blissfully happy indulging in interminable philological arguments. While he and Dashiell were throwing Sanskrit roots at one another, Leon and I discussed the village gossip in low tones.

Dashiell was slightly impressed by the fact that I could get on with my writing in spite of numerous difficulties, of which he was unwittingly the largest. He loved to lean against my table in the sunshine, a book in his hand, reading aloud anything that he thought was interesting. He was most impressed by the fact that having written something, I did not immediately tear it up. He wanted to know how I managed to overcome all my urges to destroy or impulses not to work. I found the best way of overcoming them was to sit down at my typewriter and type. Maybe the destroying impulses should then be allowed their heads, but at least the result is not negative. Another inhibition of Dashiell's was about censors. He said he always knew that they would not pass anything he wrote, and therefore he could not write. I suggested he should wait until they did refuse to pass something before he got too neurotic about it.

One day Dashiell sat down and wrote. He stayed up all night; he was unapproachable all day, and after two nights' hard work he produced a masterpiece. It was later published in the *Nation*. All the serious American periodicals anxiously demanded more articles. It was entirely criticising conditions in enemy territory.

Dashiell was a destroyer, a permanent revolutionary. He was useless when it came to building up something on the ruins. He lost interest; he became immersed in his neurosis. He would have been a revolutionary for Revolution's sake except that his knowledge of sociology was superb; he would have been a communist except that communists have too much discipline; he would have been a genius except that he was afraid.

That was where I failed hopelessly with Dashiell. I did everything to facilitate the creation of the Great Work. I nearly drove him off his head. He was driven frantic trying to find new excuses for not writing as I demolished them one by one. He did not consciously realize that he was terrified that he might not be able to produce the work of genius. Once he was stripped of every excuse not to write it, there only remained the awful fact that he was incapable of writing it. At all costs he had to escape before his beloved neurosis became psychosis.

He escaped to Barcelona, and with a cautiously worded letter of recommendation from Archie became a newspaper correspondent. He became easily one of the most brilliant correspondents of the Spanish War. He came and stayed with us several times. He never mentioned his neurosis. Archie thinks we were successful with Dashiell Whidden.

11

Hitler Spoils a Party

When the Generalitat of Catalunya began to use the Casa Johnstone as one of their show places, we knew we were in for a busy time. Without committing our-selves too far, we had always had the idea that we should support the government of the country we chose to live in. We actually bought our land immediately after the 1934 rising when a Right government was in power. We chose to remain in Spain after the February elec-tions when a Left régime came in. We stayed on during an attempt at revolution, and remained under the Left Liberal government that succeeded it. We were inno-cently bewildered when four British destroyers tried to remove us; we were amazed when British friends of ours in Barcelona were ordered to leave under threat of hav-ing their government pensions stopped. There was no way of compelling us to leave, and when it was realized that we were not to be scared away, we were left to stew in our red juice. We realized later that it was annoying to have middle-class British property owners living un-molested among the wild hordes of blood-lusty reds. It would have been less embarrassing for the British Government to remove us.

Hitler Spoils a Party

We found that the mere fact of our existence was excellent propaganda for the Generalitat. When distinguished visitors ventured to Barcelona to 'see for themselves' they were invariably taken back to the frontier via Tossa. We were pleased to be useful to the Catalan Government and interested to see the distinguished visitors. The only difficulty was the complete inability of the Generalitat to let us know when they were coming, how many there would be, and what food they could bring with them.

In theory it was simple. The visitors would be escorted by a dozen or so officials; there would be five or six chauffeurs; a couple of camera men and several reporters. The Generalitat would bring the food. All we had to do was to provide a banquet for thirty-odd people.

What actually happened was that some frantic secretary would ring up at 10 a.m. to ask, 'Please could we possibly manage to produce enough lunch for twenty-one people by one o'clock that day.' We would say, 'Quite impossible,' and ring off. After three desperate calls, each one more pathetic than the last, we would relent and promise to see what we could find in the village and to ring back. Archie and I and Leon would then fly in different directions with baskets. The *ayuntamiento* could be counted on for permission to buy from the market gardens direct (we always did this without permission as a matter of course), but we felt there was no need to buy contraband for the Catalan Government, and the Casa Blanca could always produce a couple of rabbits; Perez generally had a cuttle fish or two concealed somewhere about his person; we had potatoes and oil. We would ring back and tell the relieved secretary that the party could start, but *they must bring their own rice*. We could give them hors-d'œuvres and then an *Arroz Catalá*, but we had not a grain of rice. If they would bring the rice we would produce a good meal for twenty-one persons.

The rest of the morning would be spent in collecting Quimeta to help; looking out table cloths; Francisca always insisted on washing the tiles in the big room, although we ate out on the terrace; Leon and I stuffed eggs, made potato salad, chopped up cucumber and beetroot, plucked tomatoes from the garden, hot in the sun, rushed down to the old charcoal woman for a lemon, made mayonnaise. Quimeta chopped up the cuttlefish and dismembered the rabbits and then I was ready to make a *frigit* of onions, garlic, cinnamon, saffron, pimentos, tomatoes in oil in a huge earthenware casuela. Then the bits of rabbit were added and fried until brown, and the cuttlefish put in last. If we were lucky we sometimes wangled a tiny bit of pork to add to the mixture. The pan was left cooking slowly with a bayleaf. The hors-d'œuvres were all arranged on their plates, the dressing ready for the salad. Then we had nothing to do but to wait for our guests and the rice.

In an *arroz* the rice is added raw and then cupfuls of boiling water. It is cooked over a slow charcoal fire for exactly twenty minutes and the *arroz* is ready, every grain cooked but separate and impregnated with the flavours of the *frigit*. It is served in its earthenware dish and should be fairly liquid.

This was roughly the menu when Prince Hubertus zu Loewenstein came to lunch, complete with press and camera men. We found him charming, and he was delighted with Tossa. When we had sent him off in good time to catch his train at the frontier, the foreign correspondents went down to the beach to bathe and the Catalan Propaganda bureau amused itself by taking a film of us and the Casa Johnstone. It was subsequently shown in Barcelona and even reached London, but we never saw it.

The Generalität never forgot the rice. They frequently brought a dozen or so extra people; they always arrived two hours late, but we enjoyed having them. Every distinguished visitor said to us first of all: 'Will you be sure to see we leave in time to catch the train at the frontier? You know our hosts are charming, but they haven't much idea of time.' The last thing the Catalans said to us, as they paid us enormous sums of money, was always, 'Thank you so much. We shall come again soon'. Then confidentially, 'Tell us, Mrs. Johnstone, did you really make that marvellous *arroz* yourself? You must have Catalan blood.'

We were occasionally asked to go into Barcelona to help with foreign deputies and to show round visitors. This was Elizabeth's great work, but she sometimes needed help. We avoided going into Barcelona as much as possible. I was frankly scared stiff at the idea of air raids. Archie rather liked the excitement of a raid, but he hated leaving Tossa. Archie was passionately attached to the Casa Johnstone. He adored our small dog Beetle. He had never had a house or a dog of his very own before. I was more lofty. I had twice been severely uprooted and I had lost several dogs. I vowed I would never become too attached to anything again.

We were useful in Barcelona as interpreters and I always felt mean when I refused to go in to help. But soon my conscience was clear. Prince Loewenstein's mother-in-law came to Barcelona.

She was a magnificent old lady. I do not know her age, but she must have been over seventy. She was frail, but indomitable. She spoke English with a touch of Irish brogue, and she spoke about twenty other languages with the greatest of ease. I never knew what her own language was.

She had no fear of air raids. The only thing about them that disturbed her was her own rage. Every one adored her in the propaganda bureau where she worked. La Suegra, or Mother-in-law, she was called affectionately by every one. She tottered from her hotel, well within the bombed areas, to the propaganda bureau every day, and in her lunch hour she went off to the Blood Transfusion Station. She was annoyed because they refused to take her blood every day. 'I have plenty to spare, you know,' she would tell them.

The discovery of the Catalan doctor, Duran, that blood could be preserved under certain conditions revolutionized the old ideas of rushing the donor to the patient's bedside. Dr. Duran was a charming man, far too modest. When a foreign doctor claimed his discovery for himself we were furious.

'You must do something about it,' we told Duran.

He smiled and shook his head. 'I am far too busy,' he said. 'And anyway, what does it matter? The important thing is the discovery, not the discoverer.'

The blood was taken in Barcelona at a special receiving centre. There was an enormous list of donors who were tapped at regular intervals. Dr. Duran found that by keeping the blood under pressure at a certain temperature it could be preserved for over a month.

Special blood transfusion vans were fitted up with small refrigerators and the blood was taken up to the front line hospitals. Dr. Duran also found that by mixing certain classes of blood in special proportions he could make it available for patients of different blood classes.

The only drawback to La Suegra in an office was her talking. She loved to talk and people liked listening. Unfortunately Elizabeth also loved talking. A visit to the propaganda bureau soon became out of the question if one had anything else to do in Barcelona. By the time one got past La Suegra in the first office, one fell into the clutches of Elizabeth. Half the conversation of both was devoted to complaining how much the other talked.

The Catalan propaganda bureau was incredibly inefficient. The actual typography and layouts of their propaganda were excellent and the printing was superb, but the matter was deplorable. They produced a beautiful monthly called *Nova Iberia* which was a work of art. It was admirable as an advertisement of what Catalan printing could be, but from a propaganda point of view it was useless. The office was supposed to issue bulletins in various languages. The French one did come out sometimes only a few days late, but the English bulletin usually was delayed for weeks. When it did appear no one had had the sense to cut out the topical references which labelled it as out of date.

The Central Government propaganda bureau, just up the street, had better material. From a purely propaganda point of view it was not too bad. But it lacked the beautiful typography and printing of the Catalans. The obvious solution did not commend itself to anyone knowing the situation between Catalunya and Central Spain. The Central Government bureau could not work under Jaume Miravitles, the head of the Catalan bureau, and the Catalan bureau was determined to keep the Central Government from interfering in its affairs. So the two bureaux worked side by side in the Diagonal despising and loathing each other. We had friends in both. We invited them to stay on different week-ends. There was a certain rivalry about entertaining their guests at the Casa Johnstone. On the whole the Catalan bureau, trained by us, gave us more notice and got in first, but once the Central Government, helped by Hitler, scored heavily.

The Catalans had fixed up a week before for a lunch party to entertain the French Embassy. A fortnight previously Jaume Miravitles had told us that Hitler would enter Austria the next week-end or the following one. Catalunya was better informed than the British Government. The day before the diplomatic lunch the Central Government bureau rang us up to ask if they could bring the American author, Rhys Williams, for the week-end. Regretfully we said no. They insisted and finally persuaded us to allow them to come out for the week-end if they disappeared during the diplomatic lunch. On Saturday morning the Catalans rang up to say the lunch was cancelled because the French Embassy had to 'stand by'. Hitler had gone into Austria. The Catalan propaganda bureau would, of course, pay for the lunch. The Central Government party, aided by a hungry Basque family in Tossa, ate it.

The Basque family were a problem for us. With the best intentions, the Spanish Government had decided to employ refugees wherever possible. They found, after two years of war, that it might be a good idea to remove the Tossa telephone from the ministrations of the Right telephonist (she was a relic from the days of the Dictatorship) and to put some one in charge who knew how to work a telephone exchange. They put in Marcelino, an intellectual Basque, and with him came his cousin, Maria, her two small children and her husband, Juan.

Marcelino looked like an early nineteenth-century poet. His favourite reading was Aldous Huxley. We thought he was consumptive until we saw the rest of the family showing signs of consumption after a month in Tossa. Then we found it was merely starvation.

I often hope that Tossa was not a typical Catalan village, but I am afraid that in its attitude to *forasters* it was not unusual. A *foraster* was anyone not from the village or nearby farms. It included people from the next village or from Madrid. *Extrangers* came from abroad and were treated kindly. *Forasters* were heartily disliked.

The Basque telephonist and his family were *forasters*. They would have been unpopular in peace-time, but they would not have cared. In war-time it meant that they were unable to buy any food.

Unemployed Basque refugees received a ration from their own government; Marcelino was working as a civil servant and therefore qualified for the Spanish Government's rations. In Tossa no rations were issued; it was a question of every man for himself. There were few families who had no fishermen or farmers among their relations, and they all helped one another. They helped us because we were *extrangers* and, although for the duration of the war, *extrangers'* stock was low, we did talk Catalan and we interfered with no one. The Basques talked Castilian and no one would sell them anything. The whole question of buying had become a matter of begging, pesetas in hand.

There was nothing to be done but to feed the Basque family ourselves. We were already feeding Francisca's family (she was a *forastera* because she had come from Estramadura seventeen years before, and Pepito, her husband, had come from Gerona twenty years ago). Thanks to our good friend Perez we could get fish at reasonable prices; the Casa Blanca and Antonia could be counted on for vegetables; there was still meat occasionally and Leon's pet butcher-woman always kept some for us; Molí Lluns, a farm out in the country, could sometimes spare us maize flour. We still had our oil from Gerona. We clung to our belief that the Spanish Government would organize rationing before the winter.

Things were much worse in Barcelona. There was some attempt at rationing, but *intercambio* or barter was the only method of getting anything. Government officials and anyone receiving a regular ration could obtain everything by *intercambio*. The Central Government talked about the corruptness of the Generalitat, and the Generalitat accused the Central Government of taking the food out of the mouths of the Barcelonese. I do not know whose fault it was that shops still sold crystalized fruits and chocolate creams at exorbitant prices when there was no sugar to be bought.

It was possible to get a good meal in a restaurant if one could pay for it. There were also restaurants for syndicalized workers and co-operators. How the other people in Barcelona lived at all was a mystery. Another

mystery was how clerks whose salaries were fifteen to
twenty pesetas a day could manage to eat day after day
in restaurants where a single meal cost fifty pesetas.
The only explanation was that every one was doing
intercambio in their spare time. But that was like the
Black Bourse, there seemed to be some economic un-
soundness or even impossibility somewhere.

Nikolaus was leading an odd existence. The old, lazy,
fat Nikolaus had disappeared. He was still a fine figure
of a man in his Barcelona suit, but he was full of energy
and guile. He would pick up a reasonable little typewriter for seven hundred pesetas and sell it again for
eight hundred. He would buy, through some intricate
process of his own, five litres of oil. This would be exchanged for twenty kilos of chick peas. He would then
promise twenty-one kilos of chick peas to some one in
exchange for a week's board and lodging. Three of the
twenty kilos would be exchanged for two kilos of flour.
Then, with a heavy sigh, he would walk steadily up the
Bonanova to the very top, where there was a woman
who would give him four kilos of chick peas for two
kilos of flour.

When Nikolaus entered the 'Ritz' bar, the Death
Merchants looked up eagerly. Death Merchants look
strangely like Death Merchants. One instinctively felt
ashamed that one had no possibility of producing a few
thousand rifles or a couple of aeroplanes to start negotia-
tions.

Nikolaus would say: 'Well, gentlemen, it is up to
you. They will have to be delivered at Barcelona and
then the responsibility is yours.'

'I suppose we shall have to trust you,' said one of the
Death Merchants sadly.

'You will. But don't forget that I am also trusting you. I think we are mutually interested enough in the whole thing not to do each other down. Of course this is all between ourselves. If any one official knew about it——'

'Of course, of course.'

'Well, that is all. I will keep my side of the bargain. Good evening, gentlemen.'

Nikolaus went slowly towards the door. He was hailed by a pretty girl sitting alone.

'Nikky, come over here. Tell me, have you got it for me?'

'Let me see, typewriting paper, wasn't it? Yes, I have got it. Have you got the coffee?'

The girl pouted. 'Oh, Nikky, how horrid you are! Don't you trust me? I haven't the old coffee here, but of course you shall have it. It's all the fault of the police. I was arrested twice last week and poor Henry had to get me out. Aren't I lucky to live with an American journalist? That Czech could never get me out under a fortnight. But I must have the paper, Nikky darling. I promised Henry I'd get it for him.'

'You get the coffee and then you can have the paper. No coffee, no paper.'

As he went up the stairs of the 'Ritz' bar Nikolaus collided with a Bulgarian acquaintance. He drew Nikolaus aside.

'Look out for the Black Bourse,' he muttered hoarsely. 'Ullstein has just been pulled in. Had three hundred Swiss francs on him. Don't take any chances.'

Nikolaus looked at him coldly. 'I never play the Black Exchange,' he said.

The Bulgarian mopped his brow. 'Lucky fellow. Silly game. Wish I didn't. Good-bye!' .

Nikolaus continued his way to the Plaça Catalunya. He had had a fairly successful day. He knew a man in Valencia who could provide a hundred kilos of rice for a thousand pesetas. The man was nearly sure he could get the rice as far as Barcelona. Then it was up to the Death Merchants. They were buying the rice in exchange for a thousand pesetas, two old typewriters, a suitcase, a box of Camembert cheese and a quire of typewriting paper. Even Death Merchants must live.

100 Ways of Cooking Cauliflower Leaves

The winter of 1938 was grim. There were no young men left in Tossa. Boys of eighteen and men of thirty-five were called to the army. The older men sat gloomily in the café reading the papers to see if a new *quinta* had been called up; the younger boys whistled and clowned hysterically in the streets. Golden-haired Emilio of the café was in Madrid; his mother sobbed quietly all day. She howled when there was no letter from him and cried her eyes out over it when she got it. Little Alfonso, our singing plumber, was a prisoner; Juan, the champion tango dancer, was dead.

The women had only one thing to say. It could not go on. It must be stopped. They were not interested in politics. Their one idea was to stop the slaughter of their menfolk. It was not only the menfolk who were slaughtered. Many Tossa people lost relatives in the big Barcelona air raids; others had friends and relations killed in the smaller raids along the coast. Any day they themselves might get blown up. It could not go on. But it went on.

The attitude to England changed slowly. Even then it was not a hatred of England and the English that was born. It was a deadly loathing of Chamberlain. Chamberlain became the worst swear word in the Catalan language. Children calling each other *chamberlains*, in a fit of temper, were hushed by their mothers. They did not curse each other as Hitlers or Mussolinis. These were invaders, hated and feared as such, but they were not guilty, in Spanish eyes, of the unforgivable betrayal of a friendly people. It was unfair, because it was hardly Chamberlain's fault that the Spaniards duped themselves into thinking that he did not mean to betray them.

The food shortage was becoming acute. In Barcelona even the expensive restaurants were forced to close down and it became impossible to get a meal without a union card. Private people could hardly obtain anything and spent most of the day waiting hopelessly in queues. In Tossa the people had no notion of what a real food shortage could be like. Nearly every one had some source of food. There were a few families who suffered, but no one was near starvation point. The Basques at the telephone, Francisca, two or three other families and the Reifenbergs were the only ones we knew about who really had no possibility of getting enough food to enable them to live.

We had to have parcels sent in from France. Loon's mother arranged it for us from Paris, and Félix Potin parcels came through fairly well. I could not say they came with any regularity—they were sent off weekly, but sometimes there would be a month between parcels and two or three would arrive in a bunch—but they did arrive. We managed to keep ourselves and our friends alive throughout the winter.

The Casa Blanca were well off because they had their farm and plenty of land. They were always good to us, and we could count on getting something in a crisis. Little Carmen, Quimeta's niece, suddenly went down with pneumonia and there was great excitement. There was no doctor in Tossa whom one could trust. The only doctor went mad during the war, but unfortunately no one did anything about it. The Casa Blanca felt it would be certain death for Carmen to call him in, but they thought she would die if they did nothing. Luckily I remembered we had a huge Jaeger blanket. I whipped off the child's clothes to the horror of the family and wrapped her in the blanket. They were still more horrified when I removed the sheets off the bed and plonked the child under more blankets with two hot-water bottles. She had a temperature of 105. The Jaeger blanket had hardly touched her when she began to sweat, and the next day she was out of danger. I produced a bottle of malt and cod-liver oil and was able to order invalid foods from Paris, and from then on whatever we said was law in the Casa Blanca; and if the Casa Blanca had food, we had food.

In spite of our parcels and our kind Tossa friends, there were bad moments that winter. It was hard to make people in England realize that we did not want chocolate, sweet biscuits, and tins of potted meat. We wanted rice and haricot beans and macaroni and, above all, flour. It is hard to imagine an existence without anything farinaceous, but we went through it. We could sometimes get fish, there was a little meat, an occasional egg and green vegetables. It sounds ideal, but one takes bread, flour, rice, potatoes, for granted. We had none of these things. We did occasionally get a tiny amount of ground maize. At first we were terribly hungry, then, as our stomachs shrank, we became fairly satisfied. The frightening part of it all was that one never knew from day to day what might still be available. That is why any system of regular rationing, however small, is better than the gradually running out of one thing after another.

We had to own that we were completely wrong in having faith in the Spanish Government. The Tossa food-hoarders were justified. Luckily our friends had for once not taken our advice, and they were able to help us occasionally. We had one big advantage over people like the Reifenbergs, we could afford to pay if there was any food to be bought.

During that whole winter we only had ten days of real hunger. We were expecting a parcel and we had scraped together our last supplies for our dependent families. The parcel was delayed even longer than usual. There was nothing to be got anywhere. The sensible Tossencs were living on their hoards; even the Casa Blanca was on short commons between crops. The only thing we could get were cauliflower leaves.

We had them boiled with salt and pepper; we braised them with a drop of our precious oil; we put them through the mincer and had them with vinegar; we had them *en branche*; we tried them raw for a salad; we cooked them and ate them cold, hot, lukewarm. Then we had a gala day. We found a turnip in a field and mixed it up with the cauliflower leaves. The day after our parcel at last arrived and we had eaten corned beef until we could eat no more, a small child came up with a present. It was a real cauliflower. Creamy and frothy, it was something we had dreamed of for days. When we tried to eat it we were defeated. It tasted like its leaves.

We had other uses for our parcels besides feeding the Tossa families. It was Nikolaus who found that Magda was in the Correccional de Mujeres in Barcelona. Nikolaus had become, in his spare time, a sort of watchdog for his compatriots in Barcelona. All the people who had deserted him during Max's persecution were now relying on Nikolaus. He was naturally kind-hearted, but he must have derived enormous pleasure out of helping those whom Max had let down. It was Nikolaus who saw poor bewildered Mark safely off to join the International Brigade at Albacete. Max had lost interest once Mark was committed. Nikolaus found him wandering about Barcelona wondering how one got to Albacete. Nikolaus put him on the right train; found him a seat among the mass of soldiers; discovered at the last moment that Mark had not thought of bringing anything to eat during the two-day journey, and procured some sausage and tomatoes. His last view of Mark going to the war was of a gentle, silver-haired old gentleman with the expression of a bemused sheep, surrounded by gay Spanish soldiers and clutching a paper bag.

Frau Mark retired to bed in Barcelona. It was Nikolaus who looked after her and brought her food. She was not ill, she just was bored. She found that it was simpler to stay in bed.

When Nikolaus told us that Magda was in prison, we felt we must do something. We had never known her well and since the POUM rising we had heard nothing about her, but we felt that she was a victim of circumstances. She was one of the many who had got swept into the POUM and who clung to it in a frenzy of mistaken party loyalty. Before the war she was a nice, healthy, good-natured girl with one idea in her head, and it was not politics.

We sent her in parcels of food and finally went to Barcelona to see if we could do anything about getting her out.

Magda was smouldering in a model prison. It must be a great refinement of torture to put a revolutionary into perfectly organized surroundings. It would be hard to find anything to revolutionize in the Correccional de Mujeres in Barcelona.

The immediate impression was one of friendly comfort. The wardresses were young and peroxided, with smart frocks and lipstick. They seemed to have many friends among the visitors waiting in the beautiful prison garden. There was a queer mixture of visitors. Old Catalan women, just back from the market, were heartily discussing food prices; two or three obvious prostitutes walked eagerly round looking at the flower beds; several Catalan business men stood about looking like Catalan business men, but oddly naked without their cigars; some sinister-looking foreigners prowled uneasily, controlling themselves with an effort from offering every one eight hundred pesetas to the pound; one or two family parties had brought the babies; a few lofty-looking young ladies, wearing hats and real pearls, kept carefully aloof among some elegant young men of military age.

No one was at all overawed by the prison precincts. They joked and laughed and behaved more like relations going to a school half-term than people with their friends in gaol. Every one seemed to know every one else. Only the hatted young ladies and the beautiful young men kept themselves to themselves.

The entrance hall was gay with flowers. Through the big windows of the visitors' room we saw a huge enclosed garden with seats and tables under shady trees. A fountain was playing in the middle of a paved court surrounded by flowering shrubs. It was the prisoners' garden. The visitors' room brought a sharp reminder that the place *was* a prison. It was divided longways by a solid table with narrow benches on each side. The doors were locked after us. The prisoners trooped in with shrieks of joy and excitement and sat on one side of the table. The visitors sat down opposite. At least that was the original intention—the table was to prevent contact—but every one leant over it and embraced and wept and laughed and patted each other, Catalan fashion, on the shoulders. The prisoners wore no uniform; their hair was waved and shampooed; they used make-up.

Magda looked thin and she stared at us with burning eyes. When I suggested the prison did not seem so bad, she shouted above the pandemonium of Spanish and Catalan voices: 'Not so bad! We are seven here, seven of the POUM! Why should we be shut up with this crowd? Why should we be mixed up with fascists, spies, traitors? Why, there are relations of Franco here! We all sit in the same room. We have nothing to do but talk. The only people we can speak to are the criminals.'

'It seems a pity to do nothing but quarrel all day. Is there no work of any sort to be done in the prison? What about knitting for the soldiers or something?'

'You cannot trust these fascists to do anything,' said

Magda gloomily. 'They would sabotage everything.'

I had an awful vision of Franco's relations unravelling during the dead of night the jerseys knitted by the POUM during the day. Even that seemed better than hand-to-hand battles. Magda went on telling about the POUM hunger strike.

'We did not eat for ten days. "We will not touch food until we are questioned," we cried. It caused a sensation. Spanish women have never hunger-struck in history. The Governor of the prison promised that we should be interrogated this week. If not we start another hunger strike. For the moment the POUM is sending us food.'

'So the POUM still exists?' I said.

'Of course it exists. It is still officially no crime to belong to the POUM. We must get free and work again. As long as we remain united, Kaete says, we seven of the POUM here in the prison can——'

Magda talked for a long time, but I was not listening to her. I was watching the other prisoners and their visitors. It was absurdly easy to pick out the different types. The fascists were lounging across the table as if they were taking a morning coffee in the 'Ritz'; the prostitutes were talking shop; there were a very few sullen, hopeless faces, probably suspected spies and, equally probably, innocent; the old *habitués* seemed rather overcome by the influx of oddities in their prison. They cheered up when they saw their old friends and soon were shouting bawdy Catalan stories across the table. Magda was the only representative of the seven revolutionaries. The POUM did not get many visitors.

Magda and I shouted at each other in German. No one seemed to mind. The wardresses wandered up and down, sometimes playfully slapping a stout Catalan behind, sometimes joining in a discussion between visitor and friend. I passed Magda some cigarettes, some of Archie's precious last hoard. A pretty wardress saw me and smiled.

'Make them last,' she said to Magda. She turned to me. 'She smokes far too much,' she confided. 'And when she hasn't got any she gets so cross!'

Magda allowed a ghost of a smile to light up her dark face. The pretty wardress went on: 'We do have some terrible rows here, you'd never believe. These politics are awful. Goodness me, give me a few of the old timers for peace. We sometimes have to call them in to help break up the quarrels. They don't like it, you know. They feel the place isn't what it used to be.'

A whistle blew. The wardresses began to call above the babble. It was time for the visitors to leave. Immediately the Spaniards and Catalans burst into tears. A few moments before they had been laughing and joking; now, at the moment when the average English person feels laughter and jokes a necessity, they gave rein to their feelings. The wardresses patted them on the backs and tried to console them. The fascists swept out first, the criminals, who did not know that in the eyes of the law and the Spanish Government all men were equal, respectfully allowed them to pass through the narrow door. The old timers pushed and shoved among themselves, but hastily made way for Magda as she stalked out, brooding darkly. They seemed positively scared of the POUM. I felt sorry for the old lags of the Correccional de Mujeres.

We got Magda out of prison. The authorities seemed glad. She immediately resumed her Poumist activities and was rearrested. We again sent her in food from time to time, hoping that if she was busy hunger-striking the old lags might profit by it.

Safely back in Tossa, still having missed an air raid, we found a telegram from Mexico City:

GOIG VINGUT BONAMENT. FRANK.

After some time we came to the conclusion that Frank Jellinek was the proud father of a son. This was confirmed later by a letter from Margueritte:

'Dear Nancy . . . It was rather difficult as I seemed to have calculated all wrong. I quite thought Goig would arrive next month, but he decided to make his entry into the world just as we were between two houses. You can imagine the muddle. I went into a hospital in Mexico City and left Frank to do the final packing. So of course I was in the hospital without even a toothbrush.

'Goig is rather nice—his other name is Roger—he looks exactly like Frank when he is asleep (when Goig is asleep, not Frank), and then he opens his eyes and looks like me. Frank is disappointed because he can't talk. Says he is no use because he never answers when Frank talks to him about the coming invasion of Czecho-Slovakia. Frank can't think why we bothered to have him at all.

'You would like this place, although I think to enjoy Mexico you shouldn't see Spain first. When we get settled it'll be a good place. At the moment it is rather difficult as I have just come out of the hospital and find that Pepe, the new gardener, has been sabotaging the maid. He wants a cousin of his to have the job. I came back to the new house to find Maria (the maid) in tears and the cousin also installed. It was all rather awkward. One doesn't feel like battles after having a baby. But I can't very well throw out the cousin for Pepe is such a good gardener. At least he isn't such a good gardener exactly, but he always remembers to put hot water bottles in my bed.

'I know you don't approve of Frank and me having Goig, but I think you would like him. Did I tell you he looks like Frank when asleep? Oh yes, I did. Won't that surprise a lot of people in Barcelona. . . .'

13

Next Door to a Bomb

Nikolaus was feeling happy. He had arranged everything at last. He was going to be a stretcher-bearer. A friend of his, head of the Swiss Red Cross in Spain, had fixed everything for him and it was only a question of getting an O.K. from the PSUC. Nikolaus knew that Max was back from seeing a Paris heart specialist. He also knew what was common knowledge in Barcelona, that the specialist had advised Max not to overeat because his stomach pressed on his heart. But what really encouraged Nikolaus was that the head of the unit had written a personal letter to Max demanding the O.K. There were limits to Max's authority.

Nikolaus went up to Max's office in the PSUC building. He wanted to be a stretcher-bearer more than he had ever wanted anything. He had grown to love Spain and he understood the difficulties of ever being allowed to do anything without his papers in order. As a stretcher-bearer he would be given papers and he would be helping Spain. The head of the Swiss Unit had impressed on Nikolaus the shortage of stretcher-bearers. There were many casualties in the medical units in the days of totalitarian warfare.

Max was sitting at a desk. He looked thinner and his face was an ugly grey colour.

Nikolaus smiled. He felt quite friendly towards old Max.

'I was told to report to you for the final arrangements,' said Nikolaus easily.

'What arrangements?' said Max coldly.

'The final papers for me to go to Albacete.'

Max stared. 'Why should you go to Albacete?' he asked.

'Why, to take up my job with the Swiss Medical Unit. It is all arranged. There only remains your endorsement to the papers enabling me to go to Albacete. You have had a letter about it from the head of the Unit.'

'I have had no letter,' said Max.

Nikolaus stared at him. Max looked steadily back at Nikolaus.

'But you must have got that letter,' said Nikolaus.

Max said: 'It is a regrettable fact that letters frequently get lost between here and Albacete.'

'It was posted here in Barcelona.'

Max smiled. 'I know nothing of any letter.'

Nikolaus felt himself sweating. 'But you must have got it. It was from Heinz. It was arranging everything. He wrote it here before he left. He posted it here because of the unreliable posts from Albacete. You must have the letter. Can't you ask some one if it has got mislaid?'

'I am not at all interested in the letter.' Max tapped gently on the table.

Nikolaus stared at him. 'So that is it. You are determined I shall not be a stretcher-bearer.'

Next Door to a Bomb

'I have not the slightest objection to you being a stretcher-bearer. I told you long ago that you should go to the front. I haven't altered that opinion to-day. I still think that you should go to the front—to the front-line trenches. After six months in the trenches with a rifle, I shall be delighted to facilitate in any way I can your wish to be a stretcher-bearer. Until then I am afraid the Albacete posts will remain deplorable.'

Nikolaus could hardly believe it. He realized that Max was obsessed. He had decided that Nikolaus should go to the front, and he must go to the front or be hounded out of Barcelona. Nikolaus must learn that Max was a god.

Nikolaus went slowly out of the PSUC headquarters. He looked back at the Gaudi building, but he did not see it. The wavering lines, bulging walls, crooked windows with their jungle ironwork, melted into the rest of the Paseo de Gracia. All Barcelona seemed sinister and Gaudiesque. The tall buildings towered triumphantly over him; windows seemed horrid eyes mocking at his discomfort; the huge office entrances gaped at him. Nikolaus hurried down the street towards the Plaça Catalunya. He stopped to watch a convoy of troops going off to the front. They stood up in the lorries, singing and shouting. They were all very young. Nikolaus sighed. He knew that Max would not rest until he had driven him out of Barcelona. In the meantime he must live. He hurried down the Avenue de Pavlov, once the Puerta del Angel, and cut through to the Via Durruti, once the Via Layetana. He had to see a man about some beans.

Nikolaus need not have worried about Max. It was not Nikolaus who was driven out of Barcelona.

I should have known it was tempting Providence, or the fascist planes, to go to Barcelona without Archie. Leon and I went in for three days. We stayed thirty-six hours and got in for eighteen raids. Barcelona was raided every two hours for forty-eight hours.

As an experience it was interesting. It was hard that both Leon's and my first experiences of being bombed should have been so violent, but it gave us both a good idea of our respective reactions. We were both completely calm. Mine was the calmness of paralysis; Leon was just calm.

The first time we were in a building next to one that was struck we were in a little restaurant off the Plaça Urquinaona. The proprietor had been trying to get his customers to leave because he assured us the place was not bomb-proof. The first raid had left us pleasantly reassured. I remembered all that Archie had said about mathematical chances; I realized that there was comfort in the thought that there were nearly two million people in Barcelona and I was only one. I was surprised at the comparative lack of noise; even the anti-aircraft guns were quieter than I had expected, and the sirens hardly noticeable. I did think it odd that distant bombs caused such concussion. The proprietor was gloomy and said they must be unusually large bombs. He implored us to take refuge in the Underground before the planes came back again. We were polite but firm.

Leon swears he heard the sirens before the next raid, but I knew nothing about it at all. I found myself lying flat on my back somewhere up against the bar. Leon was coughing nearby. The air was thick with fine dust and a choking smell was making every one gasp. I was certain we were being gassed.

Next Door to a Bomb

There was an odd silence except for the coughing of various people lying on the floor. People began getting up and walking about. Someone picked up a table and put it straight. Leon was busily talking to me, but I was not interested. He says he was only asking me if I was hurt, but it sounded as if he was reading extracts from Thomas Mann. Presently I decided we were not being gassed, and shook the plaster out of my hair. Leon insisted on going out to see if the raid was over. He came back and reported with triumph that the house next door had disappeared.

It looked as if a giant knife had cut a slice out of the row of buildings. We heard afterwards that the bomb was a type that penetrates and then bursts upwards. The debris was so fine that it all settled comfortably in the cellar to the height of street level.

It was after this series of raids that Barcelona gave up trying to hide its scars. It had been almost miraculous the way scaffolding was run up to cover the indecency of a house with the front wall stripped away exposing the private taste of the householders in wallpaper, furniture and bedding. Glass was replaced or the bits tidily removed. Piles of wreckage were hastily cleared out of the streets and dumped in disused lots on the outskirts of the town. After the March bombardments there was nothing to be done. The Calle Cortes was left showing nakedly its gaping gums. The Barcelonese hurried through the streets picking their way over heaps of rubble and coughing out of their lungs the fine dust that had been ten-storey buildings.

I do not know where Leon and I spent all the raids we were in. We had business in Barcelona connected with work permits and we sometimes found ourselves in Government offices, cowering against trembling walls while seemingly unconcerned officials assured us that the reason every one was shaking even between raids was purely physical reaction. They told us that the bombs were a new type, far heavier than any used so far against Barcelona. Sometimes we waited hopefully in massive doorways with other people caught in the streets. They were extremely controlled. It seemed generally admitted that nothing on such a scale had happened before; the only people who seemed slightly hysterical were some of the well-to-do who were not used to having their part of the town bombed. Certainly the planes seemed to have lost their class-consciousness. They flew tremendously high and let loose their loads indiscriminately. We gave up the doorways when the glass covering the top of one lift shaft was shattered by the concussion of a bomb in the neighbourhood.

We tried to go down to lunch in our hotel near the Plaça Catalunya. One of the minor problems was how to get an undisturbed meal. On our way down the corridor leading to the stairs, the hotel gave a lurch, leaped lightly in the air and then settled down again as an hotel. We picked ourselves up from the floor—I was relieved that there was a floor—and shook off the broken glass that had fallen from the doors. Leon was badly cut in the hand. We tied it up and went on down to lunch. Lunch was delayed because the staff were a little disorganized. The kitchen was temporarily out of order because the bomb had dropped on a house across the court at the back of the hotel. It was a comparatively small bomb. There were presumably others dropped in that raid, but one tends to become centred on one's own particular bomb.

La Suegra was also waiting for lunch. She was so angry that she was incoherent in twelve languages. She had recovered her poise and we had started our soup when the house actually adjoining the hotel was struck. La Suegra was magnificent. She tottered round the wrecked dining-room, patting whatever part of people's anatomy projected from under tables saying '*Tranquilise-se*' in the clearest tones. I lay for a while under my table pondering on the absurdity of the Spanish language. Leon came up smiling, shaking bits of plates out of his front curl. We were nearly all asphyxiated by the dust and the half-pungent, half-sickly smell of the explosive. I did not much care if it was gas. Archie might be good at mathematics, but these airmen obviously could not count. I decided that whether the Tossa bus left or not that day, I was going to leave Barcelona.

The Tossa bus left on time. All the passengers except four were sitting in the bus a good hour before it was due to start, but the driver, although white and shaken, insisted on waiting until the scheduled hour. It was unpleasant because we waited in the newly wrecked station yard. A bomb had dropped through the restaurant. It was gutted except for one iron girder projecting ineffectually into space. From it hung an enormous glass chandelier, intact. It swayed gently in the smoke rising from the debris on the floor, tinkling merrily. Underneath it the firemen were dragging out their grisly finds.

At last the four passengers arrived. They leaped into the bus, the driver let in the clutch and we tore out of

Barcelona. As we dashed through the suburb of Badalona we heard the Barcelona anti-aircraft guns once more.

I had satisfied myself on several points. One was that air raids were much worse than I had imagined even in my worst moments. Archie pointed out that I had chosen the most violent series of raids and therefore they proved nothing. He still stuck to his theory of the mathematical chances, and declared that the dangers of air raids per person were much over-rated. I almost had to agree with him. Even after forty-eight hours of bombing, on a huge scale, the Barcelonese were still holding out. But I think that another forty-eight hours would have finished the war. The very concussion alone of these great bombs paralysed people. It seemed to me that after five or six days' continual bombing, using high explosive bombs, an army could just walk into any city and encounter complete apathy. An edifying thought in our age of civilization.

Nikolaus showed heroic qualities in the raids. He confessed he was scared, his feelings were not stunned like most people's, but he ran about between raids and looked after his friends. Frau Mark was still in bed; various old ladies of the German Jewish colony were prostrate; Gretel was ill and abandoned. Nikolaus must have enjoyed being a ministering angel to Max's woman. Max would trouble Nikolaus no more. He left Barcelona after the first day of raids. He never returned. Paris was more suited to an overloaded stomach.

Back in Tossa I watched Leon closely for any re-action. I had heard that these brave people crack up sooner or later. He was boyishly excited about his adventures and the village streamed up to listen to his accounts of a real air raid and to see his war wound. I listened to him from my comfortable *chaise longue* on the terrace. I felt like a wrung-out dish-cloth. Leon whistled at his work and sang as usual unless stopped. Then one day he sat down to write a letter. It was a long letter, it took him the whole morning. It started, 'My dear Mother, I have been bombed.'

14

And there was Light

'Seen Swire?'

'No, he isn't back from the front yet.'

'No more news?'

'Not until Swire gets back.'

'I've sent off the black-out story.'

'Funny, we've got light here.'

'Oh, well! This is the "Ritz".'

'Swire is a great guy.'

'By God! he earns his pay. Every day lying about on rocks hoping not to get machine-gunned. Filthy job, Reuters. Thank heavens I'm on a nice quiet weekly.'

'I think he enjoys it. He is interested in military matters.'

'It's very convenient for us having first-hand news every night. Nice to know where one is.'

'Where Franco is, you mean.'

'Hell, do you think the war is over?'

'I don't know. Funny people, these Spaniards. Never can tell what they'll do.'

'The fall of Lerida was bad enough, but now they have cut the light and power.'

'Damned annoying. I fought my way on to a tram and the blasted thing went dead on me.'

'Look at those bloody Death Merchants over there. A lot of use they are.'

'Oh, I don't know. I was talking to the Gangster to-day. He assured me that arms were coming in.'

'Like hell. By the way, I forgot to tell you. You know that pretty little Asturian girl who is staying here?'

'The one who used to live with that American?'

'Yes. Damned embarrassing. She was sitting right next to me and the secret police pulled her in. Apparently she is a dangerous spy.'

'That is absurd. She obviously isn't a spy.'

'Don't tell me you can be deceived by a pretty face.'

'Of course not. But if she really was a dangerous spy the police would not have arrested her.'

'Oh, they must strike a bull's-eye sometimes. Law of averages, you know. Good God!'

'What's the matter?'

'There she is! The Asturian girl. They've let her go.'

'Ah! then she may be a dangerous spy after all.'

A large man walked into the bar, rubbing his hands. He was a Bulgarian.

'I feel like God,' he remarked, and commanded that a drink be brought.

'Why?' asked some one.

'I have just given Barcelona light and water,' he said complacently. 'Just a little matter of adjustment. We have been expecting this to happen.'

'Wasn't there any water?' asked some one. 'I wish I'd known that. Headline stuff.'

'A wonderful story altogether. Panic-stricken Barcelona. Without Light or Water.'

'Yes, but Barcelona doesn't seem to be very panic-stricken.'

'No. It never is. But it should be. England expects that every Barcelonese shall be panic-stricken.'

'The trouble is that Barcelona is quite used to being without light and water.'

'Why was there no water? I know that the fascists have taken the power station near Lerida and have cut the light.'

'Well, there actually *was* water in the street fountains as usual. It was just that the electric pumps weren't working to pump the water into the high houses.'

'But there is water now?'

'Oh yes, there is now.'

'And light?'

'Oh yes, there is light.'

'And the trams working and everything?'

'And everything.'

'Rather wise of the Barcelonese not to get panic-stricken.'

A correspondent called Salter strolled up to the table. He produced a packet of cigarettes and handed them round with easy nonchalance. No one hesitated. Cigarettes were so scarce that if anyone threw away a butt it would never reach the ground. But no one ever threw away butts. They had to be unrolled and mixed together and rerolled almost indefinitely. If any one received a cigarette from a friend he was in honour bound to return the butt. The group of correspondents watched Salter's elegant figure as he went up the stairs. An American journalist asked:

'Does anyone know anything about that chap?'

'Yes,' said some one. 'He is fond of dogs.'

146

The fragrant English tobacco smoke curled softly into the air of the 'Ritz' bar.

Someone clattered down the steps.

'They've cut through to the sea,' he said.

'What, again?'

'No, this time it is true.'

'So what?'

'Where the hell is Swire? He ought to be back by now.'

'Perhaps he is trapped in Tortosa.'

'Seriously, has Tortosa fallen?'

'I don't know. But they are certainly through to the coast.'

'Here is Swire at last.'

Joseph Swire walked into the 'Ritz' bar. He clambered heavily down the stairs in his thick field boots. He looked tired to death, but he smiled his usual charming smile through his black moustache.

Everyone shouted to him at once. He looked wearily round and raised his hand.

'I must get off at once for a bath and then bed,' he said. 'I'm off to the Tremp front at dawn. No, of course they aren't through to the coast. I've just come from Tortosa. They are holding splendidly.'

Archie and I were watching the dancing in the 'Ritz' supper room. We were with Miguel and Concha. Why we were there at all, none of us knew. We did not feel like dancing. Having got there, we found it was impossible to leave. There was an atmosphere of such unreality that we, who are sick of realities, clung hysterically to our chairs. We knew that Tremp had fallen; we knew that Tortosa was bound to fall, even if it were but a dead shell that the fascists captured; we knew that the road from Barcelona to Valencia would be cut, thus dividing loyal Spain in two. But we sat at our table in the 'Ritz' supper room, watching the dancing couples, the opulent diners; wondering when the next raid would start; wondering if by any chance the fascists had already taken Barcelona and were celebrating their triumph in the 'Ritz' supper room.

I came to the conclusion that this was not the case. The dancers and diners certainly looked fascist enough, but there was a tenseness in the atmosphere in spite of the careless air of make-believe. I felt that we were all waltzing determinedly in the St. Petersburg Embassy while the mob howled at the gates. I expected every minute to see the grave, white-haired figure of the Ambassador and to hear the well-known, 'Keep calm, ladies and gentlemen. Whatever happens the dance must go on.'

My mind was dwelling on embassies and it was natural to be a little bewildered about whether we were on the side of the mob or the ladies and gentlemen. I had only that day visited the British Consulate at Caldetas.

A week previously the American Consul and First Secretary to the Embassy, embodied in Mr. Douglas Flood, called at the Casa Johnstone. We had heard about the Americans. They had clung to Barcelona long after the other consulates, headed by the British, had taken refuge in Caldetas, a little village with an hour's run if you had a car; six or seven hours by train. We found, judging by Mr. Flood, that rumour had not lied when it was said that the Americans were grand people.

Mr. Flood was sad. Washington was insistent that the Consulate and Embassy should move out of the bombing area. The question was, where to? Caldetas was out of the question, it was now a British colony. Mr. Flood had hankerings after installing the American Consulate and Embassy in the Casa Johnstone.

'We would be willing to pay in any currency you liked,' he said. 'Have you any idea about the rent?'

We had no idea.

'Well,' went on Mr. Flood. 'Roughly I should think we could offer 350 dollars a month.'

We asked what that was in pounds.

'A bit under seventy pounds.'

'A month?' we asked.

'Yes, a month.'

We stared at each other.

'But that is ridiculous,' we burst out together.

Mr. Flood looked hurt. 'I couldn't undertake to offer more without consulting——' he began.

We hurriedly explained. We meant it was far too much. Mr. Flood must have thought we were a little mad. Finally we agreed to take fifty pounds, if the house should prove suitable. It suited Mr. Flood personally, but, after asking us some questions about the time taken by normal means of transport from Barcelona to Tossa, it did not suit Mr. Flood, American Consul and First Secretary to the Embassy and representative of the American citizens who might have to visit the Consulate from Barcelona. In the end they took a house near Caldetas, but outside the British zone.

We had consistently avoided visiting Caldetas. There were many rumours about the fascists that clustered under the shadow of the Union Jack. We had, however, one rigid rule. We refused to believe rumours until we had substantiated them. We kept an open mind about the reported Badajoz massacre because we had no evidence; we believed that refugees were machine-gunned because we had seen women and children with bullet wounds. Similarly we gave the Government the benefit of the doubt about nun-rapings because we had only met un-raped nuns, but we condemned openly and loudly the habit of arresting the wrong people and keeping them months without a trial.

We applied our rule to the stories about the British Consulate. Then we saw for ourselves.

We went to Caldetas to ask Consular advice about the situation in Spain. That will show how we obeyed our own rules. The first impression of Caldetas was upsetting. We stepped straight into an atmosphere of happy holiday crowds. Beautifully dressed Catalan girls tripped about swinging tennis rackets; young men of military age lounged on the beach; straight-backed elderly British matrons sat reading the banned *Daily Mail*; their public schoolboy sons, with jobs in the Consular service, strolled about the front. No one discussed the war. One party was arranging to go over to Arenys to the cinema that night; another complained that there was no tennis court free.

We got on beautifully at the Consulate. For the first ten minutes we discussed our mutual dislike of terror. Then slowly a terrible fact became glaringly clear.

We were talking about different terrors.

I must say they controlled themselves admirably. It was an unprecedented situation. Instead of crawling at their feet, imploring to be saved from the reds, here were two British subjects suggesting that there might be a fascist terror.

* * * * * * * *

And there was Light

Barcelona was plunged in unreality. The Aragon retreat went steadily on. Every one talked about the arms that were supposed to arrive. Rumours became wilder and wilder. The Barcelonese were calm. They decided that they might as well enjoy life while they could. There were no air raids. They danced, they drank when they could get anything to drink. For the first time I saw one or two drunks in the streets. We caught the prevailing nightmare atmosphere. Nothing was tangible. We expected to waken to find ourselves back in the warm, sun-baked realities of Tossa.

There was one reality which needed all our attention. The problem of Leon was acute. His parents were in a state of panic. They sent wires imploring him to go to Paris. Leon did not want to go. In the end we all decided he must go. In face of these frantic demands our responsibility was too great.

It was not so simple just to go to Paris. There were stamps and documents to be obtained. The usual Catalan conspiracy to prevent one from getting even a plain stamp was in full swing. They arranged with fiendish joy so that two queues, one of people wanting passports stamped to leave and the other of people wanting permits to stay, should converge at the same door. For the permit to leave there was a list of questions to be answered, all of which had to be copied on official paper, with several stamps and a photograph. The cunning Catalans had pinned up a copy of the questions *inside* the door, so that one had to take turns in the queue with the people wanting permission to stay; get inside and copy out the questions; rush into the town to buy the official paper and stamps, have a photograph taken, and then go back and stand in the queue all over again.

When it became known and people started merely copying the questions from those in the queue who had already obtained them, the Catalans subtly altered the questions from time to time. Actually the Catalans were completely innocent of guile. It simply never struck them to organize things better.

Leon naturally got all his permits with the minimum of trouble. He even obtained his French visa without waiting all night in a queue. We were never seriously concerned about his ability to get his permits, but we did wonder how he was going to get out of Barcelona. Transport was an acute problem. It was impossible to get on the few trains; lorries were all being used to rush men and such munitions as there were to the front. Leon smiled at a French truck driver who had brought in food supplies, and he took him all the way to Paris.

We had one more contact with the Consular service.

In the ante-room we found a destitute British seaman; and any bitterness I may have felt towards the officials evaporated when I talked to him. He was a wild-looking young man in dirty dungarees and a jersey full of holes.

'What do you think you will get out of the British Consul?' I asked, thinking of my own lack of success.

He laughed. 'I know just what I'll get,' he said. 'I'm used to consuls. Know 'em all over the world. They 'ates me, but they 'as to do something for me.'

He explained that he had deserted from a merchant ship. He had stowed away on another ship in Marseilles without knowing where she was bound, and he had found himself in Barcelona. He thought Barcelona was a fine town. He had been there a fortnight.

'Didn't you have any trouble with the Spanish authorities?' I asked.

'Bless you! I ain't never seen any. I slept down at the docks. I 'ad three pounds and I'd like to tell you what I made those three pounds do! Cor, what a town!'

What a town, I thought. What a war, when any one can land off a ship and spend a fortnight sleeping at the docks and no one the wiser.

He went on happily. 'So 'ere I am for them to send me 'ome. They 'as to do it, you know. I've been sent 'ome D.B.S. from every port in the Mediterranean at one time or another.'

'This Consul will be unpleasant,' I remarked.

'They always is. But it don't matter to me. 'Oo is this bloke? Oh, I know '*im*. Sent me back from Alexandria. Well, well, ain't it a small world.'

'Good luck,' I said as I left.

'Thanks, but I don't want no luck. They 'as their orders. They 'as to do it even if it 'urts.'

15

Spanish Customs

There was a fascination about Barcelona in those fantastic April days. We were forced to stay by the mere fact that values changed from minute to minute. Rumours flew round; the war was lost; some one had seen a thousand Russian tanks with snow on their boots; Moors were galloping through Sitges; Italians were chugging towards the doomed city; there were truckloads of ammunition pouring through the Pyrenees; the road to the coast was cut; the road to the coast was not cut. Back in Tossa we knew we would hear nothing of all this; we would remain in a rosy haze of ignorance until the crisis was over and newspapers and telephones became normal or the first Moors clattered into the market-place. We felt we could not leave Barcelona.

Our papers for leaving were in order. We had only to demand a Generalität car and we would be at the frontier in under four hours. It was their gesture of appreciation of our efforts to entertain their important guests. For some time we had been facing up to the necessity of a visit to England. We had not been back for over three years; we needed more money; we needed to settle various business arrangements impossible to deal with from Spain. We had arranged everything for our hasty departure in the face of danger, but we could not bear to depart until that danger became urgent. We lingered in Barcelona, staying in Elizabeth's flat.

Rosita was optimistic. She was convinced that a last-minute miracle would happen. The whole question was the shortage of arms. Soldiers were walking away from the front. They saw no sense in standing still to be mowed down by machine-guns from aeroplanes. They were willing to go on fighting, but they wanted something to fight with. One half of Barcelona was convinced that no arms would come; the other half was expecting them hourly.

It was through Rosita that I got a car to take me out to Tossa. Archie had to see about the last formalities about leaving in Barcelona. Francisca was marvellous. I had seen her prostrate with toothache, hysterical about Pepito, her husband, worked up to a frenzy by Tossa gossips, but she was perfectly calm in this major calamity of our leaving. She seemed to shrink to even smaller dimensions and her black eyes looked larger than ever, but she did not let a whimper escape her. She helped me to pack things away; she assured me that she would tidy everything later; she sorted and arranged with desperate efficiency. Little groups came up from the village; they wanted the latest news from Barcelona. I was optimistic with the majority, those who had nothing whatever to fear from a fascist victory. I was truthful with the few who wished to leave if things got serious. I promised to send word somehow if we had to run out of Barcelona.

Quimeta had the clearest grasp of the situation.

'If we get no arms in a few days, then we go to France,' she said. 'We will wait here until we hear from you. We trust you absolutely.'

In between packing and advising I was trying to find out if we owed any money. I put word round the village that I wanted to settle all bills. No one responded except the owner of the café. He came panting up the hill in great excitement. He was the only man in the village who *owed* us money. We had lent him 500 pesetas to buy a stock of coffee.

I went back to Barcelona the same day. I took Beetle in case we had to leave suddenly. This was the last straw for Francisca. She did not say a word, but huge tears poured down her cheeks. She made no attempt to wipe them away. She knew I would hate her to cry, and she thought that her ignoring the circumstantial evidence would somehow minimize the effect. We left plenty of money. We left stores of food for the Basques and the Reifenbergs. I leaped into the car, Beetle clutched in my arms, and we drove madly away from the little circle of anxious friends. As we circled the hill behind Tossa I strained for a last glimpse of the Casa Johnstone. The Californian poppies had never made such a show.

Back in Barcelona there was a diversion from the interminable discussions about arms. Beetle did not care for Elizabeth's flat. It was not so much the flat as the presence of Elizabeth's small dog. Beetle declared that it was no dog, or rather bitch. Elizabeth herself had her doubts so she called it Pussy. Pussy was sleek and black and walked better on her hind legs than on all fours. She was never still and seldom silent. Beetle loathed her. Pussy welcomed Beetle with a frenzy of affection. She was an exceptionally intelligent little dog, but she never learned that Beetle could not bear her. She showed off her best tricks. She would pretend to want to go out and rush in a frenzy of urgency to the terrace door. Once outside, she would shriek with laughter to be let in again; it was all a joke. Beetle thought she was mad. Pussy would leap over the backs of the tallest chairs with effortless ease and look, her beautifully shaped ears cocked for approval, at Beetle. Beetle was disgusted at these low circus tricks. Pussy even produced her most treasured trick, that of dressing herself up in an old torn shawl which she draped cunningly over her head and trailed behind her like a train. She was delighted with the effect and called shrilly to Beetle to admire. Beetle put on her frog face which denoted utter boredom. I knew that never would Pussy win over a little snob like Beetle, but Elizabeth was determined that they should be friends. The more she devised means to throw them together, the more obnoxious Beetle became. Finally even Pussy's spirits were damped and she gave up.

It was Nikolaus who discovered Marianne practically dying in a flat, and rushed her into the Hospital Clinic. She had pleurisy and no one thought she had a chance. I went at once to see her. We managed to bring her some eatable food—the hospital was reduced to giving her chick peas—and she recovered, but she was desperately weak. Ulrich suddenly appeared from the Tortosa front. He told us that Tortosa had fallen. He had come back to be on the same side as Marianne. He looked wretchedly ill. It gave us a diversion from hanging about Barcelona. Somehow we had to get Marianne out of Spain. Nikolaus began to show his mettle. He intrigued here and threatened there, and among us we got an ambulance to take Marianne to France. Ulrich went with her to the frontier. We wired for money to be sent to the French frontier to enable her to reach friends in Paris.

In the excitement of getting Marianne settled, we had almost forgotten our own situation. We finally decided to leave. We could not bear the Barcelona atmosphere much longer. Archie's cheek-bones were showing—he had to avoid them when he shaved—and I was looking plain and haggard. Elizabeth was almost insane trying to make up her mind what to do.

It was in the Via Durruti, when I was taking a manuscript to the censor's office, that we first saw the planes. They were unmistakable. Shining, new, the red paint fairly dripping off them, they flew in perfect formation. The first squadron was followed by another, then still more. Little Xatos, chaser planes, buzzed round them like bumblebees, swooping low over the roofs. Soon there were two hundred planes flying over Barcelona.

People went crazy. Perfect strangers embraced, women laughed and cried. Every one clapped and cheered. The silver planes, their red-tipped wings glinting in the sunshine, dropped showers of leaflets. The fluttering paper sank slowly to earth; crowds rushed to grab the cheering message. Arms and munitions were coming through. At last the Spanish people could make a stand.

At the censor's office everything was confusion. The censors were all on the balconies staring at the sky. At last some one took my manuscript, neatly tied up in brown paper.

'What is this?' he asked, as he sealed it in various places without undoing the parcel.

'It's the manuscript of a book. A book about the war.'

'The Spanish War?' asked the censor, leaning back to get a view out of the window.

He wrote on the parcel that it was a manuscript about the Spanish War. Then he handed it to me and dashed for the balcony.

On our way back to Elizabeth's flat we danced into Rosita. She suggested running us out to Tossa for the week-end. We rushed back to the flat, packed the bewildered Elizabeth, the protesting Beetle and the hysterical Pussy into the car and went to Tossa. As we rounded the last corner and the Casa Johnstone burst into our view I noticed that the Californian poppies were better than ever this year.

The next week we spent talking. We had to repeat the story of the aeroplanes a dozen times a day. The philofascists in the village grew daily more gloomy as the Aragon defences grew stronger. Rumours exaggerated the supply of arms until the French Army had been seen marching through Gerona. Those who had clung to their belief in England's friendship nodded their heads sagely. It was obvious that England and France would never betray loyal Spain. Even the cynical Johnstones began to think that the tide had turned.

We decided that we would go to England for a month or two. We had battled to get our permits; we might as well use them. We were reluctant to leave Tossa in May, but we were pleasantly excited at the thought of seeing some of our friends after three and a half years.

Francisca did not want us to go, but she was far hap-

pier over this parting. We told her to keep the house
open for any of our friends who brought their own food.
As the Consul had not bothered to send the notice for
the front door, we told Francisca to dig up some of our
store of wine for any marauding soldiery that might
pass that way.

The Generalität sent a magnificent car to take us to
the frontier. We almost forced Elizabeth into it; she
still could not make up her mind to leave Catalunya.
We packed in our small suitcases and Beetle and Pussy.
Tossa turned out in force to see us off. Opinions were
pretty evenly divided. One idea was that we were fleeing
from the fascists; the other that we had been thrown out
by the Generalität.

The drive from Figueras to Port Bou was through
wild country. At unsuspecting corners carabineros
sprang out and challenged us. Pussy poked her head
out each time and was a success. Usually one carabinero
leapt across the road with his rifle at the ready, but by
the time Pussy had rolled her beady eyes a few times,
several others came up and chatted while the challenger
read through our documentation. Needless to say, our
documentation was good.

Once a carabinero was asleep as we passed and woke
up in a frenzy of zeal. He tried to fire a shot after us, but
the bolt of his rifle stuck and we left him standing im-
potently in the middle of the road, banging the butt of
his rifle in the dust. In a small village we came across
the only disagreeable carabinero I have met. He was
elderly and sour. He eyed Pussy's blandishments ston-
ily. The driver got bored with his scrutiny of our excellent papers.

'Oh hell, get a move on, you old half-wit,' he said in

effect. The carabinero jerked up his rifle and poked it through the window at the driver. Elizabeth drew in her ample bosom non-interventionally to allow him better aim. The driver thought it all very amusing.

'You are a brave fellow,' he said, and used some Catalan oaths signifying his intention of performing certain bodily functions in extremely exalted quarters.

The carabinero had the same idea, but expressed it in fluent but s-less Andalucian which left us baffled. Elizabeth, still compressing her chest into the smallest possible area, kept saying, 'Pussy, do your stuff! Pussy, pretty Pussy,' but Pussy started screaming hysterically. Beetle woke up and swore. Then she pretended it was cats and joined in. The carabinero was startled, but undefeated. He still had his rifle. He jerked it back through the window of the car in order to take better aim. Then he changed his mind. It was hot and one never quite knew with these foreigners. He handed our papers to the driver, and we drove off with the dogs in an uproar.

We twisted round the desolate coast road to Port Bou. It was always a dreary stretch of gaunt cliffs and untidy boulders, but barbed wire entanglements against landing parties did not add to its attractions. We looked down on the abandoned village of Culera, tucked into a valley spanned by a railway bridge. The bridge was intact, but Culera sprawled roofless in the sunshine, like an indecently-exposed corpse.

We had little time to feel depressed at the sight of the devastation in Port Bou. We met an old carabinero friend who had been stationed the previous summer in Tossa, and he gave us a great welcome. He told us that the last raid had been three hours ago and they were not expecting another for at least two hours. We had luncheon in the carabineros' quarters and they escorted us through the customs.

The customs' examination was the high spot of leaving Spain. The carabineros detailed off to search baggage must have been chosen for their love of American films. They felt all seams, opened every box, including a private box of Archie's which caused them some embarrassment; unwound a ball of wool, and swooped triumphantly upon twenty copies of the Casa Johnstone folder.

Our carabinero could not read English. He ran his finger along the lines of print, muttering under his breath. He studied the map on the cover; he audibly admired the photographs of Tossa. Then he laid down the first folder and picked up another. I assured him that they were identical. He gave me an amused look. Why should he believe me? He could not read English. He went systematically through the twenty folders.

Occasionally the thorough search was broken by one of the carabineros holding up a blouse of Elizabeth's or a coloured scarf of mine for his colleagues to admire. They chatted with us throughout the search. They emptied the suitcases and turned them upside down to be tested for false bottoms. Then they packed everything in again, disdaining our offers of help. They packed beautifully; occasionally there was an argument about the exact place to put certain things, and other carabineros were called in for consultation. In the end our cases were tidily closed and relocked. They were marked with chalk. The carabineros looked through our handbags and marked them also, although, one of them remarked, the handbags could be looked at when we had our personal search. Why, of course we had to have a personal search. Yes, Archie could be searched right now, but the señoras would have to wait for the station matron. Archie made some ribald remark which they thought not in the best of taste. The carabinero detailed to search him hastily stopped him taking off his coat: '*Nada de eso!*' (None of that!) he said firmly, patting Archie's pockets.

I took the opportunity to transfer some pound notes that were in my coat pocket to my chalk-marked suit-case. I did not know the regulations about taking out foreign money, and we wanted to make sure we could get to Paris.

We were searched more thoroughly than Archie was, but the matron was so enthralled by the two dogs that her mind was not on her work. Beetle slept throughout in her travelling bag, in reality a knitting bag. No one thought of looking underneath her for concealed whatever they were searching for. I did not like to ask what it was that must not be taken out of Spain in the seams of a pair of trousers. I felt that the chances were that the carabineros did not know.

Our cases were put in the Cerbére train and we were walking back through the station from the town when it struck us that we need not have gone through the customs at all. No one stopped us as we walked through the station. Various wiser travellers were walking straight on to the train, suitcases in hand. There was no check on friends seeing people off and handing parcels through the windows. But we were glad we went through the customs. We had given enormous pleasure to the customs officials who obviously did not get much custom, and we had yet another glimpse of

that strange childlike simplicity that is Spanish. We
hated leaving Spain. We shouted to our carabinero
friends that we would be back in two or three months.
They promised to have a reception for us on our return.
As we pulled out of the long tunnel into France we
heard the rattle of anti-aircraft guns and the heavy thud
of bombs. Port Bou was being raided again.

16

English Interlude

'How *did* you get out?'

Wearily we explained for the twentieth time that we had crossed the frontier in the ordinary, everyday train. No, we had not had our baggage stolen; no one insulted us; our house had not been commandeered by the Spanish Government nor captured by Franco. Yes, we left Spain of our own free will; yes, we were going back. No, the war was not yet over.

Except in so far as it affected us the people we met in England were not interested in the Spanish War. They were not interested in the Chinese War. They had anæthetized that part of their minds that could react to a newspaper bill stating baldly that a thousand people had been killed in Canton. They read it because it stared at them from every street corner, but their well-trained minds rejected its significance. If the fact that a thousand had been killed seeped in through the layer of protective tissue of their minds, they could counter with, 'But after all, they are only Chinese. Look at the awful things that happen to them in earthquakes and things.'

It was only slightly different with Spain. Spain was much nearer than China. Spaniards, while only just removed from negroes, were Europeans. There was a faint apprehension that if planes could bomb Barcelona, might they not also one day bomb London? Therefore let us ignore the Barcelona bombings, the horrible reminders of our own danger. Let the Spanish War end as soon as possible, no matter with what result. Obviously it would end more quickly if the fascist advance were not held up. Therefore we will refuse to believe that the advance *is* held up. Let any qualms about the betrayal of a friendly legitimate government be smothered under the smouldering menace of the Red Terror. After all, there must have been *something* in all those awful stories. If Franco was a real gentleman he would win the war at once and the perplexed British middle class would know where they stood.

Having lost two old friends because our outlooks were so utterly opposed, I realized that I had been foolish to attempt to penetrate the sticky ooze of British self-protection. They had as much right to cover their secret terror with dollops of ready made justification as I had to prefer to live in Spain where values had more reality. So I learned to smile pleasantly and to produce automatically the Frightfully Amusing Stories of Spanish incompetence that were expected, without a reference to the competence of the German and Italian airmen.

I paid a short visit to Cornwall, which is my home county. It was like living some horrible fantasy. On one side there were ruined fishermen, areas of unemployment, starving miners. On the other, a charming but anachronistic gentry, still unaware that they were the ghostly survivals of something that has ceased to have any meaning. They led exemplary lives; their tenants were contented; they supported the County Ball and subscribed to the Hounds. They took it in turns to lend their grounds for open-air performances of the Shakespearean Society. One knew where one was with a fellow like Shakespeare. They were quite upset to be told that St. Day, right in the middle of the hunting country and with the kennels in the district, was a Special Area. It must be these communists who were responsible for all this chaos in the country.

The fishermen, miners, china clay workers are doomed. So are the landowners. There is a third-class in Cornwall who are the life-blood of the county. They are the caterers for the tourist trade. The small farmer no longer relies on Lady Bountiful with her little basket to feed his family in bad seasons; he takes in paying guests. Unscrupulous but shrewd building firms specialize in doing up fishermen's cottages and letting them at exorbitant prices. The fishermen, unable to pay the new rents, slink away to find homes further inland, only to encounter the tourist invasion all over the county. This new class is vigorous and thrifty. It runs up monstrous little houses and bungalows; it tames the wild magnificence of the cliffs by planting little red flags and calling the landscape a golf course; it buys up as speculations little snippets off this estate, a slice or two off that. The gentry are doomed like the miners, but their big useless houses will never be left standing bleak and desolate like disused engine houses. They will be turned into country clubs, restaurants and boarding houses.

Archie was working hard. He went back to his old

paper, the *News Chronicle*; refused a job on a paper whose politics he disliked, and got a Sunday job as well. He was still at work at the *News Chronicle* office when the Sunday job came unsteadily up the stairs to our flat and rang the bell. I had just finished my bath and answered the door in my dressing-gown. A tall figure swayed gently on the door-mat and asked for Archie. I said politely he was out and, having acquired Spanish habits, immediately asked the caller to come inside. There is nothing so rude as parleying at the door in Spain. The figure rocked into the sitting-room and sank thankfully into a chair.

'You know, I'm very unpopular downstairs,' he said emphatically.

'Are you?' I asked politely.

'Yes. Very unpopular. In fact'—he leaned forward confidentially—'I am unpopular.'

I struggled with my Spanish politeness.

'I am afraid you are going to be very unpopular up here,' I said. 'I am just going to bed.'

The young man looked at me sadly. He was pleasant-looking, but he was shrouded in an alcoholic mist.

'Will you tell me what you want?' I said firmly.

'Why, of course. I want Archie Johnstone.' He laughed in a silly way. 'At least *I* don't want him. He is wanted by the *Sunday Graphic*.' He tried to lean forward again, but gave it up. 'They want him like anything,' he finished up.

'I'll tell him to ring them up,' I said soothingly. 'Now you must go.'

'Must I? You know, I live down in the flat just below. But I'm not at all popular down there at the moment. Do you think I had better go? Really?'

'Yes, really,' I said firmly, supporting him through the door.

He turned back on the stairs and looked at me plaintively.

'You know, I'm not a bit pop——' he began, but I shut the door.

The next Saturday Archie was chief sub. on the *Sunday Graphic*.

I was finishing my book. We hoped to earn enough money to enable us to go back to Tossa as soon as possible. We had met my publishers who were charming, very public school and Rhodes Scholar, but human for all that. They wanted the book finished as soon as possible. I have since learned that it is merely a publisher's formula. They never expect any writer to deliver a manuscript to date. However, I said they could have it by June 30th.

It was hard work writing in a stuffy little Chelsea flat instead of sprawling on a sunlit terrace, but it had compensations. Although there was an almost perpetual clatter of aeroplanes over London one knew they could drop nothing worse than their trailing advertisements. We found the arguments for and against bomb-proof shelters and the whole chit-chat of A.R.P. simply incredible. It was also criminal, but we were just a little bit inclined to be indifferent what happened to the British citizen with his carefully wadded mind. We felt it would be interesting to see if a nice bomb, quite a small one of course, might blow out the wadding.

I escaped to Cornwall again to do the last chapters. This time I used the British cotton-wool technique with some success. I stayed in a delightful house perched alone on the cliffs. I revelled in the charm of the local inhabitants. I knew just what the charm was worth, but it made no difference. I like people to get into a bus and say, 'Good morning, all!' as a matter of course. I refused to accept the plain facts that pointed to the exploitation of even this paradise. It was perfect if one kept the wadding well rammed home.

I rushed back to London to deliver the manuscript of my book on the appointed day. During the next month I flew round arranging to turn the Casa Johnstone into a children's colony. It was a question of finding an organization to provide the food. I wanted to give the house and our services to some non-Spanish organization who could guarantee sufficient food supplies. We eventually fixed up with the International Solidarity Fund. We knew their London representative and she seemed a thoroughly efficient person.

The idea first came to us when Leon arrived from Paris to stay in our tiny flat and promptly got a job as director of a Basque Children's Home. Our flat became a sort of clearing station for Bad Basque Boys being sent from one home to another. The whole situation was full of complications. The boys had learned that if they were naughty they were sent to embarrassed friends in London, pending a decision as to their future. The friends invariably took the children to the nearest cinema and otherwise tried to keep them entertained. The children naturally behaved like angels. I asked one very intelligent boy why he behaved so badly that he was expelled from one home after another? He raised his delicately pencilled eyebrows and real surprise at my stupidity looked out of his melting brown eyes.

'Why, I have seen England!' he said simply. 'I have been everywhere, even to Scotland.'

English Interlude

The problem was the bigger boys who, by Spanish standards, were no longer children but grown men. They were only fifteen or sixteen, but nearly all had black growths on their upper lips and men's voices. They were far too intelligent to be contented with blind-alley occupations like hacking down trees. They wanted to be trained engineers, chemists, doctors, accountants. They demanded to be apprenticed to garages or laboratories. They never believed there were difficulties about arranging this. They decided to make the lives of their friends a burden until they got what they wanted. It certainly was a fact that if, after superhuman efforts, a boy was found an occupation that he liked, there was no more trouble.

The small but faithful group of Londoners working for the Basque children were thankful to find another resting-place for their charges. Poor Archie never knew how many innocently sleeping bad boys he would find on mattresses on our sitting-room floor when he returned from work in the early morning. They never were the slightest trouble. Among friends speaking Spanish, sure of his welcome, the worst Basque boy became angelic. He would admit with an engaging grin that he could be a fiend, but always added, 'Only when people were not *simpático*.'

Leon took over a home that had been badly managed. The boys were disgruntled and there was no idea of organization. Leon had been there two days when a rich patron said plaintively: 'If you can let me have a list, say in a week or two, of exactly what is needed in the way of linen, I can get it at once.'

Leon clicked his heels and reeled off a list of sheets and pillow-slips and towels. The kind lady nearly fainted. She had been trying to give the home its linen for over a month.

It was a job for a superhuman, but luckily Leon is superhuman. He had to run the whole place single-handed. The boys were supposed to help, but they were suspicious and unwilling. Leon found himself doing the cooking, the secretarial work, the catering, the accountancy, and was invariably involved in long Spanish arguments with the boys until midnight. There was an English teacher who learned his Spanish from the boys and who had vague leanings towards Boy Scouts. He had no patience with interminable discussions and periodically resigned in despair, but there seemed to be some strange fascination that kept him from actually abandoning the little wretches. That seemed to be the prevailing attitude to Basque children among those who suffered for them. One might sometimes feel that it was useless wasting time and energy on such ungrateful, selfish and incorrigible children. Then there would be a flash of Spanish charm, a spontaneous gesture of affection, a glimpse of brown seraphic faces with guileless dark eyes and one sighed and spent agonized hours trying to work out some solution for the future of the poor little angels.

I was sorry we could not take the biggest and baddest boys back to Tossa. They would have been no trouble in their own environment. But the thought put the idea of running the Casa Johnstone as a home for other refugee children. Barcelona was crammed with refugees many of them in the poorest and most bombed areas. We knew better than to offer our house to the Spanish Government. Already, when I mentioned the idea of the colony, people suggested that we were forced by the

Government to give the house. The International Solidarity Fund seemed to offer a solution.

In all the excitement of fixing up about the colony and the thousand-and-one odds and ends to be tidied up before we returned to Spain, I had forgotten about my manuscript at Faber's. There were reminders from time to time about details of one kind and another, requests to Archie for publicity matter, etc. It was not until a week before we were due to leave for Spain that I remembered that we had had no definite word of acceptance. Had they even read it?

They had. I rang them up and was asked to come to see them the next day.

There was something indecent about upsetting the orderly calm and rhythm of a London publishing house. Not that I saw any sign of an upset. The girl downstairs still greeted me by name as if I were the most famous of Faber's authors; we were ushered upstairs by the small lift boy who had not yet become unduly impressed by the place; we sank into the deep leather chairs as if the world was in its right place. But the vibrations were not normal. I felt, as if in a dream, the atmosphere after that manuscript had been read. I had a moment of horror thinking that perhaps even afternoon tea had been forgotten, but I realized that was an exaggeration. *We* certainly got our usual tea and biscuits as if nothing had happened.

They were very kind. There was not much for them to do, but they tried their hardest to explain their inability to publish the manuscript. A very interesting experiment in style—perhaps rather a difficult construction? Personally I like it—but readers have every right to expect—I don't suppose we would lose on it, but your public expects—after the other book—I am very glad to see you doing something different, but when people expect a sequel——

We munched our biscuit and went away. There was nothing more to be said. There was nothing more to be done. We had to leave in three days, and even I, with my ten pages a day, cannot rewrite a book in three days. In any case, I did not want to rewrite it. I thought it was a lovely book. Actually Faber's were perfectly right. It was an extremely bad book, and they would have been woolly-headed if they had published it.

Luckily Archie had earned plenty of money. Although I had let the firm down, we still had enough to go back to Tossa and live there a while. We left England with few regrets. We had lost a few friends, we had gained some new ones, and we had always the rock of Me-Ant as a foundation. Me-Ant, or my Aunt May as she is never called, needs a whole book to herself to do her justice. It was she who found rooms for us when we rang her up from Victoria Station on our arrival. She found the rooms first and then expressed her surprise. She then found our flat, near her own, and somehow managed to furnish it out of her own possessions. It would take too long to list all the things Me-Ant has done for us, but she is unique.

If Me-Ant could always be counted upon to provide the necessities of life for us in Spain, La Rudd was the general purveyor of necessary frivolities. La Rudd was the uncrowned queen of the Casa Johnstone during her visit to us; we found that this is her natural sphere wherever she is.

While Me-Ant sent us parcels of heavenly rice and beans, it was La Rudd who slipped in *pâté de foie* or

chocolate creams. While I relied entirely on Me-Ant
for loans of mackintosh and umbrella while in London,
it was La Rudd who suddenly discovered that she had
always hated a certain adorable blouse that would
exactly go with my coat and skirt. It was La Rudd who
introduced us to Bucky Taylor.

It seems strange to put anyone so useful as publicity
manager of Lyons' in the luxury class, but Bucky was
a luxury to us. He was one of the bright spots in an
exceptionally sunless English summer. Our raw feelings were soothed by Bucky's sound common sense;
our faith in humanity feebly raised a dying head when
Bucky made one of his inimitable aphorisms; even the
sight of Bucky, impeccably clothed with just that well-
thought-out air of carelessness, made one feel that there
was still hope for the human race if only other people
could have a tithe of Bucky's brains. But it seemed that
there were no other Buckys in England, so we turned
joyously towards Spain.

The French, with their usual air of bewildered, ill-
used helplessness which is their protection from the
accusation of utter incompetence, had granted holidays
with pay, but had forgotten to put on extra trains. We
journeyed across France in the first week of August in
conditions that were reminiscent of wartime trains in
Spain. The chief difference was that I prefer masses of
Catalan humanity to masses of French humanity, but
they smell much the same. Beetle, retrieved from her
visit to Leon's parents in Paris, went into a trance and
lay for dead in the bottom of her travelling bag. Archie
and I soon passed into a state bordering on unconsciousness. The French holidaying families grumbled at the
lack of accommodation, but still kept the windows

closed. When I have paid for a second-class ticket I sometimes indulge in futile arguments about windows, but never in third-class.

We arrived at Cerbère to find the French anti-aircraft in full blast. Cerbère was nervous of any planes in the vicinity. It had once been bombed by error.

The first person we saw on the platform was our old carabinero friend from Port Bou. We had a wonderful reception. He escorted us into Spain and examined our baggage himself. He persuaded sundry severe-looking officials to pass all Archie's store of tobacco. He assured them he knew us personally and he knew also the many Tossa friends who were expecting tobacco. He insisted on giving us an enormous lunch at the carabineros' barracks. Our delight in being back among really friendly people was augmented by the presence of the new Turkish Ambassador and family, *en route* for Barcelona. He was not what the Port Bou officials considered *simpático*. He had to pay heavy duty on his tobacco. We met him later wandering round Port Bou, his wife picking her way delicately over the bomb holes, holding a large picture hat precariously on to her head, looking for a restaurant.

We were escorted to the Gerona train by most of the carabineros in Port Bou, and given a send-off. The Turkish Ambassador looked at us with interest. He probably thought we were red royalty.

The Gerona train became crowded. We piled up the market baskets and babies on our laps. We managed to find a bit of room for a wounded Catalan who had been sent back from the Ebro front. He told us all about crossing the Ebro. We sat there, smothered under huge market women and their live chickens and rabbits, and we revelled in being back. When we got to Gerona we had to get out by the window.

We got to Tossa in the evening. No one was expecting us. Marcelino of the telephone exchange saw us first and rushed to greet us. Presently Francisca came panting up. She was so overcome she could neither speak nor cry. She just stood with her mouth opening and shutting noiselessly. Beetle saved the situation by greeting her hysterically. On the way up to the house, followed by all our friends in a procession, I told Francisca that once more I had kept my word. I had said I would be back some time during the first week of August. It was the sixth day.

As we sat over our omelette and lettuce on the terrace looking over Tossa Bay with the old towers shining in the moonlight I thought of the words the British Foreign Office had written in my passport:

Valid for a single journey to Spain—Holder is returning to her home.

17

Back to the Land

Tossa seemed indescribably lovely after our three months in England. August is not the most attractive month, but this August was superb. The Californian poppies were just over, there was a patch or two of yellow among the green and some of the new crimson ones still flourished, just to show us what we had missed, but larkspur and cosmos were in full bloom. The oleanders were heavy with blossom, and even our eucalyptus trees surprisingly produced some more of their feathery white flowers. All the trees had shot up amazingly in the last months. They could now be termed trees without our usual apologies. The delicate new leaves of the eucalyptuses were well above the top terrace. But two unwilling little trees still remained exactly the same. They were also eucalyptus and were planted at the same time as their brothers, apparently the same age and in the same soil. But while the others shot up heavenwards so quickly that one could almost see them grow, these two sulked in the soil and refused to do anything at all. They didn't even die. They just remained green and fresh and the same size. We would be disappointed if they ever made up their minds to grow up.

Back to the Land

One minor blow was our vineyard. I had left instructions with Tonet to look after the fruit trees and vines, and gave him permission to plant potatoes in the vineyard. By the look of the jungle that took the place of orderly rows of well-trimmed vines, Tonet had harvested his potatoes long ago and had not been near the place since. It was very annoying, because it meant a small grape harvest, and we wanted as many grapes as possible for the children.

The vineyard was a small matter. It was important for Tonet because we decided to cultivate the ground for ourselves.

There is something satisfying about digging and turning over the soil. There are even people who find pleasure in weeding small flower-beds and rockeries, but after three months of England, with its stifling atmosphere of shocked horror at the first signs of liberal tendencies, give me an acre of vineyard with weeds waist high, tangled vines laden with sweet grapes and a blazing sun beating down. All the frustration and helpless feeling of being caught in a heavy pudding slowly sweated out of me as I cleaned up row after row between the vines. And I did sweat. Three months of living in London had made me soft and flabby. The first two days of work nearly killed me. Then I began to enjoy the rhythm of swinging the heavy two-pronged pick to loosen the earth and then the immense satisfaction of hauling out the monstrous roots. If Spain produces wonderful flowers, she does her bit over the weeds as well. I think our vineyard was growing practically everything that can grow in hot sun on sandy soil. Some of the creeping things were rather beautiful. There was one fat plant with juicy green leaves and

179

bright red stems that lolled about under the vines. Practically every leaf and every inch of stem put down tiny roots into the soil. Unless one carefully pulled out each root, the next day there would be another fat plant with juicy green leaves and bright red stems. There was even more satisfaction in removing something like a young tree with roots like horse radish that seemed fixed for ever in the ground, but which yielded with no effort at all.

It took me a week to clean the vineyard and another week to dig over enough to make it worth while planting potatoes. Then Miguel of the Casa Blanca came over and watched me with a grin on his face. He suggested he should come along on the Sunday with the mule and plough and finish it off for me. A week earlier I should have refused, but by this time I had worked off my hate. Miguel ploughed the vineyard and Archie and I and Francisca planted the potatoes. Archie's reactions to his English visit were not of so violent a nature that he felt the need of actual digging or weeding. He enjoyed the back-breaking business of planting potatoes because he loved to think of six potatoes growing where only a quarter was before.

With all the excitements of greeting our friends and of gardening, we still remembered our plans for a children's colony. The first letter we wrote was to Enrique Santiago, the Spanish representative of the International Solidarity Fund in Barcelona. We sent him all particulars of our house and of a second house which a German friend had left in our care, and which we needed in order to run a colony. We asked Santiago to arrange everything as soon as possible. We wanted the children while the bathing was good.

There was a slight hitch because a new chief of police had come to Tossa during our absence and had established himself comfortably in our friend Oskar's house. That meant we would have a certain amount of work to dislodge him, but I did not doubt for a moment that this could be managed. Other people in Tossa said I was mad to think that it was possible to move the chief of police, and Comas, the town secretary, told me frankly to give up the idea. It seemed inconceivable to me that any man, even if he were the chief of police, could prevent fifty children from being saved from starvation and bombardments just because he wanted to live in a certain house. In any case, it seemed to me that the International Solidarity Fund could do something about all this. All I had to do was to pay a polite visit to the chief of police and put the matter frankly before him.

The chief of police was rather a shock. We were used to various kinds, from the twitchy psychopathic ones to the genial, unshaven type who look as if they had just finished murdering their mothers and were slightly regretting the necessity for it. But Sr. Massana was yet a new type. He was tall, handsome, with silver hair and piercing blue eyes. He was dressed in the whitest of white drill. His collar was starched. I noticed that from under the ends of his beautifully creased trousers there appeared white *alpargatas*. The man might be human after all.

He appeared extremely busy when we entered his office. He waved us to chairs and scribbled away on a small pad. He dipped his pen many times into a silver inkpot and blotted things busily with a silver blotter. It would have been more impressive if the paper he was using had not been headed with Oskar's name, and if we hadn't recognized the inkpot and blotter as being also from Oskar's house. However, he did his best, and no doubt it all impressed the local Tossencs.

He listened courteously to our story. Archie and I have a method on these occasions. I do the talking in my fluent and very ungrammatical Spanish and Archie comes in weightily at the right moments with slightly hispanified Scotch. This always works. I can argue and get worked up to a good Spanish frenzy because I talk so much faster, and, when the bewildered listener turns to Archie for help, he bludgeons the remains into unconsciousness with some blunt argument.

Our arguments this time were very blunt. In brief, if the chief of police did not move out of Oskar's house, it meant that the children's colony could not materialize. Sr. Massana skated round this for a time. He advised us to put all idea of using Oskar's house right out of our heads; one felt he implied, our pretty little heads. He would do everything to help us find another house. He went deaf when we explained that Oskar's house was the only one within a quarter of a mile of the Casa Johnstone. He stared into the village square in a trance when we explained further that we needed the house because it had a big wash place in the garden and also that we had to have somewhere to unload the lorries of food. No lorry could possibly get up our hill. He came to only when I said that as a matter of fact he had no right whatever to be in the house at all. The house had been, according to the notices put on the doors by the former police, '*tancada*', which means shut. There was never any question of commandeering the house.

Back to the Land

Sr. Massana reared himself up in his chair and fixed a steely blue eye on me.

'I am', he said in resonant tones, 'El Jefe de la Policia de Tossa.'

'Yes,' I said expectantly.

But that seemed all there was to Sr. Massana.

After another hour during which Sr. Massana did most of the talking but which had not shifted us one inch, he finally said we must write him a letter setting out our claims. He had learned a lot about 'our good friend Sr. Oskar', who was obviously a fascist agent and therefore deserved to lose his house. I pointed out that there was not the slightest proof that he was a fascist, and the house had been searched by the former police. We left Sr. Massana fully determined to stay in the house. We were also quite determined.

There was an interval of ten days before we received a polite note from Santiago thanking us for the offer of our house and accepting it with gratitude. He said he would visit us shortly to settle up final details. We wrote a most formal and elegant letter to the Chief of the Tossa Police setting out our claims to Oskar's house and delivered it in person. Then we sat back and waited.

There was plenty to do in the interval. All our personal things had to be sorted; some were to be taken with us down to Oskar's, others to be stored in the Casa Johnstone. We decided to keep Leon's small room as a store-room, but we thought our bedroom and sitting-room would be useful for the teachers. The sitting-room could be used by all the personnel as a rest room, leaving the big room for the children. The small single bedrooms which could not possibly be made to take two beds, came in very well for the staff, who could each have a room to themselves, but would be within easy reach of the big dormitories.

It was difficult to plan Oskar's without actually walking round the rooms, but we provisionally decided to use the studio as a food store; the big living room for classes; the big bedroom as a dormitory for ten children and the smaller room for ourselves. We found that we could take forty to forty-five children with comfort in the two houses, and hoped to have a staff of three Spaniards, including teachers. The fact that we had stipulated for the children to be between the ages of eight and fourteen would simplify everything enormously. We began to get excited at the thought of actually having the children in our care. We personally would not have a great deal to do with the actual controlling of the children, because obviously the teachers would know far better than we how to deal with Spanish children, but we had pleasant memories of the Basque children in England and both Archie and I felt we would willingly take over control for an afternoon if the teachers wanted a holiday. We realized that, while we had beautiful theories about the upbringing of children, we lacked practice and also that our Spanish was distinctly comic.

We thought it might be a good idea to get into training, as it were, for our young visitors. This was simple. Almost with the same suddenness that foreign visitors discovered Tossa before the war, the youth of Spain had descended on it during our absence in England. We had left the Tossencs faintly grumbling at the few adult refugees seeking shelter there; we came back to find the village seething with fury at the youthful invasion.

Back to the Land

There was a children's colony in Ferrer's huge house on the front; another one, some hundred strong, in the old building near our hill which had been a summer holiday home for schoolchildren before the war and then was converted into an hotel a few months before the rebellion started. The International Solidarity Fund had already started one colony in Tossa, in a commandeered house in the village. The Tossencs went about muttering about the bread being taken out of their mouths, although the colonies were entirely self-supporting. The war was being brought home to Tossa at last.

We felt we were not adding to our popularity by taking yet more children. We had stipulated that milk should be given by the Solidarity Fund to the local school children every day and this was started a few days after our return. The Tossa mothers were impressed for a while and then they began to think that a bread ration should also be provided. Why should Castilian or Basque children be fed while Catalans starved? Well, if they were not actually starving they were on short rations. Oh yes, they knew that the people in Barcelona were probably far worse off for food than in the villages; but, after all, Barcelona was ninety kilometres away. In fact, it soon boiled down to the simple idea that really the one aim of the whole world should be to feed Tossencs first. Quite naturally the people in Lloret thought the same, only substituting Lloretencs for Tossencs, etc.

While the general opinion in Tossa was against children's colonies, our own friends were delighted. The Casa Blanca put themselves and their farm at our disposal; Antonia offered to plant anything we liked

185

especially for us if we could get the seed; Perez, pushing his check cap on the back of his head and looking more like a stud groom than ever, offered to *give* us all the cheaper fish and to sell us the more expensive ones at beach prices; Maria offered to cut the children's hair free of charge; the old shoemaker suggested mending all their shoes if I could possibly get him some nails, thread and leather from England; Tonet decided to forgive me after all for the affair of the vineyard and said his services were at our disposal, but he refused to admire my young potatoes which were just beginning to push up through the tidy earth.

Francisca was still not quite sure about this colony idea. She was terrified at the idea of a mob of wild children clattering all over the house. I did nothing to allay this terror when I said happily that I liked naughty children so much better than good ones and that I hoped they would send us all boys. She recovered a little when I assured her that she need have nothing to do with the children. I explained that we should be living at Oskar's and that she was to be there simply to run the place for us and perhaps make ten extra beds and clean the dormitory. Francisca is not afraid of work. She would willingly have made all forty-five beds if there was a guarantee that no child would suddenly pop its head round a door. She cheered up a lot at the thought of living what she called our normal life at Oskar's, although she did not quite approve of the children turning us out of our own house. I promised that she should have nothing at all to do with the children. Poor Francisca!

Our practice with children started almost immediately. The big colony on the beach was called the Forty-

Third Division after the division which held out in a pocket of the Pyrenees and was an obstacle to the fascist drive towards Puigcerda. This colony was supported by the Spanish Government and had a peculiar director. He was a wonderful teacher and the children adored him, but he had very little idea about running a house. The place was dirty, the food was badly cooked, the children's clothes were in rags. The children themselves were comparatively clean because they spent most of the day in the sea. They were the happiest children in the world. They rushed to the beach in the mornings and wandered in for lunch when they felt hungry. They always seemed to get something to eat, and they had such appetites that they were indifferent about the cooking. The bright moment of the day was when the director came down to the beach. He was immediately surrounded by children trying to drag him into the water, clamouring for stories, or just fighting to get near him.

Our popularity really depended on the fact that I could do the crawl. Lo Reifenberg had taught many of the children to swim in the early summer, but before she could teach them the crawl the fishing season started and Lo and her mother were far too tired after hauling in the nets to come to the beach. So I was heaven-sent. Although not up to Lo's standard of machine-like perfection, at least I could get through the water at a reasonable speed which gave me a status among the young enthusiasts. Archie stood on his own feet because of his ability to stand on his hands for hours.

This was our first experience of Spanish youth *en masse*. We had mistrusted our impression of Basque

boys because we had the idea that perhaps Basques are
exceptionally nice people. But these hundred children
were from all parts of Spain and even included a number of Catalans. Archie succumbed to the Asturians
with their shocks of fair hair and blue eyes. It was their
toughness he admired. I fell with a thud for the Madri-
leños; the boys with long black lashes and delicate olive
skins and the girls with their heart-shaped faces and
charming manners.

18

Grapes and Morals

Francisca's worst fears were realized when I brought the boys up to eat grapes.

We had learned a great deal about the colony of the Forty-Third Division. There was the Tossa opinion which cannot be adequately conveyed without a generous sprinkling of Catalan oaths. It would have gladdened the heart of those who fear that there is no religious sense left in Catalunya to hear the Tossencs appealing to the rites of their Church and all its appendages to save them from these children. It appeared that, owing to certain inevitable mistakes on the part of those responsible for supplying food for the colony, there were times when there simply was no food. There may be children who take this sort of thing lying down, but certainly not in Spain. A Spanish child has a simple, logical and reasonable mind. If those in authority fail, a Spanish child will fend for himself. This was exactly what the children of the Forty-Third Division Colony did. They slipped out of their dormitories on the ground floor—all the windows had the usual bars, but it takes bars very close together to stop a hungry child —and ravaged the countryside. That is to say, a few children would scrape some potatoes out of the ground; others would shake locust beans off the heavily-laden trees; they would dodge in and out of the fields of maize stripping a corn cob here and there; they even uprooted turnips and ate them raw. A hundred-odd children do manage to get away with a fair quantity of stuff.

Our house was in a position to observe the comings and goings of the children. The first time I saw them foraging I ran down and asked them why they were doing it. They explained that they were hungry. It seemed reasonable to believe them. It was not likely that anyone would eat raw potatoes from choice. I saw the director and he said that the food lorry from Barcelona had been delayed and there really was no food. The children were truly hungry. I said I thought it was a pity to enrage the Tossa people, especially as one could understand their point of view. They were in a panic over the general food shortage and the fact that no rations were ever issued for the village; at least the colonies did have some system of rationing even if hitches occurred from time to time. To my surprise the director, who struck me as being a mild intellectual, suddenly grew tight-lipped and fierce and proceeded to tell me a few facts about the Tossa people and the town council. I found it almost incredible.

The Tossencs had been so furious about the colony coming to Tossa that the first thing the town council did was to cut off the water supply. The director thought that there was no water in the building and the children hauled inadequate supplies from the open wells in the vegetable gardens. At last it came to him that something odd was going on and he investigated and found that the water supply had been cut off. It took a Government official from Barcelona to settle the matter. Then the director found it became impossible to buy anything from the neighbouring farms. The town council had forbidden anyone to sell anything to the colonies. In every possible way the Tossencs had fought against the children coming and now that they were there things were going to be made as unpleasant as possible. The director turned to me with a smile softening the grimness in his eyes.

'I *could* put netting over those bars,' he said. 'But I won't.'

I went a stage further. I had a talk with the town council on the subject of children's colonies. They were quite frank in their hatred for them and quite unreasonable. They would not understand that they could not lose anything by having children in Tossa. Their own children were getting a daily milk ration which was entirely due to the colonies. The same old cry went on: Why should these strange children be well fed while ours are hungry? I would have had much more sympathy if the Tossa children *were* hungry. But there was practically no hunger in Tossa. There was so little hunger that the pine nuts were allowed to rot on the ground and, while refugee children wolfed acorns in the woods, one never found a Tossa child gathering them except occasionally for feeding the rabbits.

After my talk with the *ayuntamiento*, I had a conversation with some of the robber children. I did not moralize or lecture. I just explained which land belonged to friends and which to enemies.

But my own morals went astray over the grapes.

Francisca, although she still adores me, has never felt quite the same about me.

It was a good year for melons and peaches, although the latter were not yet ripe. Melons and pumpkins were ripening in the fields, and some of the poor starving Tossencs simply had no time to pick them before they rotted. Naturally the logical refugee children had to do something about this. A few of the Asturian boys would slip out in the early morning and hide a water melon or two among the weeds outside their dormitories. I used to see them doing this occasionally, and while I felt it was wrong because by this time the food lorry had arrived and the children at least got enough food to keep their bones from rattling, somehow fruit always seem to be fair game, especially when on a diet of dried beans and chick peas. However, the general impression among the children seemed to be that I did not quite approve, and I was not taken into anyone's confidence on the subject of stolen melons.

I was on my way down to bathe when there was a frantic scurry as I turned the corner by the wall of the colony. I was just in time to see a group of boys hastily depositing something in the dirty weeds against the wall. They stood about looking so guilty that I felt for every one's sake I had better investigate. I found some filthy pieces of melon, clogged with sand and dirt, and a few very green, hard peaches. I was annoyed about the peaches because it was such a waste not to wait until they were ripe, but the grimy slices of melon really seemed too horrible. It was then that my moral sense deserted me.

'For Heaven's sake throw these grubby things away,' I said. 'You had better all come along with me and eat some grapes. There should be some quite ripe.'

I must explain that the only really sacred fruit in a wine-making country is the grape. All boys steal fruit, but no one touches the vines. Even the hungry refugees had a certain respect for grapes.

The children stared at me.

'You mean, come with you and eat *grapes*? All of us?'

There were about twenty in the group. I gave up my bathe. We all trooped back along our road. I pointed out the vineyard with the young potato shoots.

'Don't go there,' I said. 'There are plenty of vines growing up the hillside. Just help yourselves.'

For a moment they still did not believe it. Then they fell on the loaded vines. Unfortunately the grapes were all red ones. I have never seen anyone eat grapes as those children did. They scrambled up the slope and wrenched fat bunches off the straggling vines. Then, still slipping on the gravelly hillside, they would cram them into their mouths with both hands. Juice poured down their chins and on to their ragged clothes and dripped through their fingers on to the ground. They looked as if they had been through some frightful carnage.

I left them to it and went up to prepare Francisca. I was too late. I found the house barricaded and Francisca cowering in the kitchen. Francisca, who had grown so brave that she would defy the secret police, mock the *ayuntamiento* and even allow the International Brigade to sleep in the house during our absence, was terrified at what she thought was an invasion of hooligans. Even when I explained that I had brought them there myself she was not reassured. I left her in the kitchen, convinced that her worst fears of children's colonies were realized.

When I got back to the children they were practically full. One, a charming blond who looked like the best type of English public-school boy, smiled at me through the red stains.

'Are these grapes yours?' he asked politely. It added to the general surprise when I assured him that they were.

The children then wished to see the house. I suggested that the grape-eating should be finished first, because I didn't much care for blood-like stains all over the house. They agreed, but decided after a pause that they really could eat no more. We then went up to the house. Francisca did not appear.

'Can we go anywhere we like?' asked one of them.

'Yes,' I said, 'only don't fall over the terraces because it would spoil the garden.'

I put no other restrictions on their explorations. They went into every room and opened every cupboard. I did shout up to them to be sure to turn off the taps. The bathrooms fascinated them. They swarmed up the terraces and did gymnastics on the iron ladder. From the very top they yelled to their colleagues in the colony down below. This caused great excitement. Several of the girls from the colony started to come along the road towards our house, but they were driven back by the flood of abuse which greeted them. It seems that Spanish girls and boys have no love for one another. Presently they exhausted the house and I was amused when one of them poked his head into our quarters. He was immediately hauled out by his friends. 'Can't you see that that's private, *burro*?'

On the way down the hill they looked again with longing eyes at the grapes. I said, no; they had had plenty and it was a good idea to leave some for another batch of children. One small boy tried to snatch a bunch as he passed, but a big boy slapped him and made him drop it.

Francisca came out to watch them go.

'Poor little things,' she said. 'They really aren't so bad.'

'Ours will be much worse,' I told her. 'I am asking for really bad ones.'

For the first time she had a little confidence in my abilities to deal with children.

'I believe you would manage them,' she said. 'What made you ask them up?'

When I told her, any confidence she may have had vanished.

'That is encouraging them to steal,' she said.

'They won't ever steal anything from us,' I said.

We had most to do with the Forty-Third Division children because they were so near us, but we tried to take the same interest in the Solidarity Fund colony in the village. This colony was under the care of Señora Santiago, the wife of the Spanish representative of the Solidarity Fund. She was the *Administradora*, and another woman, a large, fussy person, who seemed to have charge of the children's education, was called the *Directora*. We saw more of the latter than of Señora Santiago who seemed to find administration a whole time job. I was sorry because I liked what I saw of her; she seemed very direct and to the point and full of enthusiasm for her work. I found the *Directora* affected and one somehow got the impression she was as hard as nails under her

gushing manner. I had a feeling that the two did not
get on too happily together, although they called each
other punctiliously by their Christian names. I felt it
was a pity that it was the *Directora* who brought the
colony up to tea with us, leaving Señora Santiago busily
sorting out the stores.

The children of this colony were all little things
from five to seven or eight years and none of them could
swim. They wanted to learn and they all had bathing
suits, but, until I took to joining them every day on the
beach, they had not been allowed even to paddle. The
Directora told me that neither she nor the stout Basque
girl who helped her direct the fifteen children, could
swim, so they dared not let the children go near the
water. Archie and I found a peaceful pool and the children were thrilled. After two or three days the Basque,
who came from Bilbao, decided she would like to learn
to swim too. She appeared in a black bathing suit of the
kind that General Franco allows for mixed bathing, a
dank garment with half-sleeves and a thick skirt well
below the knees. For some reason she let down her long
black hair and wallowed in the shallow water uttering
odd cries, looking like a stout, black octopus. When
she grew really daring and started ducking the nervous
children I had to interfere. I held her large red face
under the water for quite a long time. She gave up
bathing.

The children learned quickly. In a week three of them
could swim alone and all the others could paddle along
with corks. The poor *Directora* ran up and down the
beach with anxious clucks as first one and then another
of her brood went out to sea. Then suddenly the children stopped coming to the beach. They went for

walks, two and two. I asked why. The *Directora* told me that the nervous strain was too much for her. Also she confessed that it was dull for her on the beach. She preferred a nice walk.

They all came to tea. We arranged the tables in one row and put out the gayest table cloths and decorated the large room with masses of heliotrope and carnations. The colony brought its own milk and biscuits. The fifteen had become twenty-eight by this time and they filed slowly up the hill like little children going to their first communion. The *Directora* (whom we had nick-named 'the Mo'ca', because of her funny Andalucian way of dropping her s's, and *moscas*, or flies, were one of her pet subjects) sailed slowly ahead of the crocodile burgeoning in navy and white foulard and wearing a pair of navy blue gloves. We felt it was only by the greatest self-control that she had not worn a hat.

If the poor Mo'ca had suffered on the beach, it was nothing to the agonies she went through in our house. It had never struck us before, but danger lurked every-where. There were terraces just arranged for little children to fall over; if they managed to control themselves sufficiently to escape that, the hillside yawned slippery and dangerous under their little feet; behind the house towered jagged rocks which had waited four years to fall and crush good little girls and boys in their best suits; while all around were wild-looking woods, tempt-ing even well-trained little boys to horrible orgies of tree-climbing. The Mo'ca never ceased to admonish her flock. Obviously they had all been given such a lecture before they came that they were practically stunned, but the Mo'ca never let up. We tried in vain to brighten the atmosphere. Archie offered to take the boys into the woods; I suggested showing the girls the house. At last I had an idea. I could not bear the sight of these wretched children standing stiffly to attention while the Mo'ca twittered at them. I decided to make a real sacrifice.

'Won't your little flock entertain us with some of their pretty little songs?' I asked the Mo'ca heroically.

I knew what I was doing. I had already listened twice to bored children singing Spanish nursery rhymes in dreary voices. The Mo'ca looked pleased. It took a little while to find a really safe spot where no one could fall over backwards into space or trip over a flower bed. Then she clapped her hands. The children made a ring, held hands resignedly and took deep breaths. Unfortunately they let all their breath out again because a burst of clapping sounded from the trees behind the house. The Mo'ca looked surprised and waited a few minutes. Then she clapped again. Another burst of applause sounded. The Mo'ca began to look slightly annoyed. This time she signalled to the children to start. Without the initial hand-clap they were at a loss. Some of them started vaguely, others joined in hurriedly with another song. Stung, the Mo'ca forgot herself and clapped again. Loud applause, and a short burst of cheering. With a grim look and beating time silently with a podgy little hand, the Mo'ca rallied and got the children started. I forget the song—a pretty little thing about flowers—but it was completely drowned in a spirited version of the International. There was a roll of drums, and from the woods marched a company of soldiers. They were ragged and dirty and some were still chewing the acorns they had come up to get, but they marched well, and my friend who looked like the Eng-

Grapes and Morals

lish public-school boy was leading them, beating on an old bucket. They saluted as they passed our company and grinned at me. Then they marched across the terrace and down the hill to the colony of the Forty-Third Division. I turned to the Mo'ca. It was time for direct action.

'Such charming little children, don't you think?' I asked her. 'So full of life and fun. Must you really go now?'

19

Spanish Prisoner

Santiago came out to see us at last. We had heard a lot
about him from enthusiastic workers for the International Solidarity Fund in England. 'He is really reli-
able. . . . Although he is Spanish, he gets things done.
. . . He is a marvellous organizer.' Archie, as usual,
reserved his judgment. I frankly disliked the man at
sight; but I am apt to jump to conclusions about people
and am far too ready to be influenced by personal
appearance. I instinctively feel I am going to like
attractive-looking people and I never think of looking
for hearts of gold under repulsive exteriors.

To me Santiago was repulsive. A great, gross creature with a protruding underlip and bulging paunch
came snuffling up our hill. He looked like a travesty of
a frog as he overflowed a chair on the terrace and
breathed hard. Only, I like frogs. However, I was determined to like Santiago. He did not make it easy. He
stared at us with his bright little eyes while we asked
him questions about our colony, and he muttered re-
plies through his chins, so that we could not understand
a word.

When he seemed to have recovered sufficiently from the climb, we showed him the house and told him our ideas. He grunted occasionally and seemed quite pleased. I pointed out Oskar's little house down below. I explained the situation with the chief of police. 'I suppose your organization can fix that?' I asked.

Santiago muttered something.

'Can you see about getting the house?' I asked.

He waved the difficulties away. 'That is nothing at all,' he said, almost becoming articulate. 'I am Enrique Santiago.'

'I suppose you are working with the full support of the Spanish Government,' I said, 'so that little things like taking over houses are mere child's play?'

He stared at me with his pig's eyes. 'I have no difficulties about anything.'

After we had forced a few other statements out of him he took his leave. He said he would send us a paper explaining exactly what the International Solidarity Fund was; that we could expect the beds in a few days; then a load of food and finally the children and teachers. It sounded splendid. I did just remind him that the business of the house had to be settled before anything was sent. He gave me a disdainful look and waddled away down the hill.

We heard nothing more for three weeks.

During that three weeks I had a brain-wave and we had some visitors.

The brain-wave happened while I was lying on the beach with the Reifenbergs. There had been no nets put out for nearly a fortnight, so they had leisure to enjoy the wonderful sunshine. At least they could come down and sprawl in the heat, rolling into the sea when it was unbearable, but they did not enjoy it. They were worried about the lack of work. They still had a little money saved up from the winter fishing, but it was dwindling rapidly. Also money was becoming relatively unimportant. There was nothing to be bought locally, and even the rich Tossencs who went every week to Gerona to pay enormous prices for illegal stuff were beginning to find it not worth while. Apart from the journey, either in an open lorry or on foot to Llagostera, fifteen miles away, there was now a real risk of having the things confiscated by the vigilant carabineros, and often the whole journey would be fruitless simply because there was nothing, contraband or otherwise, to be bought.

The prospects of the Reifenbergs were serious. Now that fish prices were at last controlled, the Tossa fishermen decided it was not worth while to put out their boats, and it looked as if the beach nets would hardly be used at all. Even if the Reifenbergs did manage to earn a few pesetas every day, with maize flour at twelve or fourteen pesetas a kilo when it was obtainable, they could not possibly live on their earnings.

We were discussing the situation when I had my idea.

'Why don't you and Lo come up and work with us in the children's colony?' I asked suddenly.

I elaborated the idea.

'Lo is a marvellous cook. She could soon learn to cook for forty or fifty if I gave her some hints about quantities. It would simplify everything for me, because then I could leave the store open and have Lo in charge of it. That would mean I would have plenty of time for my writing down at Oskar's. You, Fridela, could be responsible for the upstairs department, doing, in fact, a matron's job. Then, with teachers for the children, we shall be complete.'

The Reifenbergs considered. They are like that. Where other people would rush into something without thinking, Fridela likes to weigh up all the pros and cons.

'We would still live in our flat, I suppose.'

'Of course. That is the whole point. The fewer personnel we have living in the house the more room we have for the children.'

I could see Lo's eyes were shining. She adores cooking and the idea of having something to cook at last was appealing to her.

We discussed the various aspects of the idea. Fridela naturally wanted to do it. It meant, so far as food was concerned, and to all of us that was the primary consideration, that she and Lo would have no more worries. But it also meant the end of the Reifenberg complete independence. But independence on an empty stomach is not so alluring. Lo obviously was not so concerned with her independence. She wanted a sack of dried beans and some garlic and to be left to get on with it. They decided to come in with us.

I went up to lunch (lettuce, tomatoes and the remains of our bread ration for the week) feeling something had been accomplished. I had done a real good turn to the Reifenbergs, who certainly deserved it, and I had done myself a good turn as well. It meant far more freedom and leisure for me. Archie was the only one who had to sacrifice anything. He loathes a house full of women and detests floods of German. I vowed I would try to talk only Spanish with Fridela and Lo, but I knew it was hopeless. Archie was pleased at the idea of having more of my company at Oskar's, and delighted to be able to help our friends, so he soon came round to the idea. The only difficulty seemed to be to get the colony started.

Before I had time to write again to Santiago asking when on earth he was going to get a move on about my colony, we had an amusing visit.

Donald Darling wired from the French frontier saying that he and a friend of ours, Dr. Audrey Russell, were coming to Tossa and bringing a friend of Audrey's, Dr. D. J. Collier. Dr. Collier, I knew, was a Catholic who had a great interest in the Spanish people. She had known Spain well before the rebellion and, in spite of the flood of atrocity stories and the propaganda indulged in by most Catholic papers, she had always kept an open mind. At last she decided to come to Republican Spain to see for herself. Also she decided to come as a private individual, not as a guest of the Government; to bring her own car; and to remain for her visit on the footing of an ordinary tourist.

Audrey Russell was coming to Barcelona to represent the International Relief Commission. This was an organization formed by various governments who gave grants of money towards Spanish relief on both sides. As the need was greater in Government Spain, most of the money was earmarked for relief work in Barcelona and Madrid. Sweden contributed £87,000; Great Britain gave £12,000.

We expected them for lunch. I prepared the sort of lunch that can be suddenly made ready at a moment's notice—cold boiled potatoes waiting to be fried up for a potato omelette; six whole eggs wrenched from Antonia's hens in honour of '*La Católica*'; fresh lettuce and tomatoes out of the garden. We went out early and

collected enough mushrooms for a thick soup and
decided to have that and apricot compôte for supper.
Francisca was amusing about a visit from a Catholic.
Francisca had a very strict religious up-bringing, and
there is not much she does not know about the Spanish
Catholic Church. But although she had her own children
confirmed, she utterly refused to go to church herself.
She told me she had never been inside a church since
her marriage. She didn't care for the priests, she
said.

It took some time to drag the story out of her. It happened in Tossa, too. Francisca came to Tossa from
Estramadura as servant to some wealthy people who
moved to Tossa. There she met Pepito and in due course
they were married. Her señora, who was very strict,
sent for Francisca some time before the ceremony and
told her with downcast eyes that she, the Señora, could
not possibly tell Francisca that which she should know
before her marriage, but that the priest might be able
to help. Francisca, young and innocent, went gaily off
to the Tossa priest with never a thought of any out-of-
the-way revelations being made. She turned to me with
her black eyes round at the memory.

'The things that man said to me!' As she spoke I
caught a glimpse of the horrified little Francisca of sixteen or seventeen years, horrified, but still as logical as
ever. 'What I wanted to know was how *he* knew it all.
A priest knowing about things like that! I asked him
right out, "And how does your reverence happen to
know?" I asked. "It's all Nuestro Señor," he told me.
Nuestra Señora, more like, I thought, and I've never
been near a priest since.'

So Francisca did not quite approve of *La Católica*

until I explained that she was also a doctor. That seemed to balance things, as it were.

At four o'clock we gave up the idea of their coming to lunch and we prepared a good tea. They had obviously got delayed on the way and probably would have missed lunch. I made some scones out of maize meal and raisins some one had sent us in a parcel, and we sat out on the terrace in the hot sun and waited. At six o'clock I decided to hoe a few rows of potatoes and started down the hill to the vineyard. Then we saw the big car coming slowly along the road. Archie and I rushed down to greet them. It was lovely seeing Audrey again and I was delighted to meet Marguerita Comas. Don seemed very cheerful. He was sitting in front with a carabinero. Dr. Collier, a charming person with a friendly smile and amused grey eyes, jumped out of the car and said:

'We are all prisoners, you know. It is such fun!'

Every one started to laugh except the carabinero who stood self-consciously by the side of the car. He was a very young carabinero.

Don said, 'It is quite true. At least Dr. Collier was arrested at the frontier and we are being public-school and standing by her. Meet our guard.'

The poor carabinero blushed crimson. He looked at me in an agony of misery. I tried to cheer him up. 'Well, let's all go up to the prison.' I indicated the house.

'Please don't talk about prisons,' he said. 'You know this is all very serious. But I can't get anyone to be serious about it.'

We shrieked with laughter.

'How on earth did they allow you to come here?' I asked on the way up to the house.

It appeared that Don had used his persuasive powers

very adequately and the dangerous criminal, Dr. Collier, was allowed to spend a night at the Casa Johnstone *en route* to one of Barcelona's darkest dungeons, on condition that she was heavily guarded. Hence the little carabinero. The trouble was that a permit to bring in a certain number of pesetas lacked one of the half-dozen necessary signatures. There was a gang operating abroad issuing false permits, and by an unlucky chance the frontier officials had just let a big sum of money slip through and were still feeling sore at the comments from Barcelona headquarters. So, although Dr. Collier did not look like a gangster, and Donald Darling's credentials were excellent, the chief of the carabineros at the frontier was taking no chances. Into prison first and explanations later. However, luckily, there was something about Dr. Collier that inspired confidence, and he felt it would do no harm to allow the whole party (he had hesitated for a while whether to arrest every one, including Don) to pass the night with some respectable-sounding English friends at Tossa. We took it as a tremendous joke. The only annoying part was the delay after a long motor drive, but Dr. Collier assured us she would not have missed the experience for anything.

'That is one of the advantages of not coming in officially as a guest of the Government,' she said. 'I would have missed all the amusing bits.'

The little carabinero grew more cheerful when he realized how we all reacted to the situation. He began to think that these mad foreigners had a card up their sleeves. He became quite bright at supper and we had a lively meal. There was only one moment when he was a little shaken. Audrey and Dr. Collier wanted Don to take them up to the old town by moonlight. They were arranging it all quite happily when I turned to their guard.

'Will you allow your prisoners to wander off alone like that?' I asked.

The poor little man was shattered.

'I am not on duty now,' he gasped. 'Why, I have left my revolvers upstairs on my bed! Please, we are all friends while we are here in your house. See, I have no arms at all,' he insisted on getting up and slapping his sides. 'Every one can do just what they like.' Then a shade of anxiety crossed his face. 'Of course I hope that every one will be ready to start at nine o'clock to-morrow morning. I shall get into trouble if we are not at the Barcelona headquarters by twelve. I don't want to inconvenience anyone, but if we *could* be there by twelve——'

We assured him the prisoners would be delivered on time.

Dr. Collier charmed every one. She went off to Barcelona and there delivered herself to the mercies of the 'Red' police. They were furious with the poor carabinero chief at the frontier. They were profuse in their apologies. They sent her to more offices where more chiefs of police apologized. Poor Dr. Collier spent nearly a day in Barcelona being apologized to. Her carabinero guard went back to his post at the frontier in a glow of heroism. He knew all the time that the lady wasn't a gangster.

Dr. Collier paid us another visit at the end of her Spanish holiday. We had hoped that she would come for a week at least, but she could not tear herself away from Barcelona for more than a few days. She came for three days on her way back to England. She was full of plans for sending out medical supplies. She was triumphant because she had seen for herself all that she had suspected was the truth about Republican Spain. She, an avowed Catholic, had spent a month's holiday among the 'Reds'. She had been to Mass in Barcelona; she had played (with one finger) the organ in Montserrat; she had visited churches, schools, hospitals. She had motored in her own car over most of Catalunya, seeing everything she asked to be shown. She had no other document than her passport and the only document she possessed for the car was the French receipt for the deposit always required before a foreign car can go through France. She came into war-ridden Spain to see things for herself. She had hardly left Spain before several million typhus injections were sent into Barcelona, cases of aspirin, and other urgently needed medical supplies. *La Católica* was showing her appreciation of her holiday in practical form.

20

The Policeman in Possession

Marcelino telephoned up that Sr. Santiago was at the Residencia in the village and would we please come down to see him? I felt slightly annoyed, but we were so glad to get some news of the colony that we decided to go down. I could not get used to the International Solidarity Fund's way of calling children's colonies *Residencias*. In Spanish it simply means a place where one resides, but to the British mind it recalls empires and governor-generals.

We found Santiago deep in an armchair playing with his little son, Riki. He did not get up but waved us to a sofa. Señora Santiago was very friendly and started to tell us all about the trials of running a *Residencia*. There were nearly fifty children in this colony by now, all under eight years, but it seemed that the real difficulties arose among the staff. Señora Santiago whispered to me to be very careful whom I had to work with me. I asked Santiago if he had any news for us about the colony, the teachers, etc. He did not answer because he was absorbed in Riki. I repeated it again very loudly. Señora Santiago sent me a quick glance and called her son to her.

The Policeman in Possession

Santiago roused himself a little. He said calmly that it was quite impossible to get Oskar's house.

It takes a lot to defeat me, but it really sounded as if there was not much hope. If the International Solidarity Fund backed by the Spanish Government could not get the house, it did not seem likely that Archie and I could achieve much on our own. However, I reserved judgment until I heard just exactly what had been tried. Archie and I had decided privately that we would carry the matter to Alvarez del Vayo if necessary. He could at least be counted on to see the propaganda value of letting us use the house.

It took a little time to get out of Santiago exactly what he had done. Then I almost blew up. He had done nothing more than to interview the Chief of the Tossa Police in person and to ask for the house! The Chief of the Tossa Police not unnaturally said there was no possible chance of our getting the house; that it had now been discovered that Oskar was a fascist, by documents found by the chief of the Tossa police himself; that he had no intention of moving out of the house, and that the International Solidarity Fund could look somewhere else for their colony.

Even then it took me some time to believe that Santiago had done nothing more. Surely he had approached the man's immediate superiors in Barcelona? No, Santiago had just accepted meekly the decision of the Tossa policeman not to be turned out of his nice house. I took a deep breath. Before I had been speaking very long I saw a glint appear in Señora Santiago's eye. I could almost imagine it was a glint of approval. Santiago sank still lower into his chair, his under lip thrust out, his eyes completely hidden under his monkey eyebrows. He roused himself to mutter a protest when I accused him of incompetence and when that did not quell me he started to roar. It was interesting to hear the odd noises that came out of those many chins. He soon stopped roaring when he saw I was not impressed. I finished saying what I thought about him and asked him what he proposed to do. Did he still want the colony started? If so, what was he going to do about it? He muttered that of course he wanted the colony, but that he couldn't get Oskar's house. I said *I* would get Oskar's house. Slight noises from the cautious Archie. I said we would start our colony with ten children at once. I would obtain Oskar's house; we could then have the rest of the children. All he, Santiago, had to do was to send out beds, food, ten children and a teacher. I would do the rest.

Santiago agreed. He appeared slightly stunned. Señora Santiago came with us to the gate. She shook me warmly by the hand.

'My dear, I think you are just the person to run a colony. You won't let anyone put anything over on you. Take my advice and be firm about everything.'

Suddenly she dropped my hand and started back. The Mo'ca stood just behind us.

'I am sorry to interrupt secrets,' said the Mo'ca. She fidgeted with the frills on her blouse.

Señora Santiago sighed.

'You are not interrupting anything, dear Enriqueta,' she said, and her eyes looked suddenly strange and wild.

'I am so glad, Julia dear,' said the Mo'ca. Then she suddenly turned on little Riki, who was with his mother. 'You bad boy, how dare you miss your classes. Go at once to the schoolroom.'

Riki pushed out his lower lip in imitation of his father.

'I won't,' he said.

The Mo'ca slapped him. Señora Santiago did not say a word. Her eyes still had a peculiar expression. Then she said, 'Run along, Riki, there's a good boy!'

'I should say so,' the Mo'ca sent him flying with a push.

'Good-bye!' I said hastily.

On the way home I asked Archie, who was rather silent:

'Have you any idea how we shall get the policeman out of the house?' I asked.

'Not the slightest. Have you?'

'Not yet,' I said.

By teatime we had an idea. Archie wrote a magnificent letter to the chief of the Puertos y Fronteras police in Barcelona. We did not quite understand the Spanish police system, but it seemed to be divided up into sections which had no connection with each other. The black-hatted secret police were a thing apart, but Puertos y Fronteras, which was simply the police of the ports and frontiers, were the only police in our area.

We sent this letter, which was a real Archie achievement, to Donald Darling in Barcelona, asking him to put it into real Spanish. He sent us a copy. It was superb. Between the two of them it was a letter that no one could resist. The Police Chief in Barcelona succumbed with hardly a struggle. A week or so after the letter was sent a smart young man came briskly up our hill. He wore a revealing black hat, but we had lately been so free of secret police that we were unsuspecting. We talked for a while in the polite fencing way that is all part of Spanish good manners. It is rude to barge straight in with the business in hand when one has just met some one. At last he admitted that he had been sent from the Police Commissar in Barcelona to find out just exactly what was happening about this house.

We produced our last bottle of pre-war sherry and settled down to a comfortable conversation. It slowly appeared that the policeman was under an illusion. He had spoken to the Tossa chief before coming up to see us. He asked us without a glint of humour in his eye if we really intended putting fifty children in Oskar's tiny house.

In our letter to the Commissar of Puertos y Fronteras we had pointed out various interesting facts about the Tossa chief's attitude. One was that he had no business in the house at all as the property had never been commandeered. Another was that even if he was within his rights to live in a house closed by the police, surely on humanitarian grounds alone he should move to a smaller house in order to allow children to be rescued from starvation and bombs. As to his allegations that Oskar was a fascist, it did not seem relevant to the case for not using the house as a children's colony, but we hoped that the Barcelona police had seen these new proofs which had just been found, although the house had been searched twice before and nothing incriminating discovered. We then went on to explain exactly our plans for the colony: why we needed the little house in order to carry out our plans; the number of children we hoped to have, etc.

And here was the representative of the Commissar asking us if we intended to put all the children in Oskar's house while we lived in luxury in the Casa Johnstone.

'Did Sr. Massana say that?' I asked.

The policeman coughed gently. 'He conveyed that impression,' he said.

'Oh, he did, did he?'

'Of course I did not quite credit the suggestion,' said the policeman. 'It did not sound quite reasonable to me.'

We smiled at each other. We felt we understood one another very well.

When we had explained the situation a little more clearly he told us frankly that he could see no reason why we should not have the use of the house. He would put the matter up to his superior in Barcelona, but we could consider it as settled. Then, as he was leaving, he turned to us confidentially:

'Tell me your private opinion of this Sr. Oskar,' he said. 'Would you have said that he was a fascist?'

I told him my impression of Oskar. I said it was always dangerous to assume one knew people's politics, but that I would stake a lot on my belief that Oskar was no fascist.

'He is very bourgeois,' I said unkindly. 'He loves his comforts and his painting. That is why he left Spain. He was not getting his comforts and he was too upset by events to paint. I think that anyone who abandons his house and possessions deserves to lose them, but I don't think Oskar deserves to lose his on the ground that he is a fascist. I am equally certain that he hasn't strong Leftist convictions. It is absurd to suggest that Massana has found incriminating documents in the house. I was there twice when it was searched and nothing whatever was found. Have you asked Massana if he speaks German?'

'No, why?'

'Because Oskar spoke no Spanish. Therefore any written evidence must have been in German.'

'I don't somehow think that our friend Massana speaks German,' said the policeman softly. 'In any case, he has not mentioned the documents to us at all. If he has found them it is a grave offence not to report them to headquarters.'

The policeman thanked us profusely for being so helpful, and went away. He assured us that we would hear from the Commissar in a few days.

We got a lovely document from the Commissar. It authorised us to have the full use of Oskar's house and grounds for the purpose of running a children's colony. It was a mass of official-looking stamps. At the end it just said: 'You will inform Sr. Massana of this decision and place yourself in agreement with him on the matter.'

We rushed off to the Tossa Commissariat. The chief of the Tossa police was there and would see us. We determined to be magnanimous. We told him gently that we had permission from Barcelona to use Oskar's house. I am afraid there was a glint of triumph in our eyes.

He seemed very gracious about it. Of course we would allow him a little time to look around for another house. It all came rather as a surprise to him, but he had always told us that he would be delighted for us to have the house if his superiors would allow it. We felt so pleased about everything that I said of course he could have a week to move. We would not dream of hurrying him. He said he would ask the *ayuntamiento* at once about the prospect of houses in Tossa. He shook his head sadly at the thought. 'There are very few houses available, you know. It won't be so easy. But I will do my best.' I should have been warned by this, but I felt everything was so secure. We shook hands warmly and departed.

A fortnight later we were no further forward. We had not heard from Santiago, and the Tossa chief was still in the house. We wrote a rude letter to Santiago telling him to reply by return of post or we would offer our house to the Quakers to use as a colony. By the same post we wrote to the Quakers in Barcelona, telling them the situation and asking them if they would be interested if Santiago did not reply. We also wrote to the International Solidarity Fund office in London asking them if *they* were still interested. We then sat back and waited some more.

We distributed our grapes among all the Tossa children's colonies. Most of the colonies were living on a diet of beans and chick peas with no fresh vegetables or fruit. The children seemed extremely well on this diet, but they had a craving for fruit which was almost uncontrollable. It was difficult to take a hundred children for a walk through vineyards and past loaded peach trees without their breaking loose and stealing fruit. The Tossa children have always stolen fruit and were not going to stop because of the strangers, but somehow the Tossencs turned a blind eye to the doings of their own young and ranted more than ever against the refugee children. There were exceptions. The Casa Blanca invited the children to help themselves to figs and, to show their gratitude, the children never stole the Casa Blanca peaches or grapes. Antonia sent over baskets of plums to the Forty-Third Division and Molí Lluns supplied apples. But the concerted efforts of all three could not give more than a bite among so many. I began to think every one was mad or that Archie and I must be off our heads. The Quakers did not answer my letter about using our house (later we learned that our letter took four weeks to reach them in Barcelona); Santiago did not reply; the only answer was from England saying that the International Solidarity Fund were still interested and that we were not to let anyone else have the house. The immediate action was against the Tossa policeman. We went down to the Commissariat to let off steam.

This time the chief of the Tossa police abused the *ayuntamiento*. They would not help him to find another house. They were sabotaging him all the time. I happened to have seen the *ayuntamiento* about this and they had assured me that they had shown the policeman four houses, but he had not cared for any of them. I put this to the policeman. He denied point-blank that he had looked at any houses. It was a toss up which of the liars to believe, but for convenience' sake I pretended to believe the policeman. I changed my tactics.

'There is no great hurry for the actual house,' I said. 'But we must have the garden and the use of the washplace. We have been sent plants for the garden and they must be planted at once. So, if you let us put in a door in the back wall we can go in and out, work in the garden, use the studio as a store, the women can come in to do the washing and you can have the use of the house for a week or so longer. That arrangement should suit every one.'

The chief of police did not think so. He smiled condescendingly at us.

'You do not quite understand,' he said, drawing

himself up. 'Johnstones' (he pronounced this '*Hon-stoneys*'), 'you do not, I fear, realize who I am. I am the chief of the Tossa police. As such, I cannot have people running in and out of my garden. I am in an important position; it would be impossible to have un-authorized entry to my house.'

'Not the house, the garden,' I persisted. 'It would not interfere with your living in the house if we used the garden and had a separate entrance. And this door will have to be made in the garden wall in any case whether you are still in the house or not.'

The chief of the Tossa police banged his fist on the table. He started to shout, or rather boom. He boomed away for a long time. I amused myself by making sneering noises at intervals, crossing my knees and putting my feet upon Archie's chair, heaving deep sighs of boredom and even uttering a short laugh when he shouted for the third time that he was the chief of the Tossa police. This pulled him up, and he asked me why I laughed.

'Because it is funny,' I answered. I was behaving about as badly as I knew how. Archie was not quite approving of such blatant ill-manners, but was hopeful that I knew what I was doing. It certainly had the effect of making the elegant chief of police lose his self-con-trol. He stuttered with fury and crashed and banged away at his desk. The villagers in the square were wait-ing fascinated to see us come flying out of the window. At last I had had enough. *I* started banging on the desk. It had the effect of stopping him for a moment out of surprise.

'Shut up!' I said. 'You just can't frighten us. You are a silly conceited little man with bourgeois ideas and I can't waste any more time on you. I am telling you now, not asking you, that that door is going to be put in the wall and that we are going to use the garden. We shan't argue any more. We shall act.'

'*H*onstoneys!' he shouted. 'How dare you speak to me like this?'

We got up. 'We aren't going to speak any more.'

We marched out without saying good-bye. He followed us to the top of the stairs leading down into the square. He was still shouting something about not allowing us to speak to him in this way and calling us by our surname every three words. His deputies, Manuel and the Sargento, were coming up the stairs. They looked scared.

'*Salud!*' finally yelled Massana as a parting shot. I stopped on the stairs.

'I cannot say "*salud*" to anyone as self-centred as you are,' I said in a fury. Poor Manuel and the Sargento quailed under my fierce look as I swept down the stairs. Archie followed chuckling quietly.

'It was fun, but I don't think we have achieved much,' he said on the way home.

We had not achieved much. After two months we were no nearer to our children's colony and we had an enemy in the chief of the local police. No one seemed to love us or want our house. We sat gloomily on the terrace and almost resigned ourselves to living the rest of the war in glorious idleness. I eyed Oskar's house down below with some bitterness. The back garden wall stretched solid and entire, so near and so convenient.

'Archie,' I said, 'I am going to get a door put in that wall if we have to do it ourselves.'

21

Breaching the Wall

Before we had time to think any more about the police-man a lorry arrived laden with food.

Unless people have actually suffered from a food shortage it is impossible for them to understand how we used to react to the arrival of food parcels. The childish thrill of expecting to find a full Christmas stocking, the almost sickening excitement of opening a long-expected present, the glow of anticipation before the school holidays, all seemed merged into one wonderful reality that fifty pounds of solid food had arrived. The difference between the food parcel and anticipated childish joys was that never were we disappointed. The realization was even more wonderful than the anticipation. Oddly enough, we took as much interest in other people's parcels as in our own. We could watch with intense delight the gradually unwrapping of a Reifenberg parcel, they were equally thrilled to help us tear off the wrappings and delve in the shavings of our parcels.

It was a form of delightful self-indulgence to distribute gifts from our parcels; to provide necessary delicacies for a sick child; to gladden a Catalan heart with a slab of bacon fat; to produce tinned milk for a baby. It was a miracle to be in the position to keep a whole family alive. We began to understand the self-satisfaction of the lady bountifuls with their little baskets visiting their starving tenants. It seemed unkind to want to introduce a system under which tenants did not starve.

If a fifty pound parcel could cause such excitement, the arrival of a large lorry stunned us. We watched Tonet staggering up the hill with sacks of beans, split peas, lentils, rice, chick peas. Two husky Basque boys followed with large boxes of macaroni, ground rice, Quaker Oats, a packing case containing a hundred packets of milk chocolate, a case of dried milk, a barrel of oil, fifty pounds of butter, a case of smoked sausages, cases of tinned meat, boxes of sardines and tinned salmon, a sack of salt.

A South American chauffeur, called Toni, checked the lists with me. He apologized profusely for not bringing the *bacalao*, or dried fish. That would be along next week. He also had brought ten beds complete with bedding, fifty towels and a hundred handkerchiefs.

The Reifenbergs came tearing up from the village. The entire family from the Casa Blanca came running over the hill. Antonia called, ostensibly with some cabbages. Perez passed by with some fish. Various other friends suddenly remembered they had something urgent to say to us.

We all unpacked and arranged and rearranged the sacks and boxes in our old office. We gloated over the beautiful white beans with their faintly blushing tips; we let the split peas trickle between our fingers; we stroked the lentils. I wanted to give something to each of our visitors, but they were shocked at the idea. The food was for the children. I confess I had for the moment forgotten about the children. I compromised by finding a huge tin of coffee and making a great potful for all of us. We had not tasted real coffee for months; we made ours from toasted millet.

Lo spent an entrancing afternoon making lists and filling books of reference ready for the day when she started in the kitchen. I left her weighing and measuring bowlfuls of chick peas and muttering to herself. Fridela went away by herself to work out exactly how to divide a hundred handkerchiefs among forty-five children. Archie began to move large flower-pots to form spiky cactus barricades in front of the most cherished parts of his rock garden. I sat on the terrace and brooded over Oskar's virgin garden wall.

The next day Archie went to a friend of his and borrowed a mason's hammer and chisel.

We had often watched masons knocking bricks out of walls; it is a Catalan habit to build walls and then knock them down again. It looked easy. A quick blow and out falls the brick. Oskar's wall appeared to be of sterner stuff. We chipped away at the cement around a top brick and then gave a quick blow. The wall rocked to its foundations, every one working in the gardens gazed in horror, the hills echoed, but the brick remained where it was.

Our chief concern was to get as much of the wall down as possible before the infuriated policeman appeared. We had chosen the hour when he was in the commissariat in the market-place, so that his wife would take a little time to fetch him. We took it in turns to bang at the top brick. We lost caution and rained blows on it.

Breaching the Wall

We hammered until our wrists ached and our eyes were full of flying chips. Francisca and Quimeta stood like statues on the Casa Johnstone terrace. The garden workers were frozen into immobility. Suddenly there was a rending sound and seven bricks, still firmly stuck together, fell out and into the policeman's garden, nearly braining the policeman's wife.

She was a sour-looking little thing at the best of times, and she looked shaken.

'Who gave you permission to do this?' she asked acidly, shaking the brick dust out of her hair.

'Permission?' I asked. 'What sort of permission?'

'Does my husband know about this?' She tried a different tack.

'Oh yes, I told him.'

'Oh, then you have his permission?' She seemed surprised.

'He certainly knows all about it,' I said hastily. 'I told him only a few days ago I was going to put the door in this week.'

'Oh, in that case——' She moved away doubtfully. Later she could be seen peeping from an upstair window.

Archie tidied up the breach. We were elated by our success at removing bricks and thought we would make a thorough job of it. Unfortunately there was an ominous cracking and it was quite obvious that the next blow would make a large hole in the wrong direction. We patted the crack gently and decided that now was the time to leave the fruits of our labour, a nice tidy hole.

We went along to the commissariat. We felt the policeman should be told. We were shattered to find that he was in Gerona for the day.

Breaching the Wall

We ate our usual lettuce and tomato lunch, but we were not very hungry. We seemed to see that gaping hole as a reproach. We were quite prepared to get the row over at once, but we did not relish waiting for it. We began to wonder just what was the power of the chief of the Tossa police. We began to think about the laws of housebreaking. Even the congratulations of the Reifenbergs and Quimeta and Francisca failed to cheer us. Francisca had perfect faith in our ability to deal with any official. We hoped that she was right.

I have said 'we', but Archie was not really concerned. He knew from the first moment I suggested breaking down the wall that we would probably end in serious trouble. He knew that it was insane to make an enemy of the local police chief; that he would be justified in having us imprisoned; that he most likely *would* put us in prison. It was Archie's sense of loyalty that made him a reluctant supporter of my wilder schemes. He would never commit himself to any approval, but he invariably stood by, ready for the worst.

Manuel and the sergeant of police came to fetch us at a quarter to four. We knew them both; they were in Tossa before we went to England. They shuffled uncomfortably. We asked them to sit down. They eagerly fell into chairs. The conversation dragged so I offered to show them the house, already arranged for the colony. They leapt at the suggestion and out of their chairs. At last they had to come to the point. Would we please come down to the commissariat at four-thirty to speak with the chief? We said we would come with them right away. Oh no, that would look too much as if we were being compelled to come. They would prefer us to come down later by ourselves.

Breaching the Wall

We insisted on accompanying them down. Francisca followed, determined to wait in the market-place until she knew the worst. The village rippled with excitement as we passed through the streets, each with an attendant policeman.

The Chief of the Tossa Police was speechless. His face was the colour of cheese. He could only gasp and bang his desk. He eventually found his voice and asked us what we had done. Done? Why, made a hole, we replied. We had told him we would. Next time he could believe that we meant what we said.

He spoke for about ten minutes about the laws of Spain. He told us that one could not break into people's gardens in Spain; that the laws of Spain protected innocent householders, even chiefs of police, from people breaking down their walls; the laws of Spain were good laws, designed to thwart people like us; we should study the laws of Spain——

Archie surprisingly interrupted. 'Yes, yes, the laws are the same in England,' he said impatiently.

The policeman burst into a denunciation so rapid and complicated that we could not follow it. I understood vaguely that he was complaining that we were not Spanish subjects. It seems that he could have dealt with us in a manner particularly pleasing to him if only we had been Spanish. Suddenly he recollected something and shot at us, 'Who gave you permission to do this—this outrage?' He was not quite sure of our influence with the Barcelona police. He was reassured when I answered blandly that we had acted entirely on our own initiative.

I grew tired of listening to these long, high-flown speeches. I wanted to know the worst. I banged on the desk. I had found by experience that it was the only way to interrupt the flow of infuriated rhetoric.

'Shut up!' I shouted. 'Listen to me, you silly old man,' and words to that effect until he was quiet by sheer surprise.

'Listen,' I went on quickly before he could recover. 'It is a waste of time all this noise. There are only three possibilities; one, you can be sensible and let us put in the door without all this fuss; two, you can get a mason to brick up the wall, but I tell you we shall immediately knock it down again; three, you can put us both in prison. Now, make up your mind.'

The moment I said the word 'prison' I knew that we had won. He suddenly changed his tone.

'Prison? Well, really, *H*onstoneys, we won't talk about prison. After all we don't need such desperate remedies. No, no, we won't mention anything so unpleasant as prison.'

'Of course we will mention prisons,' I said indignantly. 'You will have to put us in prison. We insist on being put in prison.'

He looked positively hunted. 'Really, *H*onstoneys,' he protested, but Archie interrupted him.

Archie had been getting whiter and whiter. It is always a sign that a deep Scots rage is slowly coming to flame. He rose and stood over the seated policeman.

'How dare you?' said Archie, in his best Aberdeen Spanish, 'how dare you think you can keep fifty children in Barcelona to be bombed and starved? Of course we shall put in that door.' He subsided slowly into his chair.

The chief of police was finished. He smiled a sickly smile.

'Now do you think that is really the best place for the door?' he asked ingratiatingly. 'I had thought of putting it in the other wall, near the studio.'

Archie and I spoke together, as though we had been rehearsed.

'The laws of Spain', we chanted, 'say that a door can only be put in a wall where there is a public thoroughfare. There is no public thoroughfare where you want the door, but there is a public thoroughfare where we have made our hole. You should study the laws of Spain——'

The next day I answered the telephone. A well-known voice said, 'Casa *H*onstoney?'

'Yes,' I answered.

The voice became dulcet. 'Ah, is that Nancy?'

The chief of the Tossa police had decided upon a policy of appeasement.

It took us ten days to complete our victory. We let loose relays of children from the Forty-Third Division Colony in Oskar's garden, ostensibly to weed and collect snails, but really with orders to make as much noise as possible. In an amazing way the houses offered by the *ayuntamiento* became highly desirable residences. The chief of police moved rapidly into one of them. We had Oskar's house.

After three months' hard work we had achieved the accommodation and the food, but still no children. I wrote another rude letter to Santiago. This time I did not threaten to offer the houses to the Quakers who apparently did not want them either, but I said that if the children did not arrive in a week I would distribute the food among the other colonies.

Señora Santiago could not understand the delay. She assured me that Santiago was overworked; that he had not visited her for over a month. I thought she herself looked overworked. She was very thin and had a twitch in her eyes. She said that the work was not so bad, but she found the atmosphere very trying. I thought she referred to the dampness of the village. She suddenly clutched my hand and drew me close, whispering hoarsely, 'I'm surrounded. I can never get away.' I saw the Mo'ca approaching us, a look of fury on her face. It cleared when she saw me looking at her.

'Julia, dearest,' she cooed, 'am I interrupting? I don't want to interrupt secrets.'

'No, no, Enriqueta, no secrets,' murmured Señora Santiago, dropping my arm.

We were sitting with the Reifenbergs on our terrace when we saw the children arrive. A little group of black figures rounded the corner by the beach. Each carried a small bundle. There was something indescribably forlorn and helpless about the nine small figures trotting after one large stout one. Nine children and a teacher had arrived. We prepared to rush down the hill to welcome them. Archie went on ahead to help with the bundles; Lo rushed into the kitchen to fling macaroni on to boil; Fridela and I followed Archie more slowly. Fridela was glowing with excitement. She suddenly embraced me. 'I do hope it will be a success,' she whispered. I was too occupied scrutinizing the advancing children to answer. They seemed very small, but perhaps that was just because we were looking down on them. Of course it would be a success. The teacher looked peculiar; he was so very fat and unintellectual in appearance. Archie was talking to him. He suddenly wrung Archie's hand and walked rapidly away across the gardens. Archie was left helplessly laden with bundles, with nine incredibly small children clustered round him.

They were extremely unprepossessing. They were dead tired after the long journey from Barcelona; they were surrounded by extraordinary foreigners; they wore the oddest assortment of clothes, mostly black. There was one small boy in a miniature edition of a real flash Barcelona suit. He looked ready to burst into tears. A bossy small girl, in draggled black chiffon, assured us that her name was Maria Josefa and that the other little girl in black chiffon was her five-year-old sister, called Carmen. Maria Josefa added that she was seven. A larger black-clad figure detached itself from a smaller one and introduced itself as Josefina, aged thirteen. Josefina was very plain, with crimped, permanently waved hair and spots, but she radiated good nature. We turned to her with one accord. She could help sort out the mass of small children and unpack their bundles. We all trooped up to the bedrooms.

Francisca had retired to the kitchen. She was secretly relieved that the children were small and of both sexes. She felt sorry for the poor little things. As long as Francisca could feel sorry for anything she was no longer scared. '*Pobret*,' she would cry about large dogs, bad children, or policemen, and thenceforth they would hold no fears.

Upstairs we tried to sort out the children. We had arranged rooms for ten children of unknown sex, finally hitting upon an arrangement which seemed to satisfy mathematics and the segregation of sexes. We rapidly assimilated the children's names. José, a white-faced boy of fourteen, shared a room with a view over Tossa Bay with his brother Ramón, an engagingly ugly child, and Miguel, the owner of the Barcelona suit; Miguel's minute sister, Pepita, a devastatingly pretty child of about four, and Carmen, were put into one of our best single rooms, facing south; Maria Josefa, Pilar, sister of José and Ramón and pleasantly stolid, Josefina and her small cousin, Maria, a terrified white-faced object with enormous sad eyes, were put in a big double room with a view over Tossa and the surroundings hills. We left them unpacking their odd bundles or *bultos* and told Josefina to wash the little ones' faces for lunch.

We were silent while we laid the tables for lunch. No one dared say what was in every one's minds. Francisca's '*pobrets!*' seemed all that could be said about them. We grimly laid the tables and prepared a large meal in the sunshine on the terrace.

Josefina brought the smallest ones down; the older ones raced down by themselves. They seemed less unattractive. They admired the view; they said they liked macaroni; they said they liked the house; they implied that they were going to like us. After lunch Carmen gave us a song. Her sister said Carmen liked singing, but was not to be encouraged too much, it became boring. We sent them up for a rest with the promise to take them to the beach before tea. We heard them shrieking with laughter in their bedrooms. We washed up the plates and became happier. Perhaps after a few weeks, with a bit of sunburn and good food, they might look almost human. We planned how we would compel the International Solidarity Fund to take back the ones under eight. It was far too dangerous to have such small children on our hillside with no one to look after them. Also we decided to have a word to say about sending the children without a teacher. In the meantime we would do our best to cope with them. It would be fun to show them the beach.

22

Children's Hotel

It was surprising how those children changed in a few days.

We had to tackle the clothes problem at once. Archie found José triumphantly in one of his shirts; other shirts disappeared and reappeared as two small ones, conjured up magically by Sebastiana, a diminutive dressmaker in the village. We made over the old hotel bed-covers into frocks for the girls; the small flowered pattern looked fresh and attractive and laundered easily. Archie's aged flannel trousers were ruthlessly cut up; the Reifenbergs produced derelict towels to make into face cloths and bath flannels; I handed over all my summer frocks. Sebastiana came up every day and sat in the sun sewing; we embroidered numbers on every garment, having conjured scraps of sewing silk from all our friends. Sewing materials, including ordinary white or black cotton, were nearly unobtainable. There were no needles, but I had brought some back from England.

We dug out our last supply of coke and coal and put on the hot water. Then we bathed the children. They had never been bathed, but they were all country children, used to bathing in rivers in the summer and swilling themselves under the pump in the winter. They had been unable to do much washing in Barcelona, living in overcrowded houses with no soap. They were extraordinarily dirty. We found we had to keep the boiler fire going for two days. One bath only scratched the surface.

The older children liked their baths. They appreciated being clean, they soaped themselves eagerly and ruthlessly, hair, eyes, everything. The smaller ones were more anxious. Pepita, aged four, screamed lustily. She was obviously pampered at home and she was determined to do exactly what she liked. She was extraordinarily pretty, with fair curly hair, a pink and white skin and deep blue eyes fringed with long black lashes. She sat in her bath and yelled. We hurriedly put Pilar, stolid and phlegmatic, in the bath beside her. She hit Pilar a resounding blow with a small fist and cried harder than ever. I decided that she was not frightened and let her scream. I started to wash the calm Pilar. Pilar, aged five, told me that her brother José could swim. She wanted to learn. Did I think she would learn to swim in Tossa? I suggested she started in the bath. We pushed the shrieking Pepita to one end, and Pilar lay on her stomach and kicked heartily. Pepita peeped at us through her fingers. Pilar and I had a fine time. Pepita slapped Pilar's backside and pushed her out of the way. She lay on *her* stomach and tried to swim. She still sobbed at intervals, but she was determined not to be outdone by Pilar. I managed to get a fair amount of washing done, and at last got them wrapped in towels and back in their rooms. Pepita was supremely happy, capering about her bed with no clothes on. She was supple as a slack-bender and could twist her limbs in any position. She was racing up and

234

down the bed on all fours, pretending to be a puppy, when the door opened and her brother Miguel looked in. He was not good-looking like his sister. He had the same fair colouring, but there was a tight, mean look about his face. He gave one look at his naked sister, blushed scarlet and hastily shot out of the room. I foresaw a certain amount of trouble with Miguel.

Miguel, aged eight, was the only one of the children who did not feel at his ease. He expressed this by being truculent. While the others were enthusiastic over any suggestion to go to the beach or for a walk in the woods, he would hunch his shoulders and say, 'I don't like the silly old beach.' He maintained firmly that he did not like it at the Casa Johnstone. He wanted to go home. We told him that he could certainly go home, but we pointed out that with the transport services what they were, it would take a day or two to arrange. We were terribly sorry, but he would have to put up with us for a few days until we could arrange things. He saw the point of this and suggested he should write to his mother asking her to come to see him. Would we please write the letter for him? We said, of course we would. At that moment we were busy, but if he would remind us later at a good moment, we would write to his dictation.

Miguel did not forget his letter. Once he asked me to write it when I was obviously busy and I put it off; another time I chose a moment when Miguel was engrossed in a snail race up the outside wall of the house and suggested doing it then and there. This gave me an excuse the next time he wanted it done. But the letter would have to be written. We knew we would have to write exactly what he chose to dictate, but there seemed to be no dishonesty in influencing what was to be dictated.

Several of the children wanted letters written for them. We collected them all together and I sat patiently pen in hand, waiting to be told what to say. Fridela joined the group. The children explained they wanted to say how much they liked it here. Then some one suggested describing in great detail their meals. We rapidly covered several pages, 'for breakfast we had two cups of chocolate, as much bread as we could eat. For lunch, beans with meat sauce, lettuce, and biscuits and jam. For supper vermicelli soup, bread and butter and sardines with salad and a bar of milk chocolate. We also had three biscuits for *merienda*.' The *merienda* always caused great excitement. It was a meal equivalent to tea, and in the summer when the days were long, children usually had a cup of milk. The really high spot of the letters was a detailed account of having eaten fried potatoes. The children had eyed their plates for a moment in stunned silence and then with one accord yelled, '*Viva la cocinera!*' Lo was thrilled.

I finished off all the letters. 'The directors, who are called Nancy and Archie, are very *simpáticos*,' was dictated to me. I turned to Miguel who had been a silent witness of the whole business.

'Now we can write your letter,' I said brightly. 'Just tell me exactly what you want to say.'

Miguel grew rather pink. He kicked the gravel in an offhand way. 'Oh,' he said carelessly, moving off to join the others, 'just write the same as the others.'

It was when Miguel wet his bed that the real crisis was resolved. Fridela came to me in despair. It was patently absurd that the five-year-olds were as good as gold and a big boy like Miguel should be such a baby. She agreed with me when I suggested that it was purely nerves and that it would be fatal to show either annoyance or surprise. When Miguel was in bed and we went our rounds to say good night, I sat for a minute by his bed. He was lying very still.

'By the way, have you been along the passage?' I asked casually. 'It is such a lot of work for us when there is an accident like last night. And, you see, you are so short of pyjamas. Of course it is a thing that could happen to anyone, but I'm sure you'll see that it doesn't happen often.' I turned to José, in the next bed. 'Perhaps José would wake you in the night,' I suggested. 'You look so comfy snuggled down in bed I expect you sleep a bit too soundly.'

José assured us he would wake Miguel. Miguel admitted he slept very soundly. We had no more trouble with Miguel. He became a cheery little boy. When we mentioned anything about going back to Barcelona he always shot an anxious look at us to see if we meant it, and then relaxed into a giggle against himself. His chief fault was a tendency to follow us round like an adoring puppy.

Miguel was the only child who really made friends with Beetle. They all tried to pet her and showed in various peculiar ways that they thought she was adorable, but she disliked them all except Miguel. Perhaps she sensed in the early days that he was lonely and shy and had a fellow-feeling of being left out in the cold, but she attached herself to him and to him only. It made a great difference to Miguel before the other children came. He was otherwise entirely forced into companionship with Ramón, and the two were incompatible.

Ramón was a tough. He had a hoarse laugh, an engaging grin and was always dirty. He was the same age as Miguel and they were nearly inseparable. This was partly because they were the only two boys, except José, who was Ramón's elder brother, and partly because there was a strange fascination that seemed to draw them together. They invariably fought; Ramón would smack Miguel on the side of the head; Miguel would pinch Ramón under the table. We were continually separating them and, luckily for Ramón, we were shrewd enough to realize that it was not always his fault. Ramón was as incapable of doing anything underhand as Miguel was of coming out into the open. They were an odd contrast. Ramón had his shirt always hanging open down the front, usually with a rip across the shoulders, his face smudged, his trousers hitched up bunchily under an agonizingly tight leather belt. Miguel, his Barcelona suit firmly hung by us in his cupboard, wore Archie's cut-downs with an air; his shirt was always buttoned at the neck and one felt he would have loved a tie. Of course he wore braces.

José was very quiet at first. He was fourteen, and old enough to realize something of the war. He had lived for six months with his family down near the port in Barcelona, and he had vivid memories of bombardments. He was a pleasant, helpful boy, and we hoped that good food and security would make him more childlike.

The little girls were like all little girls. Their one idea was to play at houses or schools; they had shrill Spanish voices and a peculiar Welsh intonation which I discovered was Aragonese. All the nine children were refugees from Aragon. Maria Josefa and her sister Carmen had actually been in a village captured by the fascists and recaptured by the Government. Carmen sang fascist and anti-fascist songs with complete impartiality. Maria Josefa came out to me when I was working in the garden and looked at me solemnly. I was in a shirt and corduroy trousers and I mopped the sweat from my brow as I paused to talk to her. She said in her Welsh-Aragon, 'Tell me, is it really true that you are the directora of this colony?'

'Why, yes,' I answered, spitting on my hands preparatory to resuming work.

'*Anda!*' she said in complete surprise, and went away. I soon learned that the Aragonese express all astonishment by this word.

Josefina was a kindhearted child. She suffered from the severe handicap of appearing at least eighteen years old. She was thirteen, but one could never remember that she was a child. She seemed to be always making beds, and I thought that we must be exploiting the poor child's willingness. I told her that she need only make the beds in her own room and then she could play in the garden with the other children. She looked at me, her prominent brown eyes welling tears.

'Please let me make the beds,' she implored. 'I *love* making beds. Don't stop me from making beds.'

I gave in. It was beyond my comprehension. Emboldened by her success, she asked shyly, 'Will you let me help with the ironing? I *love* ironing.'

Any outside observer would have said we were grossly exploiting child labour. Josefina was always to be found mending trousers, sewing buttons on shirts, making beds, tidying drawers. While the other children romped about in the woods, Josefina would be sitting on the terrace laboriously embroidering numbers on garments. Eventually I was forced to believe that she preferred it.

Maria, Josefina's small cousin, aged seven, was the least prepossessing of the children. She was all eyes, not the usual glorious Spanish eyes, but Pekinese eyes that had faded. She was pernickity about her food. Josefina told us that for months she refused to touch anything except dry bread. She looked like it. We gave her the usual amount of bread which she wolfed ravenously, but we steeled ourselves not to give her any more unless she ate some of her other food. In a little while she drank up her milk, and, for the sake of an extra piece of bread, would struggle valiantly with small portions of vegetables. It was a repulsive sight to see Maria, her bulging eyes watery with effort, masticating potato and fish pie. It took away our appetites, but it did not worry the children. *Viva la cocinera!* they cried, and ate up everything.

Pilar, or Pilarín as she was usually called, was not in any sense like her name. She was naturally plump and comfortable and no amount of food shortage would make her anything else. She had a piercing squeak of a voice which usually died away in a chuckle. She was no problem.

Pepita was another matter. She knew exactly how pretty she was. She knew exactly how to sidle up in an engaging way, casting down her tremendous black lashes and then glancing up with a pair of sparkling dark blue eyes. I had never realized just what was meant by starry eyes until I saw Pepita. When she was gazing at one, not quite sure whether she would get her own way or not, she would screw up her eyes behind the pointed lashes so that they scintillated like two stars. It took three days for Pepita to understand us. She could not believe that anyone would really question her authority. Miguel was her slave. She ordered him about ruthlessly, snatched his toys, treated him like the meanest of her subjects.

One day she began playing her favourite game, pretending to be a dog. It was a shock to her self-esteem that Beetle refused to play this game. She ran nimbly round the room on all fours, yapping lustily, pursuing the furious Beetle. Beetle threw wicked looks at me—it was all my fault that this rabble was in the house—and finally ended up against the kitchen door, protest in every hair. Francisca opened the door and Beetle fled to her cushion. Pepita was annoyed. She looked at me cunningly, she expected me to get Beetle back again. Realizing that I had no intention of fetching Beetle she started to play alone, skipping round under the tables, yelping away. After a few minutes I suggested that we had all had enough. Pepita had had a lovely game, now she could play at something else. Pepita went on yapping.

'Pepita,' I said, 'we are tired of that noise. Be a dear and play something quiet.'

Renewed yaps from Pepita who was under the table, her eyes shining defiance behind her lashes.

'The place for small dogs is the garden,' I said mildly.

Pepita, convinced that she had won, scuttled round the room, yelping lustily.

I stepped up to her and actually had her in my arms before she realized I meant it. She started to scream in earnest. I carried her kicking and yelling through the door, put her on the terrace, came back and shut the door. Miguel hovered anxiously. He asked to be allowed to go to her. He was doubtful when I said cheerfully that she would soon be all right. Pepita recovered from her surprise sufficiently to try to break the glass window of the door. She banged at it until I thought it would give under the strain, but it held firm. Pepita pressed her angry little face against it, hideous with rage, her beautiful eyes pouring furious tears. She screamed louder than I should have thought possible.

She held out for half an hour. Then there was a silence and a red tear-stained face looked through the glass and essayed a smile. She tapped on the glass. I opened the door.

'Pepita wants to come in,' she said engagingly. Then added for good measure, 'The little dog has gone away.'

Pepita was beaten but she made us pay for it. She acknowledged defeat but in no generous spirit. It was days before she would speak to me after the dog episode, and it was only the prospect of another bath that thawed her. She had decided to like baths and she also thought that my baths were the most amusing. She forgave me completely after a particularly exciting swim. We had no more real fights with Pepita, but after each loss of dignity on her part she was cold for a time to whoever was responsible. She was cold until she wanted something from the person concerned. Then the sweetest smile would break over her little face, her eyes turned up at the corners and she would rub herself against one in the most charming way. Pepita was a minx.

We had no rules in the house except those the children made themselves. When the question arose about picking the garden flowers I held a council. I pointed out that the flowers belonged to them. So far as I was concerned they could pick the whole lot, dig them up, do what they liked. Archie looked agonized. But, I went on, there were other children coming soon and they had a right to the flowers too. If they all decided to destroy the garden it was all right with us. Only we were not going to plant any more flowers and the place really looked nicer with flowers. I conveyed the impression that there would be an orgy of flower picking on the arrival of the rest of the colony.

The children were horrified. The idea of the other children wanting to destroy the flowers! José, his white face almost pink, assured us he would like to see any of them picking flowers. Of course no one would dream of touching the flowers. The elder children said that they would see that the little ones remembered. We decided that there was no harm in picking wild flowers in moderation, if they brought them home for their rooms. I left them with Archie, being told the names of some of his most precious treasures. I thought of the Mo'ca who had told me one of the greatest problems was curing the children of the urge to pick flowers. She assured me that she had been really severe about it.

We telephoned to the Solidarity Fund in Barcelona to ask when the other children were coming. We said firmly that they must be all over eight. We said that small children were too much of a responsibility on our mountain-side. We talked to the second in command, a man called Mata. He assured us that more beds would be arriving at once and, by the end of the week, thirty children, with teachers. I gave him the exact proportion of the sexes that was required if we were to fit in thirty.

243

He promised to send the exact number of girls and boys, all over eight, that we wanted. I did not mention anything about taking back the young ones we already had. It had been easy to talk about sending away the odd little grubby black-clad figures that they had been. It seemed unthinkable to return Carmen, Pepita and Pilarîn.

23

Justo misses his Pistol

Lo and I went down to the Santiago colony to find out about rations. We had been given plenty of food and nine children, but so far no one had told us when we could expect more food or had given us any idea of rations. I thought Señora Santiago as *administradora* would be able to inform us.

I knew it was tactless, but I could not resist asking the Mo'ca, who came gushing to greet us, if we could speak to Señora Santiago; our business was with the *administradora*. Dear Enriqueta could do nothing except to send a small child to fetch her. Señora Santiago approached us uncertainly. She looked extremely ill.

'You want to speak to *me*?' she said in a surprised voice.

'Why, yes. We wondered if you could be kind enough to help us out of a small difficulty.'

She turned her queer eyes towards the Mo'ca.

"Perhaps Enriqueta," she murmured.

"Oh, I wouldn't dream of troubling her," I said hastily. 'I would hate to disturb her in the middle of her classes. In any case, our business is entirely to do with the administration, so if you could spare us a few moments——'

The Mo'ca was speechless. I took advantage of it to propel Señora Santiago towards the store room. She suddenly laughed and, clutching my arm, almost ran us into the store. She slammed the door and stayed with her back against it, panting slightly. Lo and I thought she looked very odd.

She said in a breathless way: 'It isn't the work I mind. I can work all day long. But you have no idea what I suffer. No idea.' She came very close to us and peered into our faces. 'I don't suppose you will suffer like me. No, no.' Then she suddenly shouted at us, 'Where is Enrique? No one tells me anything. I tell you I am ill, very ill. I have lost weight. Look!' She pulled up the wrapper she wore and disclosed a pair of painfully thin legs.

Lo was visibly shaken. All her well-planned questions about the exact amount of chick peas per child trembled in the air and dissolved. I thought perhaps a sharp reminder of realities might save the situation. I asked if she could give us an idea of the Solidarity Fund's rationing.

Señora Santiago became calmer. She said she was sorry but she had never been given any orders about quantities. To my suggestion that she could give us an idea of the quantities she used, she shook her head.

'We have no weighing machine,' she said. 'We just guess.' She added, becoming practical, all sign of hysteria gone, 'We give as much bread as they can eat. Only that does not apply to the Catalans. They never would stop eating bread.'

We thanked her and went. Señora Santiago escorted us to the gate, chatting normally. The Mo'ca left her class of children and rushed to join us.

'Did you have a nice little talk?' she said, and her eyes were like slates. Señora Santiago pulled me close to her. She did not say a word, but her eyes clung to mine. They were light brown eyes, the whites flecked with blood, and they seemed to be bursting out of their sockets in an effort to convey some meaning that had no words. They made me think of those of a live hare, hung by its legs in the market.

Lo and I felt we would rather guess at everything connected with our colony than visit the Santiago colony again.

One of our greatest difficulties was knowing whom to apply to for information. There was a man called Angel in Lloret, where there was a big Solidarity Fund colony and depot; there was Mata, in Barcelona; somewhere there was Santiago himself. Instead of the usual shelving of responsibility these three positively battled for it. Angel declared that everything must be done through him in Lloret; Mata shrugged his shoulders when we complained that the beds had not yet arrived, and implied that it was our fault for being so foolish as to dally with Lloret instead of approaching Barcelona direct; when in desperation we got hold of Santiago, after many phone calls and rude letters, he said firmly that everything had to be done through him; it was useless to expect anything otherwise. Eventually I used to send carbon copies of my letters to all three sources, and that was satisfactory. If we sometimes got things in duplicate it was always useful. Santiago seldom answered.

We heard quite casually through Marcelino at the telephone exchange that thirty children were arriving that day. Angel had visited the other colony and, finding our hill too much for his large paunch, he had left a message with Marcelino who forgot it for a few hours. It never struck Angel to telephone us direct. Marcelino atoned for his forgetfulness by offering to come up and help if we needed it.

We did not need help. We needed beds. We phoned Lloret and told Angel we must have those beds; we put a call through to Barcelona, but the line was down owing to air raids in Mataró. We decided we would have to put our mattresses together on the floor. We prepared gallons of soup. We waited for the lorry load of children.

We were all on the beach when Archie appeared leading one small girl by the hand. She had dark straight hair, a fair skin and enormous grey eyes. Her name was Angelines. Archie told me anxiously that she and her mother had arrived by the bus.

'A teacher!' I exclaimed joyfully. A pity it was a woman teacher, but anything would do.

Archie hesitated. 'Not exactly,' he went on. 'She could not say much because she was terribly car sick. She has gone straight to bed. But I gathered she had come just to help about the house.'

I was furious. I was determined not to have the house full of Spanish women with not enough to do. All children's colonies seemed overstaffed with women and young girls, who make more work than all the children together. I had a horror of irresponsible '*responsables*'. I had already mentioned this to the International Solidarity Fund and had told them that we needed no more staff except teachers. They were naturally anxious to find jobs for the grown-up refugees, but I had made up my mind to run our colony the way I liked.

'She goes right back to Barcelona to-morrow,' I said.

'And the child. I absolutely disapprove of mothers working in colonies where they have their children.'

Francisca and the Reifenbergs agreed with me. Francisca was particularly annoyed. She was finding the Reifenbergs bad enough, but a strange Spanish woman in the house would be too much. Francisca and Beetle had a lot in common. They both resented strangers in their house; they both wanted my undivided attention. They both could be extremely disagreeable. I knew that I would have to speak to Francisca about her behaviour to Lo in the kitchen. She was being really unpleasant. Luckily I was able to discuss it with Lo, who understood the situation. I suggested giving Francisca a little more time. I also suggested we might always take care to speak Spanish in the kitchen instead of German, which was intensely irritating to Francisca. The odd thing was that Francisca resented Lo's interference in what she considered exclusively *my* sphere. Francisca had never done the actual cooking, but she could not bear to see anyone except me bustling round the stove. Naturally I handed over the whole kitchen to Lo as cook. I was ready to give a hand when necessary, but it seldom was necessary. Lo, who had never cooked for more than two people in her life, produced marvellous meals for fifteen without any difficulty. She was a born cook.

Another thing that added to Francisca's irritation was Fridela's habit of dropping into the kitchen to chat with her daughter. She would move things off the fire to heat some water to bathe a child's wound; she would occasionally stir something or add something to the soup. She knew that Lo did not mind. Francisca could not bear it. She grudgingly accepted Lo because I had pointed out firmly that Lo was complete boss of the kitchen department, but she refused to allow Fridela any rights. She became sulky and difficult. The arrival of a Spanish female to help about the house was the last straw.

I did not see the prostrate Leonor, as the newcomer was called, until the next day. I took her up some coffee and biscuits in the evening, but she remained with her head under the bedclothes. I left her for the night, telling her to stay in bed in the morning unless she felt perfectly well. I was determined that she should go back but I felt she ought to have a day or two to recover.

Meanwhile Angelines was being a success. She was an inventive little girl and soon had all the other little girls away in the woods playing shops. We found a relief in the rest from shrill Aragonese voices. The three boys always dashed to the top of the hill behind the house where Archie had fixed up horizontal bars, swings and ropes in the cork trees.

When the children went to bed, we put Angelines in the room with Carmen and Pepita. She was eight years old and they were five, but we said we would rearrange the rooms later. She said she liked looking after small children and that she would see that they got up in the night and that no accidents happened in their beds. We were grateful. Carmen had suddenly taken to bed-wetting. It was sheer laziness because she hated getting up out of her warm bed. She was particularly difficult to deal with because she simply did not care what anyone said to her. She wriggled about and giggled whenever anyone spoke seriously. She did not even care when her bossy sister slapped her. She thought it was all a tremendous joke. She also did not in the least mind sleeping in a soaking bed. Altogether Carmen was a problem unless some one got up in the middle of the night. Angelines seemed Heaven-sent.

The next morning Leonor appeared in the kitchen when I was getting the breakfast. I cannot bear anyone worrying me when I am getting breakfasts. I can have the kitchen cluttered up with visitors at any other hour of the day, but I need to concentrate in the early morning. Leonor seemed to grasp this, for she went away and started dressing the children.

We always let the children go to bed when they were sleepy, which was usually about seven-thirty. We told the older ones they could stay up longer, but they always seemed ready for bed. We decided to let them get up whenever they woke, with reservations. But it worked very well. They were so tired out with fresh air and exercise that they slept right through until seven-thirty in the morning. We told them they could get up whenever they liked, but they must go out into the garden. If they wanted to stay in their rooms they could stay quietly in bed. Occasionally there was too much noise and I would run upstairs from the kitchen and send the noisy ones outside. Only once was there a real pandemonium. They did not stop when they were asked, so they found nothing but dry bread for breakfast. I explained that the noise was so bad that I had not been able to concentrate on making the chocolate.

Leonor appeared to be a pleasant, motherly soul. She had the Aragonese dark hair and grey-blue eyes with a pink and white complexion. She said she had recovered from her terrible drive. She laughed and said it was lucky Tossa and the Casa Johnstone were so delightful because she could never face leaving in a car or bus.

We decided that she had better stay a day or two before we broke the news that she would have to go.

Toni, the truck driver, suddenly appeared and informed us that the truck, loaded with twenty beds, was stuck in the ford. He said that thirty children had already left Lloret for the Casa Johnstone.

We called up Mata. He said that thirty children had left Barcelona for Lloret and would shortly be in Tossa. We protested that the beds were in the river, but he intimated that it was not his affair. We also demanded a teacher. We wanted one male teacher at least to deal with a number of boys over eight years. He did not seem interested. We decided to write yet again to Santiago. We were not too shaken at the idea of coping with forty children; we found the ten no trouble at all. Leonor would always be able to translate our funny Spanish into suitable Aragonese. We decided not to get rid of Leonor until we were suitably supplied with teachers.

We got the lorry with the beds out of the river. The Casa Blanca sent over their mule cart and we rushed the beds up to the house. We spent the afternoon setting up collapsible iron beds. Luckily I had measured out exactly how to fit them into the rooms. Leonor was a genius at making beds; she made them look as if they were cut out of cardboard. When we had them all ready with their bright yellow counterpanes, the red tiles shining with sun and Francisca's cleaning, the rooms looked friendly and pleasant. The children brought in bunches of wild flowers for the rooms; we decorated the big room with heliotrope and chrysanthemum. Everything was ready for the thirty children.

Of course they did not come. Actually, the thirty

never came. Several days later, when we had given up the idea of ever getting any more children, a small procession wound its way up to the Casa Johnstone. Angel escorted them. He shook my hand, waved at the oddly-assorted group and fled. I realized why he ran away. In spite of all our protests and their promises they had sent us even younger children. At first glance they all seemed to be aged about five, but slowly a few older ones detached themselves. Rosa, a brown-eyed young beauty with curly black hair, was twelve; José Maria, a burly young man with the round face of a country lad, was thirteen; Primitivo, a sensitive-looking boy with a merry twinkle in his eye, was twelve; Mariano, vague and misty with his own thoughts, was ten. Two curly headed sisters were twelve and ten, they were called Pepita and Asunta. A round-faced girl, the image of her brother the country lad, called Delfina, was about ten. The other twelve children looked extremely young. There seemed to be a few little boys of six or seven; one or two small girls of the same age. Then I stopped counting. I was horrified. Hidden among the packages there emerged a round, cherubic figure. Huge, red face, broad husky shoulders in a skin-tight jersey, trousers stretched to the last agonized stitch, Justo toddled into the sunshine on a pair of diminutive but sturdy legs.

'Where's my Tato?' he demanded in surprisingly masculine tones. 'I want my Tato.'

Primitivo rushed to his side. Justo slipped a fat hand in that of his brother's and appeared satisfied. He smiled a broad, contented smile.

'How old is he?' I asked when I had recovered. Primitivo looked at him with fond pride.

'Justico is three and a half,' he announced. 'He is big for his age, aren't you, Justico? Aren't you a big boy?'

'I am very strong,' announced this phenomenon. 'I can kill anyone.'

Primitivo glanced at me knowingly. 'You see?' he said proudly.

Justo's smile suddenly faded.

'In Barcelona,' he announced clearly and decisively, 'in Barcelona I have left my pistol.'

We were thankful that we had Leonor. She revelled in the babies. We rearranged all the rooms to put the little ones on the top floor with her. There was some trouble with Justo who wished to sleep with his Tato, but we managed to persuade him to share a room with two other small boys. We put the older children together as much as possible. I had to promise a tearful Josefina that she could still help with the beds. I saw in a minute that pretty Rosa would not wish to take more than her share of the housework. The elder Pepita was obviously not a too enthusiastic worker. Her sister Asunta was the only rival for Josefina. Asunta adored doing anything that was not her business.

It was at lunch time on the second day of their arrival that I had my battle with Justo. He wished to sit next to his brother. All the tables were arranged with a purpose and his brother was sitting at the big boys' table at the other end of the room. I explained gently that his Tato was busy, but that he would play with him after lunch. Justo listened solemnly and then clambered off his chair and toddled down to his brother's table. Primitivo, knowing Justo, brought him back with a troubled furrow in his forehead.

'Perhaps I had better sit with him,' he suggested.

'Good heavens, no!' I protested. 'He has got to learn that he can't always have his own way. You run back to your place.'

Primitivo gave me a pitying look, but trotted obediently back to his table. In a minute Justo, with a baleful glance at me, set off after him. I followed. Primitivo, anxious to keep the peace, brought Justo back. This time I lifted Justo into his chair and sent Primitivo away.

'Justo,' I said as severely as I could, 'you are going to sit there and eat your dinner.'

Justo screwed up his eyes; his red face went purple and he let out a yell. He made an amazing amount of noise. I managed to get in a few words each time he drew breath. If he did not stop crying and behave he would have to go upstairs to his room. His only answer was to throw his plate at little Pepita. She was being very feminine and was protesting with hands to her delicate ears against this appalling noise. I picked up Justo. He kicked me as hard as he could and it was all I could do to hold him. I carried him out of the room. On the stairs he stopped yelling and struggling and I put him down.

'Will you behave and eat up your dinner if you go back?' I asked.

Justo signified yes. We trailed back into the dining-room. Justo climbed up on his chair and grasped his spoon. He waited until I bent over to tie his napkin round his neck, then he threw his spoon as hard as he could at Leonor who was serving the soup. 'I want my Tato. I want my Tato,' he screamed, and beat on the bottom of the table with his feet. Primitivo came rushing over.

'You know, you had better let me sit by him,' he said patiently. 'He will go on like this until he gets his own way. We have a terrible time with him at home.'

I had visions of having a terrible time with Justo at the Casa Johnstone. I explained to Primitivo through the roars of his brother that for the sake of peace in the house, I had to be firm with Justo. I picked him up again and carried him struggling violently upstairs to his bedroom.

It took me about a quarter of an hour to undress Justo. He was amazingly strong and as slippery as an eel. Twice he escaped by rolling off the bed and started to tear downstairs in his combinations, which were strained to their uttermost over his pink behind. In the end I got him into his pyjamas and into bed. Once between the sheets he knew he was beaten. He stopped screaming and glared at me from the pillow. I left him there and went to the door.

'If you behave for half an hour,' I said, breathing hard, 'I will let you get up and have some dinner. Otherwise you stay there all day.'

Justo drew a sobbing breath. 'If I had my pistol from Barcelona', he said deliberately, 'I would kill you, Fascist!'

24

Family Affairs

I do not approve of leaving small children alone in rooms. I closed Justo's bedroom door, but I did not lock it. I wanted to deter him from coming out but not to imprison him. I waited for some time on the stairs in case he came clattering down. Presently I crept back to the door and peeped in. Justo lay flat on his back, his fat cheek blowing in and out, sound asleep.

Later I woke him up and asked him if he wanted his dinner. He was perfectly friendly and trotted cheerfully downstairs. The older children had finished and were all in the garden, but one or two of the small ones were still eating. Justo climbed up on his chair and methodically made up for lost time. He did not glance at his brother, anxiously hovering by the door. When he could eat no more he pushed away his plate and leaned back happily. He started to tell me a long rambling story about something in Barcelona. He spoke very distinctly for a child of three and a half, mostly in Catalan. Many of the Aragonese children spoke both Catalan and Castilian. Their Castilian had certain characteristic modifications such as *ico* instead of the diminutive *ito*. They spoke of *casica, pequeñico,* instead of *casita*, *pequeñito*. The little girls were always building *casicas* in the woods, little houses which they furnished with odds and ends of broken china and coloured glass. Justo was invariably called Justico, but it was more a term of affection than with any reference to his smallness. Justico was not very tall, but he made up for it in breadth.

Primitivo was frankly amazed at my success with Justo. He adored his brother. That seemed to be another characteristic of these children. The older children were perfectly marvellous to their young brothers and sisters. José took almost too much responsibility for Ramón and Pilarín; José Maria, in his hulking way, was a kind watchdog for his sister Delfina and his little brother Florial; Mariano, as far as he was conscious of earthly matters, looked after his blonde, colourless little brother and sister. It was interesting to see their watchfulness as they began to have confidence in us. Miguel willingly left me to deal with Pepita and gradually the responsibilities of a family weighed less heavily on José. The children began to break up naturally into groups according to age and sex.

From the first there was rivalry between the elder girls and boys. The small girls and boys ignored each other completely. They had different interests and they did not clash. The elder ones were becoming conscious of each other and this consciousness took the form of violent jealousies. One big difference between Spanish and English children seems to be that the Spanish boys are as quickwitted as the girls of their age. The girls had no particular superiority. They had to fall back on taking great care of their personal appearance and their purely feminine talents such as knitting or sewing. The boys balanced this by their superiority on the swings and up trees. There was always trouble when one of the boys pushed the girls' fancy work off a table to make room for his carpentry, or the girls took possession of the swings and rocked gently to and fro. It seemed to us that the only way to better the situation was to get them to do things together.

This was against all tradition. The first steps seem to be to get the girls interested in some slightly masculine activity and to persuade the boys to accept some feminine pursuit. Archie started gymnasium classes and I began to give painting lessons.

We were lucky that Delfina had exactly the right body for somersaulting over bars and that Primitivo had a talent for drawing. Inspired by Delfina's superiority over the boys, Asunta and Rosita were fired with ambitions to excel at gymnastics; even Josefina made a few ineffectual attempts to raise herself off the ground. Primitivo inspired José to search through all our old magazines for pictures of ships to copy; José Maria unexpectedly developed a good colour sense. The fact that Delfina was much better than any of the boys at gymnastics and Primitivo's bold use of paint was infinitely better than Rosita's neat, wishy water colours, helped to break down the feminine versus masculine barriers. The real success was due to rounders.

Apparently Spanish children never learn to play team games. Certainly boys and girls never dream of playing anything together. Even tip-cat, introduced into Tossa by Madrid children, was played in severely segregated groups. We had to find a game which was simple to play and with few rules. Above all it had to be a game equally suitable for girls or boys. We chose rounders.

From the first it was a success. Archie and I found we had to take it seriously. We went every day to the football field, Leonor with the little ones to play in one corner, and we played rounders with the others. Most of the village collected to watch the extraordinary sight of Archie and me tearing madly round little heaps of jerseys, surrounded by fascinated boys and girls. They learned it quickly. At first there was the difficulty that the 'dead' ones grew bored and went away to play something else, but we solved that by letting them field for the other side. Not good for the team spirit, perhaps, but infinitely more amusing. Naturally the little ones wanted to play, but we told them they must practise throwing and catching first of all, and poor Leonor was kept panting up and down the field.

Rounders brought out a lot of interesting facts. Angelines, the most female creature with a passion for sewing dolls' clothes and hopeless at gymnastics, developed into one of the nippiest fielders; Rosa forgot to pat her beautiful hair and ignored the fact that her face was scarlet as she banged the ball across the pitch and tore round to make a rounder. It was interesting to see how José reacted when he was not in the limelight; he immediately became bored unless he was playing well. Beefy José Maria was in his element whacking at the ball, but his heavy, straight legs would not carry him so fast as Ramón, tearing round the pitch with his trousers hitched up and a grin of delight on his face. Miguel was in a difficult position. He really preferred to play with the little ones and Leonor and there was no compulsion to play rounders, but he could not bear to hear Ramón boasting of the rounders he had made, so he forced himself to join in. He got terribly worked up and sometimes by sheer will power and hate of Ramón would make a big score.

Rounders was so popular that several of the village boys asked to join in. Francisca's daughter, Maria Theresa, and her big son Ramón would hang about watching. Maria Theresa, aged eleven, soon joined in, but Ramón was fifteen and big for his age and he preferred to lean on his bicycle and watch. When he saw village boys of sixteen tearing round with our children he capitulated. We found we could leave them to it. The village boys were nice lads and Ramón was a young god among our children because he let them ride his bicycle, so he could be counted upon to intervene when the rules became tangled. Archie and I gladly became our ages again, but occasionally we would be on the terrace watching the flying figures on the football field, and Archie would say, 'What about joining the kids in a game?' and we would race down across the gardens, followed by Lo and Fridela.

If anyone had told me that we should find ourselves looking after twenty-eight Spanish children and have the entire responsibility for them, I would have laughed. It still seemed absurd, but it appeared to be working out all right. There must, I thought, be something particular about Aragonese children, or perhaps it is just another Spanish custom for children to be no trouble. I did know that the average Spanish child is the boss in his own home. The younger the child the more he bosses, and the less he brooks restraint. But there seems to come an undefined moment when the spoilt child suddenly develops into a charming, thoughtful adult. When and how this change comes about I have never been able to fathom. It is like the first bathe after the winter—one day one does not think of bathing and suddenly it is obviously time to bathe again.

Our older children were all at the charming stage. The strange part was that none of the others seemed to be at all tiresome. Except for the two battles with Pepita and Justo, there was no trouble with any of them. All the children were in groups, the *mayores*, the older ones, the *medianos*, the middle ones, and the *pequeños*, the little ones. Leonor was in charge of the *pequeños*, and she was excellent with them. We could not get over our luck in having Leonor. She was full of common sense and entered heartily into our ideas about bringing up children. She never made up stories to frighten them; she never told them a lie; she believed firmly in the benefits of fresh air; she helped us to wean them of their bunchy petticoats. Although she had most to do with the little ones, all the children loved her. She had a refreshing way of talking, and although she reproved the older children for their bad language, her own speech was interlarded with picturesque oaths.

Swearing was one of our problems. It was hard to know the values of Spanish oaths. Translation was worse than useless. Tiny mites lisped words which, translated, made one's hair stand on end, but which were accepted in Spain without comment; while seemly harmless phrases were frowned upon severely. Finally we decided to judge purely by repetition. When a certain oath got to the stage of being used by the entire colony every five words we would protest. We would say that the meanings of the words were not important, it was just that we were sick and tired of hearing them. Could they please think up something else? The children were most obliging. When we had run through most of the everyday expressions we were helpful in suggesting new ones. Thanks to the International Brigade our repertoire was good. The children were shocked at some of our suggestions. They could not possibly use *those*, they said, their parents would not like it. We compromised by picking on a few of the most harmless and only using those in real stress. I thought again of the Mo'ca.

'*Lo que me mata*', she had said plaintively, '*es las malas palabras.*' 'That which kills me is the bad words.'

We managed to keep rules down to the minimum. The main principle of the house was that of any community—anything disturbing the community must be avoided. The children could make as much noise as they liked in the woods behind the house, but they were expected not to scream *in* the house. We took care to provide plenty of games like snakes and ladders and ludo. If a group grew too noisy they were warned once. The next time the game was gently removed and they were sent out into the garden. They understood this and accepted it. After a while I had only to say, 'Hey!' and point to the door and the noisy group would cheerfully pack up their game and troop outside. If some of the smaller ones began chasing round the room I would send them into the garden. Generally they went willingly; if they declared they really wanted a quiet game I would suggest a race down the hill and back first of all.

We had to get used to new names for everything. The garden meant for the children Oskar's garden. It was a recognizable garden, duly planted with vegetables. Our garden, which consisted of the rock gardens, the edging to the big terrace, the gravelled space outside the front door with the big heliotrope bushes, was known as the *calle*, or street. The wild part beyond the rock gardens and behind the house was called the *bosque*, the woods. I frequently forgot these distinctions. The first day we had oranges for lunch I gave the bigger children a basket for the peel and suggested every one went out into the garden to eat them. They started trooping down the hill to Oskar's.

We had to think up some form of punishments to meet certain cases. The most satisfactory was depriving them of their *merienda* or *postre*. When Carmen persisted in scribbling in my picture books, she was by common consent not allowed the sweet course at the next meal. There was one really strict rule, against throwing stones. Unfortunately our terraces were covered with a tempting form of small, round pebbles. We always discussed the offence thoroughly and all the children agreed on the punishment. Generally the victim was one of those most interested in working out if *postre* or *merienda* should be stopped. This frequently caused confusion in the kitchen.

'Lo, remind me that Mariano and Luisa are not to have *postre* to-night,' I would remark casually.

Lo would shriek that there was no *postre* that evening.

'There *must* be a *postre*,' I would say firmly. 'I have just punished two children.'

Sometimes the fact of confiscated *postres* led to unfair decisions being made.

'I can't make up my mind whether to have the apricot tart for lunch and just a lump of sugar each this evening, or vice versa,' Lo would muse.

'Make the tart for lunch. We have docked José his *postre* because he was so mean over sharing his chalks, and I would like him to miss something good.'

Mariano was one of those unfortunate children who are perpetually in trouble. Luckily for him we had few rules and we realized that it was not his fault. Relays of children could examine my pots of small mimosa trees, but Mariano had to drop one. Dozens of children swung on the supports for the awning, but Mariano had to choose one that snapped. If he used the swing, usually the branch broke; if he absent-mindedly jumped the cactus at the corner of the drive, a practice loved by the children because it cut two inches off the corner, he had to catch it with his heel and break a piece off it. Oddly enough we were grateful for Mariano. We felt less conscience-stricken when we thought of the elaborate precautions we had taken to save our possessions from destruction. We had gradually and stealthily been bringing the mirrors back to the bedrooms; Archie self-consciously put back the glass shelves; we moved the barrier of cactuses in pots we had used to protect the rock gardens. The children simply were not destructive. But Mariano almost justified our unworthy suspicions. They might all have been like him.

Mariano was not a clumsy child. He was delicately made, with a sensitive little face and big grey eyes. The trail of destruction in his wake was the outcome of his dissociation from mundial things. He lived in a world apart. He was so used to being called stupid and clumsy that he no longer listened when he was being lectured. It took me weeks to get his attention and then he was interested to find that I had not been abusing him all this time, but that I was trying to find some explanation for his misfortunes. He began to approve of me somewhat. Fridela took a great interest in him. She realized that he must be brought down to earth gradually, and she went to great pains to see that he had heard when we let the older boys go off for walks on condition they were back in time for *merienda*, or left them alone on the beach with instructions to turn up in time for lunch. We also had to make sure that he knew why he sometimes had his *postre* stopped. I asked him once, quite by chance, why he was not having *postre* and he had no idea.

Francisca approved of Leonor. She could appreciate her immense capacity for work. Leonor was extremely tactful with Francisca. There were slight frictions between Leonor and Fridela. Fridela was invaluable with the children. She took them down to the beach in the mornings and gave them eurythmics in the sunshine with the minimum of clothes; she took the boys long tramps looking for mushrooms and firewood. But Fridela liked to be her own mistress. She liked to choose her own time to go to the beach; she took little interest in the small children, and it was the boys she took for long walks. The main thing was that she kept the children occupied, but she also was fascinated by her linen cupboard. Before we knew that Leonor was coming, it was understood that Fridela looked after the linen and made the beds. With the coming of Leonor, who was so efficient that she could have done all Fridela's indoor work without noticing it, there was no more need for Fridela to bother about the upstairs rooms. But for some reason Fridela was reluctant to relinquish her cupboard and she would spend hours taking everything out of it and putting them all back again. Leonor resented being treated like a child in the matter of sheets and laundry and Fridela thought Leonor was interfering. In the end the laundry was in such a muddle that I rushed to my typewriter and in six minutes had a timetable of days on which different items were to be changed. I made carbon copies and handed one to Fridela and the other to Leonor and a third to Maria, who did the washing down at Oskar's, so that she had an idea what work she would have during the day. I spent several days telling Leonor how useful Fridela was and telling Fridela that Leonor was really indispensable and how I could not imagine what it would be like without them both. Francisca was sardonically amused. She liked Leonor, the more so because Leonor was never allowed to do our rooms or any of my mending. Neither was I. I could darn and patch children's clothes all day, but I was not allowed to put a stitch into anything of mine. That was Francisca's business.

The first time we took our nine children down to the beach, they were reluctant to take off their clothes. We were casual about the matter, but we bathed as usual. By the time the other children arrived the original ones were splashing about in the sea in their pants and could hardly wait to get to the beach before they began stripping off shirts and frocks. We did not encourage actual bathing because it was winter, but anyone who felt hardy enough could splash in and out again. The new children watched the others for a few days. José Maria, José and Primitivo had learned to swim in the Ebro, and were all for showing their superiority, but the girls were coy and the little ones frankly refused to shed a single garment. Justo was particularly possessive. He eventually consented to take off his sandals because of the discomfort of them full of sand, but he insisted in carrying them wherever he went. He dumped them down when he wanted to play in the sand, but he never forgot them or lost them.

One day, a few days after their arrival, the older new ones asked me if they could bathe too. I said certainly, and looked out wraps and a bathing suit for the well-developed Josefina. Immediately the little ones wanted to bathe. I assured them that they all could bathe, but warned them that the water would be cold. They could hardly wait to go to the beach. I went down with them, meaning to bathe myself. When we got near the beach the little ones rushed ahead. The others followed more slowly and I paused for a moment on one of the rocky prominences surveying the beach. I saw to my horror that the little ones had not waited for me. They were prancing about in the surf with every appearance of intense enjoyment. They were fully clothed. A small boy called Vicente was dressed even to his jersey. He kept standing up and then falling flat on his stomach in the water. Justo was crawling on all fours; his trouser seams had parted as usual exposing an expanse of pink curves. His sandals were floating tidily beside him.

25

Los Abandonados

The children were no difficulty, but the village problems taxed all our ingenuity.

Although we ignored the Solidarity Fund's only
known rule, that *intercambio* was rigorously forbidden,
we could not provide food for the whole village. We
gave our friends small presents of coffee, cheese, sugar,
and in return we got fresh fish, vegetables and lettuce.
We made careful inquiries and found about six families
who had no fishing or farming relatives. We provided
for these families, but we were careful not to guarantee
any specified amounts. When we had food in abundance, we saw that the really hard-up people got their
share.

We had to have some formula for refusing other
people, so we put the onus on Señora Santiago. We
explained that the Solidarity Fund sent us the food for
the children; that we were forbidden to barter, and that
we suggested they went to the wife of the head of the
organization. If she was willing to give them something
it was no concern of ours. Naturally she, as Santiago's
wife, would not be expected to account for everything
as we were.

Señora Santiago did not know the village. We were amused to notice that many of the most importunate were people who were suffering little from the food shortage. They owned plenty of land; they had their own olives for oil; they had acres of nuts and fruit trees. But it was these who had the most pathetic stories. Their wives were ill and could only bear to nibble a little milk chocolate; they were so tired of beans, could we let them have a little rice; they would be so grateful for a few kilos of sugar, coffee lost its flavour without it. The moment anyone said to me they wanted something to brighten up some commodity which we had not seen for months, I was regretful and referred them to Señora Santiago. When they told me they were ill and must have milk, or that one of their children was consumptive, and if Francisca, the Casa Blanca and the Reifenbergs were unanimous, I gave them all I could spare.

The greatest tragedy was the colony of the Forty-Third Division. There had been a bad epidemic of scabies in the colony and, although there was some attempt at isolation, I had little faith in the director's ability to organize it. Reluctantly I had to explain to our children that they must not play with those of the Forty-Third Division. Unfortunately I had been so busy that I had no time to explain to the Forty-Third Division children why we were apparently being so stand-offish. They naturally resented it all the more because, before my children came, we had been such good friends.

I realized exactly what had happened when José, José Maria and Primitivo sought me out and asked my advice. The children of the Forty-Third Division had thrown stones at our colony on their way to the beach. The boys wanted to know if they should attack the Forty-Third Division children. They seemed to be willing to do so, although under no illusions as to the probable result. As José put it, 'There are a good number.'

I said I would see what I could do, and hurried down to the other colony. I was horrified when I saw the children. I had been so occupied that I had not noticed them except to say good-day as I passed to go to the village. I had vaguely noticed they seemed to have lost their high spirits, but I had other things to worry about.

The ones with scabies were isolated in a derelict part of the building. The windows had been patched up with rags; the wooden floors were rotten with holes; there was no water, no lavatory. The children were filthy; the fact that they had scabies seemed to alienate them from all attention of the most elementary kind. Naturally they were surly and on the defensive.

I managed to persuade them that at any rate I was still friendly. They saw my point about not allowing our children to get scabies, although it took some time to persuade them that our colony really had no scabies. The elder children and I had a discussion about means of improving their situation. I promised to speak to the director. The children assured me that if he only knew what their condition was like he would do something. It seemed that he was very preoccupied and often in Barcelona. There was a master who did most of the work. The children seemed to like the master, but admitted that he was not practical. We parted friends and they promised not to throw stones at our colony. I assured them I understood how tiresome it must be

271

to see clean, well-fed little brutes rushing gaily down to the beach.

On my way through the back of the colony to see the director, I met two Spanish women *responsables*. I told them I had been talking to the scabious ones and what a shame it was they were being treated like lepers. To my surprise the women were not at all sympathetic. It served them right. Scabies was a retribution for all their naughtiness. They were *los malos*, the bad ones.

This seemed to be the general impression. I talked with the master who was in charge in the director's absence and could not quite gather whether the badness consisted in having got scabies or whether the scabies was a result of the badness. In any case, I pointed out that it seemed a pity to deprive them of all sanitary arrangements. Our road was becoming almost unusable and Archie had to keep a shovel hidden in the bushes for the purpose of making it passable. We were anxious to do what we could to help the Forty-Third Division colony, but there seemed to be no reason why Archie should be their lavatory man.

We felt strongly about this, but we were determined that the children should not be blamed. We could sympathise with the infuriated fisherman who kept his boat in a shed exactly below the big dormitory with its rotten flooring. But, after all, if one fails to provide anything else, to what better use can one put a hole in the floor? The children did not know the boat was below.

The children had reached a dangerous stage of apathy. They were not compelled to stay all day in their quarters, but they preferred to hang about the doorway, or to sit in the sunshine in their dormitory windows. In the evening they collected outside and huddled round a fire. They did not even bother to roam the woods for firewood; they preferred to slip into one of the gardens and steal the bean sticks. They were bored, bored, bored. There was no reason why they should not have done exactly the same things as our children, except that there was no one to encourage them.

I was longing to take them in hand, but I could not risk bringing scabies into our colony. I did what I could. I found one *responsable* who seemed fairly intelligent and I got huge jars of sulphur ointment from Rosita. With the help of the older children, the *responsable* managed to keep the scabies within limits. It was impossible to cure it without cleanliness, and to keep eighty children clean without a tap of running water in the house was beyond the powers of one *responsable*. I took them in small bands to hunt for mushrooms and to collect firewood, hoping that they would get interested and continue on their own, but although they were enthusiastic when they were led, they relapsed into inertia immediately they were left on their own. They had been left to their own resources too long. At first they enjoyed the freedom of being completely on their own; now they were so bored with freedom they were imploring every one to give them lessons. The village called them the *abandonados*. Now that they were suffering, the Tossencs hearts were rung. The same people who had cut off the water supply and who refused to sell them fruit, now brought them roasted acorns and nuts. Tossencs had a hatred only for those they thought might have something more than the Tossencs.

It was while I was thinking how lucky we were to

have hot baths and running water in all the rooms, that
our pump died on us.

We were three weeks without a drop of running
water in the house, and our well was at the bottom of
the hill. There were thirty-six people. We got organized. We divided into water-carrying gangs. One gang
was responsible for filling the bath on the top floor every
day; another kept the first floor bath filled; another
filled our bath on the ground floor. The kitchen staff
drew their own water and filled whatever utensils were
not being used.

Each bathful had to wash the children and flush the
lavatories. The children were born haulers of water.
All Spanish village children are used to carrying water.
We had four big pots and we worked in relays. It took
ten journeys to fill the baths. The children enjoyed it.
The first flush of enthusiasm wore off towards the end
of the second week, but they stuck to it nobly. We had
a fiesta in Archie's honour when the pump was repaired.
The pump was brought from a Barcelona repair shop
in a lorry and dumped at the bottom of the hill. Archie
fixed it in place. We had to wait until midnight for the
light to come on—that was a Catalan way of rationing
electricity, it was turned on only from midnight until
five in the morning—and we held our breath to hear
the familiar whirr. There was not a sound. Archie
struggled down in his dressing-gown and worked for
an hour by the light of a candle. He found some screws
missing, but managed to find others to fit. I stood by
outside the house, in a draughty corner, ready to switch
on. We switched on three times and nothing happened.
At last Archie found the fault and remedied it. There
was a triumphant click and the water started rushing

into the cistern. We always swore that Archie had
mended the pump.

We celebrated with an orgy of baths. The children
had not minded carrying up the water, but they were
bitter about missing their baths. The Solidarity Fund
had so far only promised us coke, but we managed,
with a tin of meat, to bribe some one to sell us a sack,
the price to be fixed later. I had a talk to Mata about
prices. He said: 'One sack? I have no idea of the price
of one sack. We buy it by the shipload.'

'Yes, but you could give me some idea. The man
insists on leaving it all to me.'

'One sack—we really cannot bother about one sack.
You had better send it back.'

'I'll send it back when your Solidarity Fund delivers
our coke,' I said firmly. A lorry with coke was leaving
right away, according to Mata. And what about our
teacher? Oh, he was doing his best about a teacher.

We had now given up our grandiloquent ideas about
two masters and a mistress. We would be grateful for
one teacher, male or female. We were managing well
enough with twenty-nine children, but I was determined not to have any more until we had at any rate
some Spanish adult to look after them. If they had all
been about the same age, it would have been even less
work, but with the children divided into three groups
it meant three of us always on duty.

I believed in letting the children have freedom, but
I was careful to see they had no chance of being bored.
As they had no real lessons it meant thinking up plans
for them every day. Archie added to his gymnasium
classes by a 'How it works' class which covered most
natural laws. He guaranteed to answer questions about

electricity, water pressure, drains, trains, motors, aeroplanes and to show them how to put in a fuse. Lo allowed the older girls to help her plan menus while Fridela ran a first-aid section. This started purely as a class, but it ended by being a real first-aid procession every morning. The children's blood, impoverished by a year's malnutrition, reacted strangely to good living. The slighest cut or abrasion suppurated; there was almost an epidemic of tiny sores behind their ears; the few who had boils when they came to us could not get rid of them.

We were handicapped in medicaments. We managed to squeeze the last drop of iodine out of the village chemist, but there was no alcohol. After many telephone calls and letters we got some zinc ointment from the Solidarity Fund which helped the ear trouble, but Fridela was the genius who understood herbs. She culled plants out of the woods and drove the kitchen staff crazy by boiling them on the stove. Soon the whole kitchen reeked of frigola, rosemary, fennell and many unknown varieties. Every precious kitchen pot was filled with a nauseating mixture of Fridela's. The kitchen suffered but the children throve. We refused to ask advice from the insane doctor, but Audrey Russell came and looked over the children and found them healthy except for this blood germ. It seemed to be common in all colonies. Fridela determined to rid our children of it.

We had a rough time-table which varied slightly as the occasion demanded, but which was fairly constant. The children came down to breakfast at 8.15. After breakfast they played in the garden, I mean the *calle*, until they were called in one by one to have wounds dressed and their ears done. Most of them had to have some treatment, if it was only sewing on a button or changing Justo's trousers. Justo was a problem. He burst gloriously out of his trousers whatever was done to them. We were desperate for *culos* or tail pieces. When people asked me what they could give us to help, I would burst forth with, 'Please give us something to make *culos*!' At last Sebastiana hunted through all her accumulations as a dressmaker, and we were able to patch to our heart's content, or rather the content of Justo's behind.

When the first-aid was over Archie would take the older ones for his class and the others would go down to the beach with Fridela. Later the others would join them and all do drill in the sunshine in their pants. Pepita always took off all her clothes and scampered about on all fours, stark naked. It was difficult to explain to Luisa, a black-eyed stout little madam, tremendously developed for her age, that she had better run about in her vest and knickers.

They returned from the beach in time for lunch. After lunch it became understood that we all wanted peace, and they usually went off to the swings up the hill or settled down quietly to their games or painting. My painting and drawing class was a success. I found a collection of old poster paints that I had forgotten and a quantity of drawing paper at Oskar's. No one except Primitivo showed much originality, but they enjoyed themselves. I sacrificed my best sable brushes, feeling it was in a good cause.

Later in the afternoon every one went for a walk. It depended on the weather, but usually the walk meant rounders on the football field. Sometimes the boys went off alone or with Fridela to get rabbit food and mush-rooms; the girls usually preferred to go with Leonor and the little ones. They took their *merienda* with them and stayed out until five or six. It meant that Lo, Archie, Francisca and I could have a leisurely tea in a quiet house. Lo generally planned to do most of her cooking in the morning and only have to warm things up for supper.

We would play games with the children until supper-time. Often they would take it in turns to tell stories in the dusk before Archie battled with the lights. We had bottles filled with petrol and stuck in tins of sand. A piece of string threaded through a scent-bottle cork did as a wick. They smoked sometimes and were unbear-able; generally they seemed satisfactory. Archie had a knack with them. On Sundays, when the munition factories were not working, there was light along the whole coast from early evening. We allowed those who wanted to stay up and dance to the gramophone on those occasions.

The little ones were usually half asleep by the end of supper. The older *mayores* and *medianos* tried valiantly to stay up to talk with us. If it was cold we lit the fire and all sat round it on the floor. We discussed most topics, but the favourite theme was their own adven-tures when they had to leave Aragon and become refugees. They were never tired of talking about their homes; the number of chickens and rabbits they left behind; the barrels of oil they ran into the river rather than leave for the invaders. They described without a tremor ghastly scenes of panic-stricken refugees flying from raiding planes. They seemed to take a ghoulish delight in playing at air raids. José was the only one who was visibly affected by his experiences, and this made him more talkative than the others and more eager to show his indifference by discussing gruesome details.

It amazed us that none of the children seemed to be homesick. They were eager for letters and they were excited at the prospect of a visit from their parents, but if the parents did not turn up they were quite calm about it. Most of the children had one parent or guardian in Barcelona; many of them had both parents alive. This did not surprise us because we were used to the International Solidarity Fund by this time. We had stipulated especially for orphans.

26

Food, Children and Autonomy

It was interesting to meet the children's parents. We could nearly always guess the sort of people they would be. Miguel's father was an odd nervous little man, with a pretty, spoilt wife. She clasped Pepita to her and smothered her in kisses. Pepita was not enthusiastic. Her mother wept, but Pepita was unmoved. We felt ashamed when Pepita ran off to play with the other children and ignored her parents for the rest of the day. Most of the children noticed their parents only for a few minutes and then were immersed in their own affairs. The parents would usually suggest leaving for their bus without calling the children's attention to their departure. They were convinced the children would scream and make a scene. As they tip-toed down the hill we used to pray that their occupied little brats would not look up and see them and just wave a casual hand. We only once had a weeping child at the bus. Mariano went down to see his father off. He came up whistling, but with tearstains on his face. We felt he had shown a nice sense of fitness until some one asked him why he had been crying.

'I was afraid my father would take me with him to Barcelona,' he said simply.

Apart from the awkwardness of the children being so casual, it meant that *we* had to work hard to entertain the parents. They were mostly charming people, but it was exhausting discussing the same child or children for three or four hours. Luckily for us the journey from Barcelona was so terrible with the long waits for the train and the crush when once one got on it, that the parents came only once to see what sort of place it was. They all seemed satisfied at the sight of the round, brown faces of their offspring.

The children were very happy. So were we. I was already so enchanted with having a children's colony that I was making plans for a permanent colony. I thought it would be wonderful to have English children at the Casa Johnstone after the war if a fund could be raised to send a few dozen children from South Wales for three months at a time, as a return for the help given by the Welsh miners. There would be many Spanish children whose homes had been destroyed who would need to stay in a colony, and it seemed a good idea to mix the children. Archie still hankered after his hotel. He really liked hotel guests, so I was prepared to compromise by having a few guests as well to amuse Archie.

We had one terrible tragedy. The Solidarity Fund assured us that each child was inspected by a doctor before it was sent to us. I mistrusted the Fund, so we searched the heads of the first ten children with great thoroughness. I felt I had misjudged the Solidarity Fund and we relaxed our vigilance. I was very keen to avoid cutting off the girls' hair, which was the practice in most colonies. The Santiago colony had infuriated me by shaving all the children's heads except the mass of golden permanent curls belonging to the Mo'ca's small daughter. I felt that if we started free of trouble, there was no reason why we should not keep their heads clean. Rosa shampooed her lovely glossy curls; Josefina groomed her permanent wave; even the little ones took a great interest in keeping their hair nice. When the new children arrived we never gave their hair a thought. It was Leonor who mentioned casually that she had caught a head louse in Asunta's frizzy hair.

It was already too late. Several of the smaller children had caught them. We felt it was impossible to cope with seven or eight thick mops. There was only one solution. All their hair must be cut off.

I broke the news to the elder girls as gently as I could. They were horrified. Rosa clutched her black curls with both hands and swore that she had no lice on her head. I said ruthlessly that if one girl had her hair cut, they all must have their hair cut. We discussed the matter for two hours. Finally they agreed, but tearfully. I had clinched the argument by procuring one of the revolting little creatures and showing it round.

I thought the village barber would object to having a mass of lousy children in his shop, but he preferred it to coming up to us. We went down in relays. The elder girls insisted on waiting until the very last. They clung to their hair as long as possible. Actually we were extremely gay when it came to the actual cutting. Once they had made up their minds, they were determined to be cheerful about it. They laughed so much at each other that they began to enjoy themselves. We cut all the boys' hair first and sent them off for a walk with Fridela; then the little girls, who were rather pleased by the novelty. Only Angelines was tearful. Pepita was delighted as each fair curl fell to the floor. She looked even prettier with a shorn head. It was not becoming to most of them. Carmen looked like some odd little monkey, but her plain elder sister revealed a beautifully shaped head. The majority looked like plain little boys. Rosa and Josefina battled for the last place and the barber with great understanding fetched his assistant so that they could be shorn together. Josefina looked fearfully plain, but Rosa appeared as a nice-looking boy. Her eyelashes seemed even more startlingly long and curly.

The girls were relieved that no one in the village noticed them as they scuttled back to the Casa Johnstone. The boys were still out and we turned the whole affair into a fiesta. Lo produced some cookies for *merienda* and we had the gramophone on. The girls were just a little nervous about facing the boys.

I had already spoken to the boys. I did not often use threats, but I threatened them with dire penalties if they dared to laugh. They had promised to be good about it and not to take advantage of this Heaven-sent opportunity of getting back at the girls. They knew that I often took their side in disputes with the girls, who usually were more underhand in their methods than the boys, and they kept their word. They came trooping in hungry for their *merienda*, and surveyed the clipped heads without a quiver of an eyelash. The girls were astonished. They were so surprised that they began to giggle. Soon Primitivo's composure collapsed and he went off into hearty guffaws, and in a moment all twenty-nine children were shrieking with laughter. We had a most cheerful evening.

We spent the next few days scrubbing their heads with carbolic soap and madly scratching our own heads. Lo washed her thick mop about three times a day in sheer panic. We became calmer as there were no signs of trouble and soon the whole thing was forgotten. We were slightly suspicious of Archie, who persisted in still getting his hair cut at a village barber's, but we decided his hair was hardly luxuriant enough to be attractive to head lice.

Poor Archie was losing more than his hair. We ruthlessly used his shirts and trousers to make clothes for the children. They were desperate for clothes. Our hillside was not conducive to long life for garments of any kind and for trousers it was fatal. Thanks to Sebastiana we managed to get thread for mending, but all sewing materials had long since vanished from the shops. By now each of the girls had two frocks made out of our bedspreads, and all the children had jerseys provided by the Solidarity Fund. We found that a cotton frock and a jersey were sufficient, even in the winter. There were few days when the frock alone was not enough for the mornings and they put on their jerseys in the afternoons. They had no socks, but the Fund had provided stout leather sandals with rubber soles which seemed to keep them warm. We were continually agitating for clothes from the Fund, but with no result.

The Solidarity Fund was at its best over food supplies. It worried me to think how much better we were eating than the average working-class family who helped to provide our food. They supplied everything except fresh meat and vegetables, and we could get vegetables. We had tinned meat and tinned salmon and sardines; three different kinds of cheese, including an entire

Gruyère which looked like a motor tyre and was a present from the workers at Gruyère. We had as much white bread as we wanted; ample butter for eating and cooking; every kind of dried vegetable; dried plums and apricots; huge tins of jam pulp. Beside all this we had dried milk, milk in tins, cocoa, coffee and tea.

We discovered why there was no rationing system. The Solidarity Fund itself did not know what it was going to get. For a month there would be cases of cooked sausages, then there would be no more sausages but bully beef instead. There would be Gruyère cheese for a while, then cream cheese would be given. The Solidarity Fund was odd. It announced cheerfully that it gave each colony complete autonomy. It certainly did with us. Then some one at head office would have an idea. A bright intelligent idea. A few sacks of potatoes would arrive with a little printed slip:

'By using these potatoes you should not need to use so many dried vegetables. Therefore your consumption of dried vegetables should be less.'

Every now and then the Fund forgot its watchword —autonomy for all—and became positively officious. It would send a printed time-table:

> Breakfast 7.30.
> Classes 8.30–12.
> Play-time 12–1.30.
> Lunch 1.30.

I used to send the time-table back with 'Where is our teacher?' written across it.

The Solidarity Fund never let us down over food. The lorry seldom came when it was expected, but it did come and always brought plenty. That was the most important question. The children could run about in rags so long as their bellies were full.

Leonor told me that in Aragon they celebrate Christmas. In Catalunya the great fiesta is at Epiphany. We decided to make a fiesta on Christmas Day.

We had long ago realized that the only way to give these children a treat was to provide something to eat. Their minds dwelt continually on food. They kept a diary, each child writing a day, and it consisted almost entirely of menus. They were astonished when I said I was bored by the recitals of meals. When I explained that I also kept a list of menus in the kitchen they understood and promised to avoid mentioning food unless we had something especially good. It was hard work and frequently the diarist would relapse into 'for lunch they gave us a sort of fish pie with potatoes browned on top', which would be hastily scored out and 'After a nice lunch we went for a walk with Nensi and Hachi, and Vitel came as well' would be written in. It was odd that no matter how often we explained how to spell our names the children preferred their own variations and Beetle ranged from Vitel to Bill.

Christmas must obviously be an orgy of food. We decided to give them their favourite dishes with some special cakes for *merienda*. After some subtle inquiries we discovered that milk-rice with cinnamon was the favourite of all. We therefore decided to have milk-rice and cinnamon for lunch, as much as they could eat. Lo and I made hundreds of sugar buns, some with chocolate icing, others with lemon and orange icing. Lo made a fascinating marble cake each slice of which was a wiggle of different colours. This was for *merienda*. We had a light supper of sardines and bread and butter and after supper the room was cleared for dancing. Between dancing there were refreshments in the shape of sugar buns, mixed raisins and nuts and sweets.

Archie and Primitivo provided the entertainment. They dressed up as a giant, Primitivo perched on Archie's shoulders and Archie's big dressing-gown over all. Primitivo acted as the dummy in Archie's ventriloquist act. They had a mock battle, pretending to slap each other's faces while the other slapped his hands together to make it more realistic. Primitivo was a born clown. Carmen sang one of her interminable songs; Asunta surprisingly produced a repertoire nearly as long as Carmen's. Justo insisted on doing a dance. It was very solemn and consisted chiefly in lifting one fat foot with a tremendous effort a small distance off the ground.

Sebastiana brought her two small boys; the Casa Blanca children looked in and stayed until Quimeta fetched them home to bed; Francisca's children came up, and various other friends dropped in during the evening. The party broke up about eleven. Every one decided that it had been a great party. I felt the children had not much excuse to feel homesick for an Aragon Christmas.

Archie was tired because he had rashly made José a wooden gun during the afternoon and all the other boys had demanded one. We were full of theories about not encouraging children to play soldiers, but we gave up these theories for the duration of the Spanish War. The boys thought of nothing else. José was pleased with his gun and for the rest of the day Archie had to turn out others. The children helped by sand-papering the guns and nailing on their bayonets. Altogether

Archie made twelve guns on Christmas afternoon. Not an occupation exactly in keeping with the Christmas spirit, but we in Spain had given up thinking about peace. I spent a more suitable afternoon. At the suggestion of José the children had given up their chocolate ration for the past two weeks. I took enough chocolate bars down to the Forty-Third Division colony to give the *abandonados* a big bar apiece.

The International Solidarity Fund was not to be outdone. It did not bother about Christmas, but just after Epiphany a lorry arrived with several pounds of *turón*, the famous Spanish sweet that is a cross between marzipan and nougat; several indoor games, one toy revolver, a toy cart, and a large wooden horse. There was complete unanimity about Justo having the revolver.

More important, a little man called Ribas also arrived and proceeded to measure all the children for clothes. He was horrified when he saw the state of the children's clothes. He assured us that if he had only known that our colony existed he would have visited us before. He had been several times to Tossa to the Santiago colony but no one had told him that there was a second colony of the Solidarity Fund in Tossa. I suggested that that was what had happened to the dentist and the doctor who were supposed to visit all the colonies from time to time. Ribas told us that he knew that both the doctor and dentist had visited the Santiago colony. I said I suppose we must be thankful that we at least got our food supplies.

I was annoyed. If there were no clothes we would willingly have run about in rags; if there was no doctor to visit the children one would have to do without. But it was irritating to be left completely in the dark about everything and given nothing but food, children and complete autonomy, while other colonies had all these things. Sr. Ribas promised us some shirts at the first opportunity. He told us that there were stacks of lovely clothes in the store in Barcelona. He said there were clothes even for us, the grown-ups. He promised to come back the following week with the first lot of clothes.

Sr. Ribas kept his word. He turned up exactly seven days later. He asked us to go down to Oskar's to unpack the lorry because there were so many things. We rushed down, with visions of lovely shirts, socks, perhaps even a pair of trousers for Justo. We unloaded large tweed skirts, grown-up overcoats, a pair of corduroy trousers for Archie, two dozen pairs of stockings for adults, some hairy jerseys, outsize, one dozen linen aprons and six enormous white overalls. Before we could recover from the shock, Ribas smiled out of the back of the lorry. He had a real surprise for us. He handed out twenty-eight brown serge circular capes of assorted sizes. They were magnificent capes, thick and warm, and lovely if one had a colony in Alaska. I toyed with the idea of cutting them up into shirts, but dismissed it as impracticable in the Tossa climate. Sr. Ribas was entranced with his capes. He had designed and cut them out himself. They were beautifully cut, but why? There were no socks, no underpants, no sandals for those that had worn out. I could have beaten the nice little man. He was babbling happily about his capes, oblivious of my rage. The other colonies were delighted with them, just what they had been wanting. I asked faintly about our necessities and he assured me that next week he would bring socks and shirts. In the meantime we had all the clothes for the adult staff and these beautiful *capitas*.

When he had gone we had a hilarious time playing bullfights with the *capitas* and letting the boys dress up in the jumpers and skirts. Francisca was delighted with her clothes and I cheered up a little. I packed the capes away with moth balls thinking that we might have freak weather in February and use them once or twice. The next day we went to the beach as usual. The boys were bathing, Pepita running about stark naked; even Justo had been persuaded to save on wear and tear and was playing in his shirt. We were lying about in the sunshine when there was a shout from the boys. The entire Santiago colony was parading along the cliff walk, two and two, looking like odd misshapen little dwarfs, the hot sunshine pouring down on rows of brown humps. They passed the beach, wheeled tidily round and trotted away, row upon row of brown gnomes. Our children shrieked with disgraceful laughter. They lay about the sand in their underpants, rocking with ill-mannered mirth. The Santiago colony had also been issued with capes.

27

Bombs and Toothache

Just before the children came the news had been favourable to the Spanish Government. The Government troops had advanced across the Ebro and were holding their positions without difficulty. The long-heralded fascist offensive still had not materialized.

I had left my portable typewriter in England during our summer visit. I thought it would be useful to have it out of Spain in case the war got too near home and we had to run away. Although we had come back to Tossa, meaning to stay whatever the outcome of the war, neither Archie nor myself had any desire to sit on our terrace if Tossa became a battlefield.

I struggled with the standard machine for a few months, lumping it from place to place so as to write always in the sun. Then I gave it up. I sent for my portable. The British Medical Aid kindly offered to send it out to Rosita who would bring it out to Tossa. It might be anything from several weeks to several months before it arrived.

When the fascist offensive started with a big artillery bombardment on the Ebro front we could hear the guns in Tossa. They rumbled all day long. Correspondents back from the front told us that there was a systematic artillery barrage covering the whole front, with planes to fill up the chinks with machine-gun bullets. Although the Government Army held out incredibly, they were bound to give ground. When they finally recrossed the Ebro most people thought it was to take up prepared positions for a period of static warfare.

But the fascists broke through. The first positions were well fortified and strong, but there was nothing behind them. The Government Army retreated, expecting to find some line where they could make a stand. There were no prepared positions, no trenches, no fortifications, nothing. The army was beaten back to Reus, to Valls, to Tarragona. We waited every day to hear of the offensive slowing up, of a Government stand. Every day a new position fell.

Tossa was as usual divided in extreme opinions. There were those who hoped the fascists would reach Barcelona as quickly as possible and thus end the war. These people were only interested in the ending of the war. They disliked any form of government if it came from Castilians, and while control by the Central Government seemed inevitable for the moment, at least Franco's government would finish the war more quickly. Then there were those who felt it was going too far to want Barcelona to fall, but who were also anxious to have done with the war in the least possible time. Besides, if Franco were advancing it usually meant that he stopped the air raids. Air raids were always worse when the fascists were being checked. There were just a few who genuinely disliked the idea of the Government losing the war. All were agreed on one thing; if Barcelona fell the war would stop automatically. There could be no fighting anywhere near Tossa. At the very worst they might fight to Gerona, but that was along the main road, and Tossa was well tucked away in the foothills.

The Casa Blanca family was miserable. The old man would have to go if the fascists won because he had been mixed up in politics years ago, and he assured us that in Spain these things mattered a great deal. He was rather vague as to how deeply he was committed, but he was certain that he had better leave. The rest of the family could not decide. We felt we were not capable of taking the responsibility of advising people on the subject of Spanish politics. In any case there was always the chance of Barcelona becoming a second Madrid.

José was the only one of the children who took the war news seriously. We always left the *Vanguardia* for the children to read, and we had a Michelin map of the war area. José and Leonor would study it carefully. The map was also useful to refute some of the Tossa rumours; it was reassuring to find that the latest fascist conquest was sixty miles from Barcelona when Tossencs had it that the Moors were climbing over Tibidabo and looking down on the city.

Then the usual Tossa blackout occurred. This always happened in a crisis. All communications were cut off.

The telephone still worked occasionally, but it was being used so frequently by Fuerzas del Aire, the air force, that it was practically impossible to have a coherent conversation. Fuerzas del Aire look-out posts seemed to have nothing else to do except to telephone to each other from remote villages. They were given precedence over all private calls. The first time I had a call interrupted and Marcelino told me apologetically that it was the fault of the forces of the air, I somehow got it into my head that the lines had been blown down somewhere.

The telephone was dangerous as a purveyor of news because by the time a rumour had reached Blanes, been passed on to the operator at Lloret and had reached Marcelino, in Tossa, it had grown unrecognizable. We decided we would go to Barcelona at the first opportunity to try to discover how serious the situation was. Also we could visit the headquarters of the Solidarity Fund and hear what they intended to do about the children. I also thought I would take the opportunity to have a tooth stopped.

There was no way of getting to Barcelona unless we could beg a lift. We decided we would take the first Solidarity Fund lorry available. We did not realize that we had seen our last Solidarity Fund lorry in Tossa.

Rosita appeared unexpectedly on the Friday on her way to a base hospital. It was a typical Rosita week-end, and consisted of arriving Friday afternoon and leaving after lunch on Saturday. She was as usual cheerful and calm, but she said that soon there would have to be a stand. She was able to tell us where the front was; she had been down there looking for an English nurse and it was near enough. Rosita had an unenviable job. Hospitals were being evacuated with amazing rapidity, and it was Rosita's business to keep track of all the English nurses so that she was able to inform the Medical Aid in London of their safety and whereabouts. She had to borrow a car or an ambulance from Sanidad and dash off to find where the front was that day. She had terrifying escapes. The day before she came to Tossa she had been in an ambulance with her driver coming away from near Valls. They had to rush from the ambulance and take cover under some trees while a few fascist planes swooped about, machine-gunning in the vicinity of the ambulance. When the planes had gone Rosita and her chauffeur found the ambulance roof riddled with holes, but the tyres were not touched. They drove away with some speed. Half an hour later they heard that the fascists were in possession of the whole district where they had been. Rosita took that lightly. She was much more concerned with an adventure they had had on their way to Tossa.

They had reached Malgrat, about seventeen miles from Tossa, when they were forced to line up in a queue of cars to wait while a raid warning was in progress. It was always annoying to have to wait in a small village during a raid instead of being able to rush out of it, but this time it was more than annoying. Rosita's ambulance was practically touching the tail-board of a large army lorry. In the lorry were four half-ton aerial bombs.

Rosita spoke to the carabinero on traffic control, but he had his orders. All vehicles must remain stationary during a raid. She argued and cajoled, but he was adamant. She went to the police. The police chief saw the point of her argument, but he had *his* orders. She persuaded him to telephone to Barcelona; the telephone was out of order owing to an air raid at Mataró. At last she prevailed upon the policeman to order the lorry to be moved. It meant moving the whole queue, but it seemed better than risking the whole town. The bombs started dropping just as the ambulance, still with the bomb lorry ahead, got out of the village.

Rosita suggested we should come back with her to Barcelona. She laughed when Archie said there would be no raids while he was there. The fascist rule of no raids during an advance seemed to have been discarded. In any case, Tarragona was taken, after heavy raids, and Barcelona was the next objective.

We left with Rosita in the ambulance. We took with us a sack of potatoes to pay the dentist. He was a very grand dentist and really only cared about the teeth of ambassadors and members of embassies, but he would stop anyone's teeth for potatoes. I also took a long list of urgent needs for the colony. We intended to visit the International Solidarity Fund's store.

Rosita's rooms fascinated us. The Medical Aid flat had been given up and Rosita now had a separate office, besides her own rooms in a big house off the Diagonal. They were lovely rooms, but one could not see the walls for gilt frames and more-than-life-size coloured photographs of the owners of the house. Papa was there, from a small boy in full uniform to an aged, moustached gentleman still in full uniform, through various stages of his career, always in full uniform. We came to the conclusion he must have had something to do with a band. Mamma was also resplendent, from girlish white muslin and bows to a mass of bosom blooming out of wisps of tulle, the whole overshadowed by a vast double chin. There was also room for a few relations here and there to fill up the gaps, but they were only life-size. We were longing to see Papa and Mamma, but Rosita assured us that they had changed a great deal. They spent as much time as they could in the country because they were nervous of the raids.

The first raid for that day started at 8 p.m. We had

just finished cooking supper on Rosita's electric fire when the current was turned off. Rosita, ever practical, kept candles handy, and we had our supper, although Archie could not be kept from dashing out on to the balcony to look at the tracer bullets darting in patterns across the dark blue sky. The bombs were falling some distance away in a series of sharp explosions. Rosita explained that these were small bombs that burst and scattered and were chiefly useful for killing people in the streets. She told us how she had been caught in a raid the week before. She went to a cinema below the Plaça Catalunya, and just as she was leaving in her car, a warning sounded and all cars were stopped. Every one abandoned their cars and took shelter in doorways. Rosita's car was the first in the queue. A small bomb burst at the far end of the street and the blast took the air out of the tyres of the cars. They gave a whistling groan, one after another, all along the line, and the cars subsided slowly down on their rims. Rosita watched the cars anxiously as each settled down quietly, getting nearer and nearer to her own. The car before hers gave a sigh and finally lurched down on the rims; her car gave a faint surprised whistle and stopped. The tyres remained inflated. Rosita was able to drive away triumphantly.

There was another raid at ten o'clock, just as we were going to bed. I was so tired I fell asleep before it was over, but Archie insisted on watching it from the balcony. There was an ornate clock in our bedroom; it struck the hours with a particularly irritating timbre like that of a telephone bell. I started up in bed at each hour. It soon became automatic. The siren sounded almost simultaneously with the striking of the even hours—twelve, two, four, six, eight. The odd hours struck peacefully. I learned to turn over and go to sleep when I heard one, three, five and seven. The raids were not in our part of the town, but at the docks and the lower part of the town by the station. They were not particularly frightening. There was an odd atmosphere of aloofness about them that was very different from the March raids. The fact that one flight after another dropped bombs within a specified area made for a feeling of selfish security so long as one stayed outside that area. In the March bombings the attacking planes divided over the town and dropped their extra heavy bombs indiscriminately.

There were raids at ten and at twelve. As it was Sunday, Rosita had only to pay a flying visit to her office and then was free for the day. She suggested running us up to the front if she could get a car or an ambulance; there was a lost English nurse to be located. We felt we might as well be at the front as in Barcelona, but Rosita could not get a car. It was I who suggested we might take our lunch up Tibidabo. I was not so much frightened by the raids as tired of them. There was one unpleasant moment during our efforts to reach Rosita's office when we sheltered in a doorway during a raid. That seemed to be the only precaution the Barcelonese took. They ignored the siren, but when the first anti-aircraft guns began, they looked up into the sky to locate the planes by the puffs of smoke. The shooting was excellent. The planes were not high. In the March raids I did not once see a plane, but these came over slowly and in perfect formation. We stood in a doorway on the way to Rosita's office with a few Barcelonese. We watched the planes circling carefully over the port.

Bombs and Toothache

The anti-aircraft fired continuously; one particularly noisy one sounded as if its shells were a size too small. We waited to hear the bombs. It was purest egotism. The moment we heard the bombs explode we knew that for this raid at least we were all right. This time the planes suddenly altered their course. They came, heavy with bombs, straight over us. It was an extraordinary feeling, standing quite still, eyes fixed on nine bombers, head tilting more and more backwards as the planes soared overhead. I noticed that I was not afraid; I was resigned. When my head would tilt back no farther and it meant taking a step to see them any more, I bent my head, shut my eyes and waited patiently for the bombs to fall round me. I have no recollection of thinking about anything in particular. Afterwards, when the planes banked and dropped their bombs in another part of the town, near enough to shake us considerably, I realized that I at last understood how the Spanish are so stoical about air raids. Where I differed was that I could not go on being stoical for ever, I suggested taking our lunch up Tibidabo.

Tibidabo is the highest hill round the cup of Barcelona. From it we had a magnificent view of the whole town and the country round. Montserrat loomed in the distance with the Brucks, the last natural defences of Barcelona. The flat coast country stretched for miles; there were no signs of defence. The sides of Tibidabo were smooth and green; no one had attempted to fortify them.

We expected to hear the guns from the front, but there was absolute quiet. A heat haze simmered over the horizon; Barcelona lay in a peaceful, sunny dream. The only disturbing element was the raids, now becoming more frequent. They lost their two-hour rhythm at one-thirty; after that they came along about every hour. They were German land planes escorted by Meisser-schmidt chasers, coming direct from Reus aerodrome. It was the chasers that made one realize how high the bombers must be; the bombers looked huge, but the chasers fluttered in and out of the formations like swirling leaves. It was unreal, sitting in the grass watching Barcelona being bombed. We watched the planes in the distance; saw them curved over the town, circle, bank and then straighten out to drop their bombs. One after the other, great plumes of smoke rose up from the houses. The still haze was shaken by the explosions. Then the planes sailed slowly away, the white puffs from the anti-aircraft guns looking miraculously near, and the haze settled down again, darkened here and there by slowly wreathing smoke.

Towards the evening the *tempo* was increased. The raids were now every forty-five minutes. I was surprised that the sirens functioned without fail five or ten minutes ahead of every raid. It meant that the people living in the bombed areas would have time to dash for a refuge. But who could spend days running into refuges every three-quarters of an hour? I was astonished that the whole life of the city was not becoming paralysed. People went walking or driving in the streets until they were stopped by the police. Then they waited until the bombs had been dropped—a matter of from ten to fifteen minutes from the first anti-aircraft fire—and then continued their pursuits as if nothing had happened.

On Monday morning Archie rang up Bill Forrest,

of the *News Chronicle*. He was surprised to hear that
Archie had come into Barcelona.

'Are you staying long?' he asked casually. 'I would
make it short.'

'A few days. Nancy has to see her dentist.'

'Good God! Is Nancy here? Then I should make it as
short as possible.'

Bill Forrest was a good judge of the Spanish War.
He was also usually extremely optimistic.

We found the International Solidarity Fund unperturbed. We wanted to impress one thing on them.
There was a tendency to invest all English people with
supernatural powers. We wanted to make it quite clear
that we could do nothing to save the children if Tossa
became a fighting zone. We were prepared to stay with
the children in any circumstances. We would stay in
Tossa with them or take them into France. It was the
International Solidarity Fund's business to tell us what
it wished us to do.

Santiago was in France. Mata seemed annoyed with us.

'We do not consider the situation so bad,' he said
stiffly.

Patiently I tried to explain that we simply wanted to
know the Solidarity Fund's plans. We had our own
ideas about the situation. Mata would not be drawn. It
soon became evident that the Solidarity Fund had no
plans. We asked if a lorry would be going to Tossa and
if we could go with it. Mata told us that a lorry was
going to Lloret the next afternoon. That was all he
could do for us. He seemed dead with overwork.

That evening we heard that the fascists had taken
Sitges, twenty miles away. It was taken by Moorish
troops.

The next morning, Tuesday, I went to the dentist. We could not leave Barcelona until the afternoon so there seemed no point in going back to Tossa with toothache. It was purely a question as to whether the dentist would be there. He was. He was overjoyed with the idea of the potatoes and examined my tooth forthwith, apologising for having to use a foot drill because with all the raids the electricity was almost permanently cut off.

I sat in the dentist's chair facing down the Paseo de Gracia. A Government office building was across the broad street. The sentries marched up and down the pavement. The street looked perfectly normal. People were strolling about in the sunshine; others were hurrying to get to their offices; cars rushed up and down the roadway. Every half-hour, for the raids were getting more frequent, there would be a temporary loss of animation. The cars would stop. The pedestrians stepped into doorways. In a few minutes life would be resumed except for those who had been mangled to death in the bombed areas.

The dentist was apologetic about the tooth. It was a tiresome tooth. It would need treatment. The nerve must be killed and then removed. It was a longish job. He would clean it up and kill the nerve to-day; then to-morrow he would dress it and the day after we would see——

I thought of the rapidly advancing troops, now within ten miles of Barcelona. There was nothing but the little trickle of the Llobregat to hold them.

'I think you had better take it out,' I said.

The dentist was upset. Not at all, it was a good tooth. He was a good dentist. He would save my tooth. He

302

did not approve of pulling out teeth for no reason.

While he was talking I was looking out of the window. I saw the sentries outside the Government office building suddenly tuck their rifles under their arms and walk away. They did not run or seem unduly excited, but they just walked away from their posts. What was good enough for the Government was good enough for me.

'I'll have that tooth out,' I said, 'and I'll have it out quick.'

28

The Importance of being Childless

I prevailed upon the dentist to take my tooth out, but I could not make him do it quickly. He pulled, his assistant pulled, his brother, also a dentist, was called in and he pulled. Luckily the dentist had plenty of novocaine, a great rarity during the war, and, except for the fear that my jaw would break under the strain, I bore up. In between the struggles, the dentist and his assistants pausing for a rest and breathing hard, I could hear the bombs falling near the port. It was a fantastic situation. The dentist was most upset. He finally broke the tooth and had to take the rest out in pieces. It took a long time. There were several raids. When he at last extracted the last bit of root he apologized profusely. He was so upset about his professional reputation that he irritated me.

'Good God!' I said, as well as I could with my aching jaw, 'what the hell is a tooth?'

We went straight from the dentist to the store of the International Solidarity Fund. Mata looked even more exhausted. He said there would be a lorry in two hours. We had some sandwiches with us which did for Archie's lunch, and we decided to wait in the store. It was near the bombed centre, but I felt I could not face the long walk back to Rosita's rooms. She was waiting for orders to leave Barcelona; Sanidad were already moving.

By this time the novocaine was wearing off and I began to realize what had happened to the tooth. Before I had time to work myself up into a state of real misery, Mata appeared and suggested casually that we might help to load up a lorry. We had been working about half an hour when we realized that the Solidarity Fund store was being evacuated. We asked Mata if this was true. He sheepishly admitted that they were moving the store to Lloret—just as a precaution. We asked him again if there were any instructions about the children; he could give us no satisfactory answer. After much labour we gathered that Santiago was in France to arrange for accommodation for the children in that country if the situation got serious in Spain. We heard also that the Mo'ca had gone to Paris.

We worked frantically all the afternoon loading up bales of clothes. All the shirts, trousers, underpants, sandals that I had been clamouring for were there. I managed to make a parcel of the most necessary items such as sandals and a pair of trousers for Justo and firmly took charge of them. My agonized jaw had one advantage; it took my mind off the raids. They were now continuous, coming over in relays of twelve. The sirens gave up the unequal contest. Some bombs dropped close to the store, shaking the building to its foundations, but I was past caring. Holding my face with one hand and flinging parcels into the lorry with the other, I worked automatically, my mind a blank. I focussed all my consciousness on the fact that soon the lorry would leave and we could go back to Tossa.

Tossa seemed a haven. Nothing ever happened in Tossa. Once in the Casa Johnstone we could sit on the terrace and relax. Barcelona would fall; Catalunya might fall, but Tossa would somehow remain Tossa.

Archie was loading the lorry with Scotch determination. Archie always takes the worst view, and I am sure he was thinking we probably should never leave Barcelona, but he was too kind to disillusion me. Archie is always kind in the most violent crisis, in spite of the fact that it is usually I who lead him into these situations. It was I who dragged him out of a peaceful newspaper office and landed him in a war-time hotel; I who precipitated him into the offices of irate officials; I who suggested breaking through policemen's garden walls; I who insisted on his accompanying me to a dentist in Barcelona when wiser people were fleeing from it. Archie may disapprove, but he never complains.

Strangely enough the lorry did leave, and we went with it. It was Tuesday evening. We crawled into a stream of cars and lorries, practically stationary, on the road leading out of Barcelona. Pedestrians, carrying bundles of their possessions, dodged in and out among the motor traffic. Sad-looking horses drooped behind stationary lorries, their overloaded carts piled with household goods.

The exodus from Barcelona had defeated the Spanish Government. The inhabitants of Tarragona and Reus had been evacuated in Government lorries and whisked away into the country; villagers within a few miles of Barcelona were somehow helped to escape. But the Government could not evacuate Barcelona. There was nowhere to evacuate them to. So the Barcelonese were left to escape as best they could. The Government slipped away quietly, apparently hoping that the people who were in danger from the fascists would know enough to get out and that the majority of the citizens would stay where they were. There was going to be little resistance.

Unfortunately the constant raids did not encourage staying quietly at home, at least if the homes were in the bombed areas. So people streamed out along the congested roads. There are few sights more pitiable than refugees hurrying along with their few possessions, hurrying to nowhere. The only sight more horrifying is when these same refugees are machine-gunned from the air.

It was the escorting chaser planes that swooped down and machine-gunned us. The anti-aircraft were still firing, but there was obviously no chance of Government planes coming up. The fascists had captured the Llobregat aerodrome. So the chasers had nothing else to do. If they had looked like fluttering leaves high up among the bombers, they seemed now more like infuriated dragons as they dived along the road, spraying bullets and noise. I had often imagined my reactions to seeing women and children shot down, lying squealing and kicking among trampling, terrified feet, but I found that my imagination was as usual far stronger than reality. It had always seemed to me inevitable that nearly every one must be hit if bullets were flying among a crowd. I found that the casualties were surprisingly few. There was considerable panic in the vicinity of the actual wounded, but on the whole most people seemed calm and controlled. Perhaps they were wondering, as I was, how the traffic jam could be resolved so that we could get on. It seemed foolish to sit in a stationary lorry when it was obviously so dangerous.

The whole shooting match was over in a few minutes. The dragons roared away and became pretty little moths again. But there was no comfort in the feeling that for the moment the raid was over; the chasers did not have to go away for more ammunition. At any moment the light-hearted pilots might get bored and want another bit of fun.

At last the long queue of vehicles started again. We went on in a series of jerks, but we did move.

We arrived at Lloret late at night. I had hoped we could walk straight on to Tossa, about ten miles, but we were too tired. The Solidarity Fund colony in Lloret put us up for the night. They also informed us that a teacher had arrived for us and had left for Tossa that very day by the bus. A nice woman teacher, with her little boy.

The next morning, Wednesday, we walked from Lloret to Tossa. We left our packages to come by the Tossa bus later in the day. It was a perfect walk. We took sandwiches and lunched on a promontory overlooking a wide sweep of the Mediterranean. It was a typical January day, brilliantly sunny, with a soft heat haze over the tree-covered cliffs and hills. We could see the faint outline of Montjuich showing where Barcelona lay in the wreathing mists. We wondered if behind that curtain of haze, death was still being hurled out of the peaceful sky.

We had a riotous reception from the children, Beetle, the Reifenbergs and Francisca, who streamed down our hillside when they saw us appear on the bridge. They were anxious to hear the latest news. We

308

were non-committal in front of the children, but we told the Reifenbergs later that Barcelona was sure to go. In the meantime there was nothing for us to do except to wait for instructions from the Solidarity Fund.

Our colony was excited because they had been able to provide a meal for President Azaña's colony who had escaped to Tossa from Tarrasa. They were sixty strong and were under the charge of a Captain Arjona and Sarjento Bueno. Fridela said with triumph that the Casa Johnstone had provided wonderful soup and bread and that the Captain was overcome with gratitude. The colony had settled temporarily in the village and their own supplies had arrived.

We were introduced to our teacher. She looked a mass of nerves, dark, twitchy, with faint black hairs on her trembling upper lip. She asked me anxiously about the situation. She was particularly interested because *she* was in the greatest danger. She had heard that the fascists immediately shot all teachers. It was terrible for her, all this uncertainty. She was feeling quite ill. I hastily changed the subject and later managed to convey to her that I preferred all conversations about fascist terror to be strictly private. I reminded her that there were twenty-nine children in the house who were at all costs to be kept calm. She said of course she thought of the children—her own son was always in her mind.

The son was a bilious-faced child of eleven. He wore plus fours and large boots. He never ceased to grumble because he had no sandals. He took it as a personal affront because I had brought back sandals from Barcelona for every one except him. I tried to explain that I had not known of his existence at the time of choosing the sandals, but this was too incredible. He was a difficult child. He sprawled all over the table at meals and threw bits of bread at Mariano; he put his feet in their large boots upon the chairs; he bullied the little ones and teased Beetle. He was unattractive.

Ordinarily I would have looked on such a child as a challenge, but just at that moment I had too many things to think about. Also I was up against the problem of mother and child.

Leonor was so wonderful about her Angelines that I had forgotten the usual difficulty of a mother and her child in the same colony. Leonor herself had said to me that while Angelines and she were staying with us, Angelines would be exactly the same as any of the other children. Actually even Leonor was not infallible, but her maternal lapses took the form of being unduly severe when poor Angelines was in some minor trouble. Therefore I was all the more unprepared for the fierce maternalism of the teacher. She flew to her youngster's defence with the impartiality of a tigress. The other children were deeply shocked. They were also disappointed in me. They expected to see me make short work of the teacher and her young. I tried to explain the situation to the older ones.

'The teacher is ill,' I put out lamely. 'She is very much upset by the Barcelona air raids and she feels that this boy is all she has left in the world. We really ought to be sorry for her. I promise to cope with the little beast when I think it is the right moment. In the meantime be angels and put up with them both. I have a lot of worries just now and it will help me a lot. If he gets really unbearable fetch me and I will deal with him.'

I knew the children would not let me down. We had developed a most satisfying trust in each other. I knew I could rely on the children to do the right thing in all circumstances. They were delightfully gay and ran about singing whenever visitors came to see whether refugee children were being done right by; they answered inane questions about the rivers of Aragon when fierce-looking elderly women took it upon themselves to see about their mental state; they spontaneously did all their Aragon dances when fascinated English visitors came from Barcelona. They seemed to know by instinct when to creep about like mice and when to burst into *jotas*. It was by way of being a return for some of the things we did for them. It was a gratifying return.

They did their best to put up with the teacher. They did not suffer from her so much as we did.

We grown-ups were all trying to keep up our spirits. We all of us knew that things were serious. On the Wednesday night we sat with some of the older children, the Reifenbergs, Leonor and the teacher after supper. We talked about everything except the war. Then, relentlessly, the teacher brought back the subject really in our thoughts, the situation in Barcelona. We were purposely saying nothing about Barcelona in front of the children. The teacher had left several days previously to us and would ask us searching questions about the exact situation. We hedged and put her off, conscious of José's intelligent grey eyes watching our expressions. Finally even the teacher managed to grasp that we were reluctant to discuss Barcelona. She started talking wildly about some other topic, very obviously changing the subject. Just before the children went up to bed she said suddenly: 'But if Barcelona falls we are lost. The Moors will be in Tossa in three days.'

I was sorry that a nice hearty Moor could not materialize just long enough to deal with the teacher.

The next day we smuggled the radio out of the big room into our sitting-room. After an hour's tinkering and shaking we got it to work in time to hear the Empire news broadcast. Barcelona had fallen at noon that day.

We told the Reifenbergs, the Casa Blanca, and the telephone Basques. The Basques were determined to leave Spain. The Casa Blanca decided to abandon their lovely farm. There was no question about the Reifenbergs. They were completely disinterested in politics, but they were German Jews. We reluctantly agreed with them when they decided to go, but, once they had decided, we advised a move at once. There was a chance that the Government might surrender; in any case it was as well to get within jumping distance of the French frontier as soon as possible.

Once the families had made up their minds, things moved swiftly. Marcelino said that his cousin Juan could get the use of a lorry and enough petrol to get them all to the frontier. The Casa Blanca decided to go with them and the Reifenbergs. They were to start at midnight.

We waited until the children were in bed and then crept into the kitchen to get food and supplies for the fugitives. We shared our remaining pound notes among them, knowing that the possession of even a little money would mean a lot in France. We filled two sacks with eatables. A little before midnight the Reifenbergs came over on their way to the Casa Blanca. They were to pick up the lorry there. We promised to see about their flat and to pack away their possessions. The Basques had already left two large trunks with us. We said a hasty good-bye and wished them luck. We said that surely the Solidarity Fund would send a lorry for us and we could all meet in France and continue running the colony. Then Archie and I went back to bed to snatch a little sleep.

We had not mentioned the flight to anyone in the house. We intended to explain the absence of the Reifenbergs by saying they had gone to Gerona to get their papers in order in case they had to leave. We made a mistake in not telling Leonor and the older children. José heard us moving round the kitchen and woke the others. They fetched the older girls and crept up to Leonor's room. They spent a miserable night thinking that we might have abandoned them. Leonor was doubtful, but Primitivo was certain that we had not done such a thing. José did not think we had both left, but thought that Archie might be packing me off to safety. Leonor told me afterwards that while I was in the kitchen getting the breakfast the following morning she tip-toed down to the dining-room to see how the tables were laid. I always put out the bread, Archie invariably forgot it. She rushed back and told the children that I was in the kitchen getting the breakfast as usual. The bread was round the tables.

After that we took Leonor and the older children into our confidence.

We were horrified when Marcelino rang us up after breakfast. It was like hearing a ghost. He explained that he could not speak over the phone, but Maria would come right up. Something had upset all their plans.

Maria looked terrible. She was shaking with nerves.

The Importance of being Childless

We made her drink a cup of cocoa and then she told us her news. Juan had tried to steal the petrol for the lorry from the carabineros' pump. Some one had heard him and he ran away into the hills. The others were all waiting at the Casa Blanca for the lorry. They heard the shouts and realized that something had gone wrong. The Casa Blanca decided to leave in any case and went towards the frontier with their mule cart, the father, the old mother, Ramona and her two children, and Quimeta. Miguel at the last moment refused to leave. The Reifenbergs went with them. Miguel stayed behind alone in the big farm. He was fifteen and scared to death, but he could not bear to think of the stock dying of starvation. Maria, her two small babies and Marcelino went back to the telephone exchange. No one knew where Juan went.

We tried to cheer Maria and promised faithfully that when a lorry came for us we would take her family and Marcelino. She said that the Santiago colony had also promised to take them. She cheered up a little. Between the two of us she thought she would get to the frontier.

She reminded me of the other colony. We managed to telephone through to the colony at Lloret, but no one seemed to know much. They thought they were going to be evacuated. Yes, they would let us know if a lorry came to fetch them. They thought there was a possibility of the Blanes, Santa Coloma, and Lloret colonies of the Fund being evacuated in that order. Oh yes, they would advise us to have everything packed up in readiness.

This was more cheering. At least we had an idea of the Solidarity Fund's line of action. I went down to the

Santiago colony hoping that they might have more definite news.

I found the place in a panic. The children were huddled in the playground; some of them were crying. A few young *responsables* dithered about hysterically. The fat Bilbaina was prostrate on her bed. The cook had run away into the hills. Señora Santiago was in bed.

I shook a little sense into one of the *responsables* and sent her upstairs to wash her face. I had a long talk with the children. The ones who knew me from the swimming lessons had a certain amount of confidence and soon I had them all reasonably cheerful. When the *responsable* came down with the tear-stains removed I sent her out for a walk with all the children. I told her to pass by the beach and to let the children have a good look at our children playing about as usual. Then she could take them to the other beach and let them run about a bit. I purposely did not suggest letting the wrought-up children loose among ours.

I was elated with my success with the *responsable* and set to work on another one. She said she was the cook's assistant and could manage to get the dinner if I told her what to do. We looked around the store and chose macaroni and tinned meat to make into a meat sauce. Having fixed up an evening meal and by this very fact restored confidence among the *responsables*, I went upstairs to see what could be done to Señora Santiago.

She was almost out of her mind. She lay and moaned. I tried various methods to get some sense out of her, but in the end I gave it up. I suggested to the new cook, who was by now enjoying herself thoroughly, that she carry on. I also suggested that a good hearty meal might be sent up to Señora Santiago. I felt that the Bilbaina was beyond help.

Francisca was being marvellous. She undertook the entire work of our kitchen. I came up from the other colony feeling exhausted and hating the thought of having to produce a meal for thirty-odd people. I found that Francisca had done everything. Leonor was being equally wonderful. She kept cheerful, she breezed round among the children in her usual hearty way; she was perpetually on the watch to save me work. Archie was quietly seeing to things in his own way. We did not need to discuss the situation; we both knew exactly what the other was thinking. Five minutes' quiet alone with Archie was the best rest I could have, but five minutes' quiet was hard to get.

The moment it became known that Barcelona had fallen, Tossencs streamed up to the Casa Johnstone. Should they go or stay? What did we advise? Were the Moors really so terrible? Would there be fighting in Tossa?

At first Francisca faithfully tried to keep every one out. She knew I was snatching a rest in my sitting-room. The children were out with Leonor and the gloomy teacher. Archie dealt manfully with the mob, but they wanted to hear both of us. The men were content with Archie, but the women wanted my opinion.

It was an extraordinary situation. Archie and I sat on our terrace and held the fate of a few hundred people in our hands. If we said 'leave' they would pack up and leave their homes, their village, their country. They would swell the world's legions of refugees. If we said 'stay' they would stay and face a fascist régime, chances of bombardment, chances of battle. We were in a ghastly position. It was bad enough to have to decide for ourselves and to have the responsibility of thirty children, but at least we shared that responsibility with the Solidarity Fund. These people handed their fate over to us. Should they go or should they stay?

We reached the same conclusion. If anyone asked that question, surely it meant that there was no real reason for them to leave? It seemed to us madness to join the mass of homeless refugees in the world unless one's most precious principles or one's life were in danger. Then people do not have doubts about it, they go. We suggested to everybody that they stayed. If they were not definitely *destacados*, that is marked for their political activities, it seemed unwise for them to leave everything. We thought they could take the chance of actual fighting in Tossa; so far Tossa had escaped raids. It had not even been machine-gunned.

Archie and I never discussed our own position. We were no longer individuals. We were bound to count ourselves as part of a group. We were free in that we had good passports—they were even visad for France—and we were strong enough to trek to the frontier at any time if we wished. We even had a bicycle. But we were no longer Archie and Nancy Johnstone. We were the directors of a children's colony.

'Francisca,' I said solemnly as I watched her making the supper, 'do you realize that Archie and I have never had any children of our own because we always felt we might one day be in a situation like this?'

Francisca stirred the lentil soup and sniffed.

'Look at you now,' she said.

29

Half under Two Flags

The fine weather continued. We cursed the climate that produced perfect conditions for an advancing army in January. That was all the news we could get, that the fascists were advancing from Barcelona along the main road. This news was brought by refugees fleeing from the villages between Barcelona and Malgrat. Malgrat was at the fork of the main road. The main road to France through Gerona and Figueras went to the left; the coast road through Blanes, Lloret and Tossa to San Feliu and Palafrugel was the right fork coming from Barcelona. The question was, Would the fascists advance along the main road, keeping all the fighting away from the coast and just send a party of troops to mop up the coastal villages, or would they fight their way along the coast road? We thought they would probably know through their excellent espionage system that a landslide had swept away a portion of the road between San Feliu and Tossa, which meant that any advance from Tossa to San Feliu would be impossible. We expected them to continue their pressure along the main road to Gerona.

This meant that, once past Malgrat and on the way to Gerona, the fascists would cut off all retreat from Blanes, Lloret and Tossa. San Feliu people could escape up the coast towards Port Bou, but with the landslide all escape from Tossa onwards would have to be by the inland road.

It was an extraordinary feeling, sitting at the bottom of the Tossa hills, cut off completely from all communications except somewhat hysterical reports from hurrying refugees. The only conclusive fact gleaned from the processions of mule carts laden with possessions was that the way was still open. It was Archie who suggested to the *ayuntamiento* that they post some one to stop people going along the blocked San Feliu road. There was a small notice, but many of the mule carts ignored it and we saw them returning wearily hours later.

Marcelino tried valiantly to get some news by the telephone. He could still get Blanes and Mataró. The Government Army headquarters seemed to be at Mataró, twenty miles away. The Government itself was supposed to be in Gerona or Figueras. Rosita had told us she expected to be stationed somewhere outside Gerona. The Quaker relief organization had moved northwards, presumably to Gerona. Some of the Quakers stayed on in Barcelona after it was taken. Gerona seemed inaccessible to telephone calls.

Captain Arjona and Serjeant Bueno came up to say good-bye. Their lorry had arrived at last. They regretted not being able to take our large family, but they said they had room for one person if we liked to avail ourselves of the opportunity. Archie and I looked at each other. A gleam came into our eyes. We had no need to speak our thoughts. I went to find the teacher.

I had previously discussed the question of going or staying with Leonor. I told her frankly that I had no idea of her political background, if any. If she felt there was any danger for herself she ought to leave, as much for the sake of the children as for herself. The fewer *destacados* we had in the house the better. Leonor assured me that there was no reason for her to leave. She would prefer to leave if there was a reasonable possibility, but she had no intention of dragging Angelines over the Pyrenees on foot. She would stay with us. If we could get away she would be very pleased; if not, she would take her chance.

There was no question of Francisca leaving. She had no interest in politics and Pepito was only a lorry driver. She asked me if she ought to start off with the two children for the frontier, but I told her not to be a fool. I said even if there were a bloody battle in Tossa, all she had to do was to run out into the hills until it was over. It was different if one had a party of thirty to look after, some of them almost babies.

We thought of the Basques, but there was only room for one adult and perhaps a child might be squeezed in. Captain Arjona's offer seemed Heaven-sent for our teacher. She was delighted. She had packed everything in readiness for such an opportunity. Archie escorted her down to the village, carrying her suitcases. The boy followed reluctantly, kicking stones with his boots. Outside the café a crowd of refugees were huddled together, waiting hopefully for some kind of a conveyance. They had walked from Barcelona and were desperate for a lift to the frontier. The Azaña colony had gone a little way out of the village to wait for their lorry, so as to avoid a rush. Arjona and Bueno were having coffees in the café. The lorry was unobtrusively waiting up a side-street.

The teacher walked up to a haggard-looking woman sitting motionless on some *bultos*.

'Can you tell me where the lorry is?' she asked brightly.

Archie pulled her arm.

'Come inside and have a coffee,' he said between his teeth.

'No, I don't want a coffee. I want to find this lorry.' She turned to the now interested crowd. 'Doesn't any-one know where it is? I was told——'

'Come and have a coffee,' hissed Archie.

'But we've just had coffee up at the house. It is much more important to get a good seat in the lorry. Doesn't anyone really know——?'

'*You are going to have a coffee*,' said Archie grimly, as the crowd pressed closer. Suddenly the child washed out all his past troublesomeness by saying, '*I* want a coffee,' and pushing his way upstairs. When Archie explained over his untasted coffee just what he thought of the intelligence of Spanish teachers and of Aragonese ones in particular the teacher said, 'Why, yes. How silly of me!'

Arjona and Bueno strolled quietly away. Archie, with a firm grip of the teacher's arm, hurried in the opposite direction. Several refugees followed them hopefully. When they saw they were going towards the Casa Johnstone, they gave it up. They went back to the hopeless group round the café.

Archie, still holding fast to the teacher, hurried down the little road leading through the gardens to the cross-roads. The lorry was a little farther along the Llagostera

road. The children were already packed in; Arjona and
Bueno were waiting to go. Archie pushed the teacher
up over the back, hoisted up the child and breathed
again. The lorry went off, leaving three stalwarts of the
Azaña guard. They were left behind to make room.
Arjona said if there was a possibility to send a lorry to
fetch them and us he would do so, but he was doubtful.
In any case the soldiers could trek to the frontier if the
worst came to the worst. Arjona was terribly upset
about leaving us and our children. We explained that
we still hoped the International Solidarity Fund would
send to fetch us. It did not seem likely that Enrique
Santiago would abandon his wife, even if he otherwise
might not bother about two colonies. We knew that one
of the Fund's big food lorries could easily take the
Santiago colony and ours.

The atmosphere lightened considerably with the
absence of the teacher. We had all managed to acquire
a resigned attitude to whatever happened. The children
were really cheerful again; only José needed a little
watching. Leonor, having decided to stick by us and
now convinced that we would not abandon our colony,
became her own cheerful self. Francisca was suffering
from different emotions. She joined us in watching for
the lorry, but with fear in her heart. She did not want
that lorry to come.

I decided to pack up so that we could leave the
instant it came. We had noticed that the other Tossa
colonies had left in the evening or at night, so as to
avoid the plane attacks on the road in daylight. The
Gerona road was being heavily bombed; we could
hear it clearly in Tossa. The children put all their personal belongings into pillow-slips marked with their

names. They each had a blanket rolled up ready to sling over their shoulders like the carabineros. I had an old Gladstone bag packed ready with emergency kitchen equipment, including a petrol stove. Iron rations, consisting of two 'dog biscuits', two bars of chocolate and a handful of raisins, were put up for each child. We packed immediate necessities, such as bedding and food in big *bultos* made from blankets with the four corners tied together. Archie slept on a mattress by the side of the telephone. Marcelino promised to keep watch for the lorry and to ring us immediately. The Santiago colony had promised to let him know when it came.

Lloret suddenly ceased answering the telephone. Rumours flew around. The fascists were in Mataró, in Blanes; they were advancing rapidly towards Tossa; they were still in Barcelona; they were at Arenys. The only consistent rumour was that there was fighting through all the villages, in the line of the advance, the Moors being used as assault troops. There was one delightful rumour which we hoped was true. Caldetas had been bombed at last. We were not unduly disturbed by a still wilder story that the British vice-Consul had been wounded as he was about to leap onto a battleship. It seemed certain that Caldetas had undoubtedly been a scene of fighting.

We had no hope of a battle-cruiser this time. We knew our consular service too well. I rather wished one would call just to see what they would do if we asked them to take thirty Spanish children as well. They might even have taken them, in which case I would gladly have revised my opinion of the Navy. But the Navy was not given a chance.

It was just before lunch on Saturday, January 29th,

that the *ayuntamiento* sent for us. We found the full
town council in session, the director of the Forty-Third
Division colony, and Enrique Casanovas and his wife.
Casanovas was a charming elderly man, one of Catalunya's best-known sculptors. His wife we knew
slightly, a pleasant capable woman, and we had often
played with their children on the beach. She told me
that Casanovas had been giving drawing lessons to the
children of one of the Tossa colonies and that the
responsables of the colony had run away and left the
children. She and her husband were taking charge of
them.

The mayor had left for the frontier and it was the
town secretary who took charge of the proceedings.
He had been town secretary through many régimes and
one more or less would not worry him. He explained
that he had asked a representative of the Santiago colony
to come, but they all seemed to be ill. Perhaps I could
speak for that colony as well as mine. I said it depended
on what I was supposed to say.

It was then explained that the fascists were in Lloret,
eight miles away. They were expected to make a peaceful entry into Tossa that evening headed, it was true,
by Moors, but by nice, peaceful, friendly Moors.
There had been a fascist landing at Port Bou and all
escape to France was cut off. The Government was
trapped somewhere in the neighbourhood of Figueras.
This meeting had been called to discuss the steps that
Tossa should take. The main thing was to save the
children as much unpleasantness as possible. There
was a suggestion of a gala reception by the remaining
colonies lining the Lloret road and waving flags.

There was nothing to be said. Obviously the children

must be spared unpleasantness. If waving monarchist flags of red and yellow would appease the Moors, the children should wave flags. I noticed the town secretary's wife was already preparing flags by the simple expedient of tearing off the purple strip of the Republican flag, leaving the red and yellow. It reminded me of the story of the Spanish Embassy in London, after the '31 revolution when the monarchy was overthrown. Instead of removing the stone royal arms carved over the fireplace in the reception room, they hung a silk curtain over it. It took the Spanish civil war to have those arms removed. The entire fireplace was rebuilt on modern lines.

As we left the *ayuntamiento*, the town secretary called me aside. He had always been slightly nervous of me, especially so since the episode of the policeman and Oskar's house. He coughed apologetically.

'If I may suggest——' he began. He seemed very embarrassed. 'Please excuse me mentioning it——' He tried again and finally it came out with a rush. 'Please don't wear trousers at the reception,' he begged. At all costs the village must be spared unpleasantness. I assured him I had intended to sacrifice my trousers.

Breaking the news to the children was interrupted by frantic unpackings. The children seemed to take it calmly. Leonor and Francisca were too busy helping me to put everything in order. It had struck me that if we were to stay, it was as well to appear willing to stay. A house full of packages done up in blankets looked too suggestive of a hastily-planned flight that had not come off.

Archie and I went through our papers. We had nothing desperately incriminating; nothing more than an average liberally-minded household might have. We were prepared to leave everything in the house if the lorry had come, but we felt that we must be extra careful for the sake of the children. We finally got to the stage of destroying everything, even Christmas numbers of ordinary magazines, in case they contained something displeasing to the totalitarian mind. We got our central heating up to eighty. One of the last things to feed the flames was the galley proofs of the first part of a novel of mine Fabers were going to publish. I had the manuscript back for some alterations to the end. Looking at it hastily in the excitement of the moment it struck me that it was dubious. There was a communist in it, a nice, pleasant creature. I flung the proofs into the furnace. Later I found the manuscript, and flung that in too. I remembered just as it disappeared into charred ashes that I had no copy of the manuscript, but it seemed relatively unimportant at the time.

Marcelino and Maria came up to say good-bye. They were walking towards the frontier with two children, aged three and eighteen months. We gave them all the food they could carry and would have wished them luck, but it seemed impertinent. They had been hunted from San Sebastian to Bilbao; from Bilbao to Gijon; from Gijon to Barcelona via France, and thence to Tossa. Now they were fleeing again to France, but with no hope. It seemed absurd that Marcelino, an intellectual, should be hunted; it seemed still more fantastic that a harmless little body like Maria should have to face a trek of eighty miles with two small children and then to reach only something unknown. But the whole situation was so insane that one lost all sense of reason.

The same tragic scenes were happening every day in other countries than Spain.

Now that the whole business was over and we knew where we were, I felt a sense of relief. At least there was nothing more we could do. I could have snatched some sleep in the afternoon, after the hectic business of replacing everything was accomplished, but Tossencs toiled up our hill in relays. They were the same ones who had asked our advice about staying or leaving. They came this time to persuade themselves that we had been right. They were beginning to have doubts. There was nothing whatever to be done, but they felt they would like to be reassured. Had we really meant it when we advised them to stay in Tossa? There were stories about Moors——

At last I got a moment to have a real talk with the children. I explained that there was very little time, the fascists were expected at six. Allowing for Spanish and Italian ideas of time, it meant they should be in Tossa by seven. I was cheerful and reassuring. I really felt cheerful. I did not much care who walked into Tossa so long as they made up their minds. It was the hanging about in uncertainty that was wearing me out.

We waited for the fascists in the big room. We tried not to glue our eyes to the curve of the Lloret road. The *pequeños* were playing as usual. They did not understand the situation and we were careful not to show them that anything was wrong. The older children were very silent. After their first outburst of protest at the idea of welcoming in the fascists, they had not said a word. I had been amazed at their vehemence. Nothing would induce them to stay if the fascists came. They would run away to the hills, anywhere. They would not under any circumstances utter a word of welcome.

I had argued with them as well as I could in between reassuring scared Tossencs. We had been careful during the time the children were with us to discourage any violent anti-fascist feelings. Neither Archie nor I approve of bringing up children under any circumstances with pre-conceived political notions, but we did believe in making them conscious that they were part of a community and that they must behave reasonably fairly and decently within that community. It may have been unfortunate that our ideas of fairness and decency and our definition of a community differed from the totalitarian ideas. Archie and I hold the untotalitarian theory that under no circumstances should open towns be bombed; our answer to the fascist argument that no towns are open towns is stop bombing altogether. We tried to instil this into the children when they would play at bombing fascist towns. We pointed out that bombing behind the fascist lines, where there would be a number of non-fascists, would not stop the fascist bombing. The children gave up singing anti-fascist songs and they gave up their beloved game of turning our garden into an anti-fascist stronghold, but they clung to their wish to bomb behind the fascist lines. They had been bombed and they wanted to bomb some one else.

It was not surprising the hatred these children had for fascists. The fascists had killed their parents; had driven them from their homes; had bombed the children themselves. For the children fascisim stood for something loathsome. They refused to greet them when they entered Tossa.

At last I gave it up, but I did persuade the children

not to try to escape. I decided we had better let the
other colonies do the welcoming. I went down to tell
the *ayuntamiento*. On the way down I met the director
of the Forty-Third Division colony on his way up to
the Casa Johnstone. He was worried because his two
hundred children flatly refused to join in any procession.
He thought they had better stay in their houses. We
met the Casanovas in the *ayuntamiento*. They had been
having trouble with their children. Perhaps it would be
better to get the Tossa children to do the welcoming.

As I toiled back into the Casa Johnstone, Francisca
told me that Señora Santiago was waiting for me. I
found her in my sitting-room. I was dead tired and not
feeling like dealing with a mental case, but something
had to be done. Archie had nobly taken the Santiago
colony for a long walk with instructions to bring them
back at five-thirty. I gave a hysterical giggle when I
realized that there was something to be said for repress-
ing children. We could at least send the Santiago children marching out with red and yellow flags. They
would always do what they were told.

I soon felt no inclination to giggle, not even hysterically. Señora Santiago suddenly flung herself on her
knees. 'Save me! save me!' she cried, thrusting a scared
little Riki into my arms. 'Save me and my child!'

I tried to explain that I was in no condition to save
anyone. I pointed out that I was doing my best to look
after her colony. She twisted round on the floor, her
eyes glaring and her mouth working in hideous
grimaces.

'You must save me,' she spoke in a strange sing-song
voice. 'Every one has abandoned me. Enriqueta has
left me; Enrique has left me——' She suddenly

screamed and clutched my knees. 'Don't you understand? I am his wife—the wife of Enrique Santiago. They will kill me and kill my son. You can save me if you only will. Save me! save me!'

I managed to quieten her. I was sorry for Riki who looked scared to death. I patiently explained all over again how I could do nothing. I suggested she should go back to bed. I promised to look in to see her as soon as I could. I repeated that I was sorry, there was nothing I could do.

She scrambled to her feet and snatched Riki from me. She hurried to the door. She stared at me, her face twitching.

'You won't save me,' she said at last, her words coming out in a horrible choke. 'You won't save me.'

I watched her running down the hill like a mad thing, dragging the terrified Riki by the arm.

Francisca was still performing marvels. She took the entire work of the kitchen off my shoulders. It was not until after supper, when the *pequeños* had gone to bed and the older ones were clinging to us round the fire, that we realized that it was nine o'clock and the fascists had not come. We stayed up until nearly midnight, and then I persuaded every one to go to bed. Francisca and family had moved up to sleep with us. Archie ran down to the telephone exchange to see if there was any response anywhere, but reported a blank. Archie had taken over the exchange unofficially after the departure of Marcelino, his old Army training in the Signals proving to have some use.

We slept, as usual in these times, in our clothes. I had snatched sleep on the divan in the sitting-room for several nights listening for a lorry. This night I meant to keep awake in case the fascists came, but I fell sound asleep. I felt anyone could come, but I must sleep. Archie slept on the floor in the sitting-room. Some one had to be on hand to give food to refugees and soldiers making for their homes. There was a procession of boys wandering back to their villages. They had lost their headquarters and their companies and naturally made for home. Several Tossa boys came back, including Emilio of the café. Rovira appeared after various odd reports had circulated about him, varying from his having deserted to his having escaped to France. Actually he had been living in the mountains just ahead of the retreating army. Two Tossa boys appeared who had hidden in their houses to escape their military service. They had not been outside for two years. They were white and almost transparent like tissue paper.

The refugees and soldiers called at our house for food. We had received a huge consigment of food in the last lorry that came to Tossa and we were able to give something to every one. They were always polite and charming. Archie left the door open at night so that he could wake up easily, otherwise the soldiers did not like to knock. They were shy, rather ashamed of themselves for deserting, but certain that there was nothing else for them to do. We fed them all. It was not a time for arguing about rights and wrongs. We suddenly realized that we were encouraging the British Consul's pet bugbear, the marauding soldiery.

The next morning we were still in the territory of Government Spain. New rumours began to circulate. Perhaps the fascists were not in Lloret. Was it possible that the Port Bou landing was just a bit of wishful thinking? Archie suddenly announced he was going to bicycle to Lloret to see where these fascists were. He also hoped to be able to telephone forward from Lloret, if it was not already captured.

Archie says that he bicycled very slowly. He assures me that he braked hard down the twisty road and pushed the bicycle up the hills in a leisurely fashion. However, he came back like the wind. The Lloret colony had been evacuated. He had telephoned to the Army headquarters at Blanes and had asked for a lorry. Headquarters replied that all their lorries were in use for the transport of war material. Archie explained that it was for a children's colony. Oh, for children? That was rather different. There was a conference and headquarters stated that they would do their best to send a lorry. It was difficult, but if there was the slightest possibility we should have a lorry. The Spanish Army headquarters added, 'We are terribly busy, but of course children come first.'

The Port Bou landing? A story put out by fascist propagandists.

The fascists? Oh, they had not yet reached Malgrat.

30

Hotel in Flight

We packed up again. Leonor helped the older children fill the pillow-cases once more; Francisca and I rolled up as many of the Solidarity Fund's sheets, towels, aprons, etc., as would make five large *bultos* wrapped in blankets; we packed up the emergency kitchen suitcase again; we packaged up the iron rations. Archie and I had three suitcases. Beetle had her travelling bag.

Archie had reported that the Lloret colony had been evacuated by Solidarity Fund lorries. I went down at once to tell Señora Santiago that the rumours were all wrong and that there was a good possibility of a lorry coming to fetch our colonies. She refused to see me, but I talked to the children and told one of the *responsables* to get things packed up in case the lorry arrived. I saw the Casanovas and we agreed that whatever lorry arrived, we would inform each other. I told them there was a chance that an army lorry might come from Blanes and that the Solidarity Fund might send one of the lorries big enough for both our colonies. In any case we decided to keep in touch. I passed by the Forty-Third Division colony and saw the children rushing about in great excitement. Four Government lorries had arrived to fetch them. They were pathetically excited. They crowded round me asking anxiously if we would be able to escape. I said I thought it was very likely.

'Then we can all meet in France.' They spoke as if France was a huge children's colony.

I assured them that I hoped we should meet in France. We had a touching farewell; the four lorry-loads of children insisted on shaking my hand; the lorries had to wait while Archie came running down the hill. We clutched hot, scabious hands, and hugged incredibly dirty necks until the drivers said they must be off. Our children stood up on the Casa Johnstone terrace and gave them a cheer.

There were now three colonies left in Tossa; the Casanovas one, the Santiago one and ours, altogether some ninety children.

It was just after lunch that Miguel arrived on a motor bicycle. He looked deathly tired and on the point of collapse. He revived after some food and told us that he had just left Barcelona. He had not been able to get away when the fascists entered, but had hidden in the city and somehow managed to get through the fascist lines. Concha was still in Barcelona, but he thought she would be safe. He knew that he would be shot if he were caught.

The children were fascinated. Miguel was a story-book hero to them. He had to tell the older ones again and again exactly how he managed to avoid being caught. At last we intervened and put him to bed. Archie and I could not help thinking it was typical of Miguel to find a motor bicycle to escape on. We felt that whatever happened Miguel would come out all right. He was one of those people.

He told us that he had seen Nikolaus the day before
Barcelona fell and that Nikolaus had said he was coming
out to us. We had fed several hungry Germans on their
way to the frontier, and we were worried about Nikolaus. He had done so much for other people it seemed
that he ought to find some one to help him in this crisis.
The most important news brought by Miguel was that
the fascist troops were on the point of taking Malgrat.
Miguel said they were advancing without haste, but
nearly as fast as they chose. There was some resistance,
but hardly enough to delay the advance. Miguel said
that a section of the army headquarters were moving
back from Blanes to Lloret, but that the main resistance
would be in the Gerona section. He seemed convinced
that there would be some fighting along the coast. He
advised us most certainly to do everything possible to
remove the children.

If we had not already decided upon this, we certainly
would have had our minds made up by an incident during the afternoon. There was a constant procession of
enemy planes passing over Tossa, but we had got so
used to the idea that nothing ever happened in Tossa
that we ignored them. I was walking down to the village
and was just passing the now empty Forty-Third
Division colony building. I was walking under an
avenue of naked plane trees, with the long wall of the
building on my right. Nine Savoia bombers were passing slowly overhead and I was watching them through
the branches of the trees. Several chasers were escorting
them. I noticed one chaser dive low over the beach
apparently back-firing. I heard a spattering among the
trees, like the beginning of a heavy thunder shower,
but the sky was bright blue and cloudless. The spatter-

ing stopped and the plane swooped away. I realized that I had been machine-gunned. The wall behind me was pitted with holes; a battered spent bullet lay on the ground in front of me.

When we were machine-gunned in the lorry on the way out of Barcelona there was too much excitement and commotion to bother much about oneself. Although it is inexcusable, according to many standards, to mow down refugees, there was the undoubted fact that the town was about to be taken, and it might be possible to mistake a stream of carts and lorries for troop supplies. But this was too much. There was not a soul on the beach except me. I felt it was a direct personal assault. I was furious. For me it was no excuse that the pilot could not possibly have seen me under the trees; it was wanton destruction to scatter bullets about in a peaceful place like Tossa. One never knew whom one might hit! I marched back to the Casa Johnstone full of indignation.

'I've been machine-gunned,' I announced in a fury. I held out the bullet on the palm of my hand. 'Good God! They might have killed me!'

We were surprised that the lorry did not turn up during the course of the day. Then we thought that the Solidarity Fund wisely preferred to wait until it was dark. We were not perturbed. We were by now convinced that the lorry would come. I was angry with the Fund for not having the sense to announce to all its colonies that arrangements had been made to evacuate all the children and that it was just a question of waiting quietly until the lorries arrived. We would have been saved a lot of worry and exhaustion.

We made the children and Leonor go to bed, but we

decided to snatch some sleep in our clothes as usual. Miguel said he would follow us on his motor bicycle as far as the main inland road to San Feliu. He would call at San Feliu to see if he was wanted for work. Miguel was still a mystery. He should have been in the army, his class was called up several months before, but he still did his mysterious 'work'. He was a great comfort to me; it was so restful to meet some one who could look after himself.

Archie went down to the Santiago colony and offered to spend the night down there, but Señora Santiago was so peculiar that he decided to sleep in the telephone exchange. He explained to Señora Santiago and to some of the *responsables* that all they had to do if a lorry came was to run down the road to the telephone. If the lorry came to the Casa Johnstone first, I was to telephone Archie and he would inform the Santiago colony and the Casanovas in case there was a possibility of fitting them in as well.

I do not know how many times I heard lorries during the night; there seemed to be a procession of them. I was always dropping asleep and then starting up hearing gears being changed. But no lorry came. I did think I actually saw headlights moving towards the village, but I came to the conclusion I was mistaken. Towards morning I fell asleep. Leonor woke me up to say she and Francisca had made the breakfast. Archie came yawning and stretching up from the telephone exchange. He had heard nothing.

It was little Sebastiana who came running up with the news. She had run all the way from the village, and she was breathless with exertion. When she recovered sufficiently to speak she told us her news. At first we refused to believe it. The Santiago colony had left in a lorry during the night.

We were stupefied. At first we thought it was simply that a small lorry had come and that another was on the way for us, but soon we heard from eye-witnesses that it was one of the big covered food lorries that could take a hundred children. Then we found that every scrap of food and clothing had been taken. The stores alone would have taken as much room as our colony.

The children were more angry than upset. I reserved my fury until later. I would have plenty to say to the International Solidarity Fund. At the moment they were all sitting safely in France while I was landed with thirty of their children in a village that was one of a chain of villages being systematically fought through and captured; and the fighting was two villages away— just twelve miles.

We unpacked again. We decided to wait until the remnants of the Government army appeared over the hill, and then we would beat it to the woods behind the house with our children and the Casanovas colony. There was a chance that our house with its commanding position might be used as a machine-gun post; there was a better chance that fascist guns might not wait to see if it was fortified or not. There was now an almost constant stream of soldiers walking away from the front. They were mostly boys and fed up. They had no ammunition, they said, and tossed their hand-grenades away in the woods. There was a scare in the afternoon when some Tossa children spent an enthralling few hours letting off the hand-grenades. Even in our misery we could appreciate the story of the Tossa fisherman who came upon a half-buried hand-grenade with only the

pin sticking out of the earth. He drew it out, thinking
it was a cartridge which would be useful for his sporting
gun, and luckily walked away to examine it. He never
believed that the resultant explosion had anything to
do with him.

The children were being wonderful. They realized
that we had done our best and they were repaying us by
their support. They agreed to do whatever we said; they
sat quietly playing their race games, snakes and ladders
and ludo. Leonor and Francisca were marvellous.
Archie and I were worn out with nervous exhaustion,
but we could appreciate the loyalty of our household.

Francisca was secretly delighted that we could not
go. She knew I wanted to get the children away, but she
felt safe with us in the house. We had seen her through
so many crises that she knew that we could resolve this
one. I heard her singing as she prepared the supper.
She suppressed it, but little songs kept breaking
through.

We let the children stay up. No one felt sleepy. We
passed the time by practising how to behave under a
fascist régime. I kept reminding the children to talk
about 'Nationalists', not 'fascists'. They found this
difficult. Poor Francisca, having taken three years to
bring herself to call me Nancy, had to remember to
address me as Señora. I managed to persuade the children that they could shout *Arriba, España!* with the
best of them. They might mean something slightly
different than the Italian idea of a new Spain, but
Arriba, España! as it stood was an excellent sentiment.
They grew interested in this and pranced about calling
Arriba, España! Captain Arjona, as he tapped at the
door, must have thought he had arrived too late.

Hotel in Flight

We nearly died. We were expecting Mussolini or Franco, and there stood Captain Arjona. He smiled his gentle smile. He told us to hurry. There was still time to get back to Gerona if we hurried. He had a lorry down below. He had already informed the Casanovas.

We were thoroughly practised in the art of packing our belongings. In an incredibly short time we were bumping the *bultos* down the hill. Francisca's Ramón and Maria Theresa were helping; the older children staggered down with their mattresses. Beetle, who had suffered miserably by the household upsets, sank thankfully into her travelling bag. She hated travelling, but at least she knew where she was. We found the Casanovas colony already installed. It was a small lorry. It looked completely full.

I am afraid both the Casanovas and Arjona thought I was being tiresome. There was the need for haste in case the road was cut, but I insisted on taking all the children out of the lorry and repacking everything. I was willing to sacrifice the Solidarity Fund's bedding and to abandon the *bultos*; I was even prepared to leave our personal suitcases, but the emergency suitcase and certain sacks of food must go in. I had chosen carefully everything that needed no cooking—cheese, chocolate, biscuits, tins of sardines, tins of meat, a sack of bread, everything to prepare a hasty meal for both colonies anywhere. The Casanovas had packed up the lorry with their mattresses and sacks of lentils and chick peas. I was ruthless. Rice, dried milk, macaroni, flour and oil could be brought; then my sacks. Even so it looked impossible to get everything in. The Azaña guard, two strong, did their best to fix it all up. The bundles loomed up over the hood of the lorry; we lined the floor

and sides with mattresses. Then we started to pack in
the children. I insisted on putting the big ones first and
the babies in their laps. We found that Justo, wearing
triumphantly the new trousers that I had brought back
from Barcelona, had had an accident in them. Darling
Justo. Leonor tore them off and dived into the nearest
pillow-case for another pair. Justo was plunged into a
pair of Mariano's. They came nearly to his chin and we
tied them under his armpits with string. The children
began to fit into the lorry like a jigsaw puzzle. It was a
near thing. We got the last child fitted in place and saw
that they all had their blankets. Leonor was squeezed
in by the side of the lorry. She was dreading the journey
and knew she would be sick. Señora Casanovas and her
husband perched themselves on the sides. I kissed Francisca, standing silently with Beetle in her travelling bag.

'Look after Beetle for me,' I said. Francisca's eyes
opened to their widest. Beetle was sound asleep. It was
impossible to dream of taking her. 'Move your things
up into the house and live there until I come back,' I
said. 'Good luck!' Archie kissed Francisca too. I
climbed on to the side of the lorry and perched on the
edge. Serjeant Bueno hung on to the back. The front
was filled with packages. The two soldiers attached
themselves somehow to the rear of the lorry, having
handed me their rifles. Archie climbed up and clung
to the hood. Captain Arjona inserted himself among
the packages in front. We moved slowly away.

'Good-bye, Francisca,' we shouted. 'We may have
to come back if the road is cut.'

Francisca stood staring at us, Beetle in her travelling-
bag over her arm. She was trying not to hope that the
fascists had cut us off.

Hotel in Flight

I still do not know how that overloaded lorry reached Llagostera. We swayed round the terrible curves, Archie looking like something clinging to the crow's-nest of a ship. I tried to balance myself on a narrow edge, an army rifle over each shoulder. Every now and then I would shift the two rifles to one side while I dragged up some small child into the air. Leonor had collapsed utterly. The Casanovas were trying to rescue suffocating children at their side of the lorry. Serjeant Bueno's good-looking face grinned at me from the back of the lorry. God knows how he was staying on. The two soldiers seemed like limpets. The driver was marvellous. He had to hurry, but he drove magnificently. We reached Llagostera and proceeded cautiously. We would know soon if we could go on or if the fascists had beaten us to it. We were in time. The Johnstone luck was holding.

Our luck held all the way. We passed Quart and Cassa, two little villages on the Gerona road. The roadside houses had been bombed almost out of existence. We caught glimpses of the wreckage as our headlights flashed across devastated houses with no fronts. The smell of explosives hung heavily in the air. There were one or two bomb holes to negotiate, but on the whole the road had escaped. It was a dark, cloudy night, just the night for a flitting. We rattled through Gerona, deserted and debris-strewn. I wondered where Rosita had gone; if she had got out of Barcelona. It was as we passed through the silent wrecked streets, ghostly in our headlights, that I realized I had no idea where we were going.

It started to drizzle as we went along the main road to Figueras. We tried to cover the children with blankets. For some time the Casanovas on one side and I on the other, encumbered by the rifles, tried to rescue some sinking face before it disappeared below the surge of humanity, but we soon gave it up. We decided that if any children were to be suffocated there was nothing we could do about it. The small children slept; the older ones relapsed into semi-consciousness.

Presently we rolled into Figueras in pouring rain and drew up outside a large double door. Captain Arjona climbed stiffly out and banged on it. Presently he borrowed the bayonet off one of my rifles and tried to prize the lock. Eventually a woman appeared out of another door with a key. She seemed surprised to see us. The big doors were flung open and we looked in. It was the side entrance to a theatre. The stalls and pit had been cleared of seats. It was to be our temporary home.

343

31

House Full

There are certain advantages about living in a theatre. For one thing there is ample room, and when one has a family of sixty-odd, room is essential. We fitted very comfortably into the pit and stalls of the Edison Theatre.

We manœuvred the bedding successfully. There were only twelve mattresses, but by arranging them lengthways we got five children on each. Each child had hung on to its blanket and all the children had survived the trip. Poor Leonor was prostrate for hours, but she eventually became her efficient self.

For a kitchen, Señora Casanovas and I made an enclosure across one corner with rows of stall chairs. I unpacked my petrol stove triumphantly.

We had arrived about five o'clock on the Wednesday morning and just fell asleep anywhere. By ten o'clock the place had an air of organization. We made hot chocolate for breakfast. We arranged for hot milk for lunch with bread and cheese and sardines. We borrowed a broom from the woman who let us in, the custodian of the theatre, and we cleaned the place up. Another advantage of the theatre was that it had running water and two lavatories; and the *plugs pulled*. It appeared to have been some time since anyone had pulled them, but we remedied that.

If I am ever cast away on a desert island I hope that chance will cast away Señora Casanovas with me. She was magnificent. She produced everything we required, from aspirins to a huge iron cauldron big enough to cook for the whole family. Archie rummaged below the stage and discovered odd bits of wood. We found a mysterious door that led into a little garden. Señora Casanovas promptly said she would cook a hot meal for every one if Archie would help her with the fire. Señor Casanovas was perplexed. He was an artist before everything, and recent events were overpowering him. His wife and I were alike in that we temporarily only saw the advantages of our position; he, while admitting that we might be a good deal worse off, could not blind himself to the disadvantages. He saw the dust and dirt everywhere; he smelt the lavatories; he realized that Gerona had been bombed and evacuated; Figueras was the next target. He wisely set about expediting our departure for the frontier.

Our first real shock was when we realized that Figueras was apparently deserted. Actually that is misleading. Figueras was packed with refugees; there was hardly a doorstep without a sheltering family; the Rambla was full of campers round their little fires; every house and building was crammed. But we expected to find Figueras the centre for all governmental activities; we expected to find the headquarters of the Quakers, Sanidad, perhaps even the Solidarity Fund.

There was nothing. The press department was functioning vaguely in the temporary 'Foreign Office', but there was no one we knew there, and the Foreign Office seemed in a state of not knowing whether it was in the throes of being occupied or evacuated. There was no Quaker headquarters visible. No one had heard of Sanidad. We did find a building with the grandiloquent lettering of the Fondo Solidaridad International all over it, but the Solidarity Fund had deserted it. It was full of refugees. We eventually found out that one had to get Spanish passports in order to cross into France. The French were at last allowing refugees to enter. Passports, collective for colonies, took about four to five days to obtain.

It was depressing, and the rain should have made things worse. It did indeed make life harder for the refugees, but it also meant less danger of raids. The families huddled wetly over their fires preferred discomfort to death. Figueras was a dreadful sight, packed with steaming, starving people. We were told that the frontier road was jammed with traffic. It had been static for two days. Fourteen miles of massed cars, mule-carts and lorries, were unable to move an inch. At the frontier were waiting Quaker lorries laden with food supplies, unable to get in. Meanwhile the refugees sat in the rain and starved.

Our children were happy. They could not go out, but they raced round the theatre. They felt they were on the way to safety. They could not get cut off. However quickly the fascists advanced, we could get to the frontier. The Casanovas' children were a pathetic collection of skinny, white-faced little objects. They had been only a fortnight in a colony. They were refugees from all the recently evacuated towns and villages. It was easy to manage our own confident, well-fed brats, but these other children were suspicious of every one. There was a group of older boys, from twelve to fifteen, who looked as if they could be tiresome. It was essential to have strict discipline in such surroundings. I had tremendous confidence in our own colony, but I was surprised by the way they jumped to orders when they had never had more than a pleasant request from us before. Luckily I found a way to gain the confidence of the Casanovas' children. I always made a full report of our findings when we went out looking for news; I felt the children deserved to be treated like grown-ups. The Casanovas, while devoted to the children, had old-fashioned notions about how to handle them. Children were children. I could see these older boys were worried about the situation, which had not been made clear to them. I asked Señora Casanovas if I might have a talk with them. She told me in front of them that they were *malos* and did not deserve to be talked to, but I could do what I liked. I explained a few things that had been puzzling them; exactly what we were trying to do; our chances of being raided; our chances of finding an organization to help us get out of Figueras; why they could not go out and wander about the town. I gave them my Michelin map to study the probable fascist positions and our distance from the frontier. I smacked their bottoms and told them I relied on them to help in a difficult situation.

Before we went to bed that night, three of the boys solemnly offered me their share of the communal mattresses. I declined with thanks, preferring to roll up in my blanket on the floor. It was a wooden floor luckily. I found I had improved the morale of the other colony, but at a cost. I was shadowed by five devoted slaves.

José, José Maria and Primitivo were slightly disgruntled. I explained that they would soon get used to me and that the novelty would wear off.

Spanish girls are no problem. They giggle and link arms and are prepared to worship anything in authority if it is at all human. Spanish boys seem to be no problem either if one basely appeals to their chivalrous instincts.

The next day things began to happen.

The day started with a series of air-raid warnings. We could not hear the sirens in our theatre, but the lights went out. We told the children not to worry until they heard the anti-aircraft guns and then to run and crouch against the back of the pit, well underneath the dress circle. There were warnings every half an hour and soon the children became quite unperturbed.

Archie and I were walking across the Ramblas when we heard a shriek. There was Rosita. She was just moving into her new office down the road. She promised to come back to lunch with us. She was waiting for a lorry from England. She said it would probably have my typewriter in it.

We had just recovered from our excitement when Nikolaus rushed up. He had walked from Barcelona. Nikolaus was almost thin. He too said he would come to lunch; he was starving. We promised to give him provisions for his trek to the frontier. He had got a Spanish pass to go into France.

Suddenly I gave a whoop. Walking along the road, head on one side, sneezing violently, was Richard Rees, Bart.

'Hey!' we yelled; 'Richard!'

We were saved. Richard could arrange everything. He was just the man we had been waiting for.

He had a shocking cold. We took him right back to the theatre and gave him bowls of hot Quaker Oats. It was always impossible to convince the business-like Catalan that Quakers had no ulterior motive in dealing out supplies of Quaker Oats. Richard lay back in a *fauteuil* and allowed Señora Casanovas to spray his throat with one of her infallible remedies. He explained when he got the chance that the road had just been cleared and the Quakers' organization could function again. Their headquarters were at Pont de Molins, about five kilometres along the road to the frontier. The clearing of the road had been effected with that surprising thoroughness which the Spanish keep wrapped in cotton wool for moments of real crisis. No matter how luxurious a car might be or how valuable the load a lorry carried, and no matter whether the vehicle had merely run out of petrol, if it could not move under its own power it was pulled, pushed or rolled into the nearest ditch.

Of course, said Richard, he would arrange for us to be taken into France. He would also arrange about the passports, everything. We fed Richard more Quaker Oats.

In the afternoon the pit door shook violently, and I opened it with the usual effort and fell into the arms of Donald Darling. Later Audrey Russell turned up, with a charming person, Edith Pye, the only Quaker in the Quaker outfit. They were expecting a conference of Americans to arrange about money for more supplies; might they have it in our theatre?

We told the children to be like mice. I made tea while Audrey and Miss Pye wrestled with obtuse gentlemen who could not be convinced that it was necessary to remove children from Spain, despite their own obvious nervousness and anxiety to get out of the danger zone. Eventually they reached some conclusion satisfactory to Audrey and Miss Pye and I handed round the tea. Every one fell on it like something from Heaven, except one of the nervous gentlemen. He pushed his cup away.

'I don't like to drink the children's milk,' he said. You bastard, I thought, yet you would try to leave the poor little brats to be bombed to death.

Audrey, Miss Pye, Richard and Don all had to go into France, but Richard said he would be back the next day, and either then or the day after we would be taken out. Our collective passport was already in hand.

Nikolaus did not turn up again so we concluded he had got a lift to the frontier. Rosita came and spent the evening with us and Captain Arjona. Her lorry had still not arrived.

During the evening the caretaker of the theatre came in and apologized profusely because she had to allow refugees to fill the upper part of the theatre. They were only there to pass the night. We said of course we did not mind at all. The noise was terrific, the place jammed with people. They seemed very friendly and shouted remarks from the dress circle to the children.

I was making chocolate over my petrol fire and stirring it carefully. We had to make the chocolate in a huge dried milk tin and it was not easy. There was a sharp explosion and a flash. I looked up at the domed roof, expecting to see a jagged hole. It was complete and there was no debris on the floor. The children pelted for the back of the pit. We waited. Then I realized that it was not a bomb.

House Full

There was a terrific banging on the door. A man from the secret police wished to know what we were doing in there. I asked him what the hell he thought he was doing out there, and slammed the door. Later we discovered that some child in the gallery had found a hand grenade, pulled out the pin and thrown the grenade over into the dress circle.

The total casualties in that mass of humanity were one man killed, one child injured and our cocoa burned.

I was outside in the garden recovering from the episode of the hand grenade when I saw Dashiell Whidden. He was sitting in the window of a ramshackle building opposite the theatre which proved to be the back of the 'Foreign Office'. He was in Figueras looking for a story. We gave him one. He was fascinated by our theatre. We had not met for months and Archie and I were amazed at the change in him. He seemed an efficient newspaper man, with a newspaper man's impatience at the delay caused by the road block. He told us he was leaving the moment it was clear in order to send his stuff from France. He did not once mention his neurosis.

The next day Figueras seemed different. There was an atmosphere of activity. Government offices began to re-open. We picked our way over recumbent refugees littering the stairs of one office. Upstairs a man was painting a huge sign, 'Generalität de Catalunya, Commissariat de Propaganda'. In the same room a military band of sixty performers of combatant age was practising something intricate. Across the room there was a door marked Private, but the room was full of refugees. The commissar Miravitles was not there.

There were the usual warnings and a small raid on

the outskirts of the town. We took the opportunity after this raid to rush the children out into the park for a breath of air. If there was to be a real raid on Figueras, the park was the safest place. Archie stayed behind to guard the theatre. He could not leave it because if it were left unguarded it would be filled with refugees. It was while we were in the park that the big bombs were dropped. They missed Figueras and fell outside the town, luckily on the opposite side to us. The twelve planes soared over the town and let go all their load at once. There was a shimmer in the air as the bombs hurtled down, and a horrible whirring noise like a flock of birds startled out of a wheat field. The noise of the explosions was terrific. The children clung together in the park.

Archie admitted to me afterwards that he had been scared to death. He felt trapped. He had always watched raids in the open; he had never imagined he would have to sit in the dark in an unsafe theatre and listen to bombs falling.

When we got back to the theatre we found Richard had arrived; our passport was ready, the lorry was waiting. Richard told us that the Quakers had had a marvellous idea. Archie and I should stay on in the theatre and they would make it a clearing station for refugee colonies while their passports were being fixed up. I said I would willingly return to Spain once my children were handed over to responsible authorities in France, but that neither of us would care to make Figueras a headquarters for children. We should not like to stay in Figueras ourselves a moment longer than necessary. It seemed to us that Figueras was going to get hell.

Richard said it could all be arranged later. For the

moment he had collected some stray children who had run away from colonies near Barcelona. There was nearly a colony of them altogether. They would take over our stores and guard the theatre. Four older Basque boys were left in charge temporarily. As there was nowhere else to leave them, it seemed the best place.

Rosita came along to see us off. She said that her lorry had just arrived. Probably my typewriter was there. Would I care to come and look for it? I hesitated. A typewriter means a lot to a refugee writer, but I decided I could not hold up the lorry which was needed to return to Figueras. Rosita said she would look out for it for me. She knew that it was important.

We had more room in this lorry, and Leonor was so thrilled to be really leaving Spain that she forgot to be sick. The children all took hunks of bread and cheese which they munched in the lorry. It was a perfect day for a raid. As we turned towards the French frontier we heard the planes. They passed over us and circled round Figueras. We heard the rattle of the feeble defences, then the heavy, dead sound of the bombs. The first of the series of raids that were to wipe out Figueras had begun.

The drive to the frontier was unforgetable. The scenes of utter desolation were like pictures of the ravages of a flood or earthquake. It looked as if a giant wave had flung up the broken suitcases, the littered clothes, the swirling heaps of paper. Exhausted refugees flung their possessions from them as they trudged to France. Mattresses, bursting obscenely open, spilled out their entrails, overturned lorries lay nakedly revealing their innermost machinery. The country rose majestically in a series of rocky hills to the very

Pyrenees, glorious, proudly wooded. The littered road lay like a festering wound through the fertile valley. On each side it spread its poison, abandoned carts, dead mules, charred ashes of innumerable fires; a swift little stream was choked with blankets, sodden mattresses and pillows.

Nearer the frontier humans were added to the litter. The fires were alight, warming groups of human jetsam. Smoke from thousands upon thousands of tiny fires wreathed the valleys and poured up from the mountain sides. On the bridge leading into France, carabineros were listlessly poking among the abandoned clothing and pitch-forking it over into the valley below where it hung helplessly on the tree-tops.

The Quakers' lorry could not pass into France without wasting time in formalities to allow it to return to Spain, so we were dumped at the end of the bridge. Our possessions were piled round us. Thirty yards away was France and a row of black-helmeted Mobile Guard.

It took us several journeys to take everything to the frontier. A Spanish carabinero helped us. The French authorities allowed us to pass over the chain into France. Some policemen worried the children by insisting that they throw their clutched bread away. They were given crisp French bread instead. But the children did not like throwing bread away. We had to wait to see what the Quakers could do for us now, so I took all the children into a field by the side of the road. We left them with the Casanovas, and Archie and I started up the hill into Perthus village. We met Donald Darling looking for us. He had arranged for a bus to meet us. He told us that the Reifenbergs and the Casa Blanca families had crossed over safely and for a time had helped in a Quaker canteen. No one seemed to know quite what happened once one did get into France. I wanted to dump the children somewhere while I located the International Solidarity Fund. I wanted to avoid having them all put into a concentration camp. Donald told us that the Quakers could do nothing about lodging the children, but that he would see if he could wangle us into Perpignan where we could try to fix up something. In the meantime, what about a drink?

On our way up the hill of Perthus we met Dashiell Whidden strolling down towards the chain. He seized our hands.

'Congratulations!' he said. 'Do you know that your Tossa was taken after heavy fighting two days ago?'

Epilogue

For this Relief

Refugees poured into France with no thought of the future. France stood for safety; freedom from bombs and machine-gun bullets; bread in abundance.

Soldiers marched into France. They looked upon France as a stepping-off ground for Valencia and Madrid. The Forty-Third Division, who had been trapped in the Pyrenees the previous year, had passed through France on its way back to Barcelona. The retreating Spanish army expected to embark immediately for Central Spain.

Children trailed into France. They were tired and dirty, but they were confident and happy. The fascists and Moors could not get them.

France was a haven, but a hysterical haven. No one could decide who was responsible for the refugees. The Ministry of the Interior tried to shelve it on to the Army; the Army pushed it back to the Ministry of the Interior. Meanwhile the district of Perpignan bore the brunt.

We had eventually to appeal to the Prefet of Perpignan to take charge of our children. Thanks to Donald, we managed to avoid sleeping on a windswept plain at

Le Boulou concentration camp, and our bus was
allowed to proceed to Perpignan. Perpignan was
crowded out. After tremendous efforts by various interested relief workers, we camped in a ball-room while
Archie and I tried to find the International Solidarity
Fund. It had disappeared. Archie went back to Figueras on a job for the International Relief Commission,
leaving me to deal with the children. The Casanovas
dared not go out without the collective passport, and
even that was not proof against the hysteria of the Perpignan police. I managed to get bread and chocolate,
but we had no means of cooking anything; no cups; no
bedding. The Prefet was furious that we had escaped
Le Boulou, but he sent us to the Perpignan concentration camp at Les Haras, on the outskirts of the town.

We were put in the old stables of a barracks. Clean,
fresh straw was shaken down for us upstairs in the lofts.
We managed to secure a corner large enough to
accommodate us all. Sleeping in the straw was heaven.
We burrowed into it like rabbits and were soon asleep.
Other refugees were sitting up in their straw, grumbling
at their situation. They were refugees with money, who
had come out of Spain in their cars, and had friends in
France, but they had to stay in the concentration camp
until they were checked up.

I woke in the night with a feeling of suffocation. I
found that my newly acquired boy friends had ten-
derly covered me with their coats. They were deeply
touched because I chose to sleep in the straw with the
colony instead of going to an hotel. I pushed off the
coats and saw a shadowing figure creeping about among
the children. It was our Senegalese guard. He had an
adoring expression on his coal-black face, and he was

peering into the faces of the sleeping children. I was in a quandary. If a child woke up and saw that face, it would think at once the Moors had got it, and probably die of screaming hysteria. Yet it seemed rude to tell a man bristling with revolvers that his face would have that effect. Luckily the Senegalese had finished his round and crept silently away without any damage being done. I resolved to warn the children in the morning.

Les Haras was a peculiar place. The main barracks was a concentration camp for men; the stables and lofts were for old men, women and children. It was heavily guarded by French gendarmes and Senegalese troops. Our guards were civil enough, although their not very strong nerves were badly shaken by the constant stream of questions from the refugees. The guards genuinely did not know anything; they had no idea how long we had to stay there; they did not know where we should be sent; they knew nothing. The man in charge of the whole camp was a harried individual in mufti who did not know anything either. Certainly the Prefet had no idea what to do with every one.

It was to help solve this problem that a little man with a large book sat down at a table in the courtyard of Les Haras. He was a bland little man like a tourist agent; he *was* a tourist agent of a kind. He was 'selling' trips back to Franco Spain.

The women and children were treated well. The food was good and ample; the straw was clean and, if the sanitary arrangements were inadequate, one had to remember that Spaniards were not more fussy than the French. The men were treated abominably. It was not, as in the case of the big concentration camps, inefficiency on the part of the authorities, it was a deliberate attempt to persuade as many men to return to Spain as possible. Many men did so. Their families protested when they came over to our part of the building to fetch them. I asked one man why, when he had suffered so much to get into France, he now was going back to Franco. He was a middle-aged man, not yet called for his service in the army. He said, 'If I am to be ill-treated, I prefer to be ill-treated by my own countrymen, not by niggers.'

The gentle Senegalese may be fond of children, but they treated the Spanish men abominably. I went into the men's part of the camp and talked with the Spaniards and the few Germans of the International Brigade who found themselves landed there. They all agreed that tremendous pressure was being put on them to return. Those who wanted to go back got better food and better treatment. Otherwise they got a quarter of a pound of bread and a small tin of sardines per man per day. They were expected to work in gangs cleaning up the barracks and constructing latrines under the surveillance of the Senegalese. If they did not understand an order or failed to jump to it, they got a bayonet jabbed at them. I saw a man recovering from a bayonet thrust in his thigh.

I thought the men's camp at Les Haras was the worst example of misery and hatred I could expect to see. I was wrong. Les Haras was the best concentration camp in the district. The men were under cover; they had water; they had latrines.

There was nothing to complain about in our part of the camp, although some of the richer refugees did complain. I found that the children were suffering from lack of exercise, and asked the guards to let me take

them out to play in a big yard next door to the camp.
They refused. I asked the man in charge and he said it
was impossible. I could go where I liked with my special
pass as a member of the International Relief Commission, but I could not take the children. I called a re-
union of the older children and explained the dilemma.
I also put up a suggestion which they immediately
proceeded to act upon.

It was astonishing the dust a few children could
raise in that straw. The other refugees rushed out into
the tiny yard complaining bitterly. Gendarmes tore up
the stairs and coughed and choked as they ordered the
children to stop. They turned to me with streaming
eyes. 'Stop them! stop them!' they cried. 'Can't you
control your so wicked children?'

'I am so sorry,' I said. 'They have got out of hand. It
is the lack of exercise. Now, if only I could take them
out into that beautiful yard——'

The guards rushed away and came back with the
chief. He took in the situation at once.

'Take them out, then,' he snapped, and rushed away
coughing. The gendarmes remained to see if I could
regain my lost control.

'Hey!' I called above the uproar, and there was
instant silence. 'Come on, get into line. We are going
out to the big yard.'

The children trooped out like little angels. The gendarmes stared with their eyes popping.

Later in the day I called at the Hotel de France to
see if Archie had returned from Figueras, and found
that he was still away. When I returned to the concentration camp I found the children greatly excited. They

had been told to be ready to go to the station. They were being sent off to a permanent home.

I asked the chief of the camp where we were going. He did not know. I spent the next few hours with a note-book taking down particulars and notes for letters from the hundreds of refugees remaining in the camp. Most of them were separated from their families; wives had lost their husbands; no one knew where they were going to be sent, least of all the French. I was standing on a raised platform in the yard taking notes when I heard shrieks of excitement from the roadway. There stood Ramona and Quimeta of the Casa Blanca. I made such a rush for the iron gates that the black guards doubted the validity of my pass, and I had to get a French gendarme to let me through. Quimeta looked devastating in a new coat and skirt; they both looked well and happy. They had an extraordinary story, but somehow it was not surprising.

When they had finished with the canteen job, they found themselves in Le Boulou. Quimeta sat her family at the side of the road while she went to find a telegraph office. She had friends in Perpignan. On the way a man accosted her. He was a charming middle-aged Frenchman, and he asked her if she was a refugee and if she would like to be adopted by him and his wife. Quimeta dimpled at him and said she had her father, mother, sister and two small children with her. She explained she wanted to telegraph to some friends to come to Le Boulou to help them. The man promptly offered to run the whole family into Perpignan. Quimeta asked him if he would not get into trouble. The man smiled. He was of the French secret police.

He took them to Perpignan. He found their friends.

He arranged their papers, and the fact that Quimeta's father had been born in France enabled him to get French papers for the whole family. He found a job for the old man; he was getting one for Quimeta. Quimeta told me the story outside the iron gates guarded by Senegalese. She often passed by the camp to see if she could find any of her friends in order to help them. Quimeta was a French citizen.

My meeting with the Casa Blanca family was cut short because children had to go to the station. We filed through the streets of Perpignan. The Casanovas colony went first, ragged, white-faced. Passers-by commiserated. 'Poor little things.' Some one pressed a hundred-franc note into Señora Casanova's hand. Others rushed off and bought bags of sweets. When our colony brought up the rear, their round faces shining above their *capitas*, people looked puzzled. 'You know, they don't look so bad!' That was why we had arranged that the other children went first.

In the train we settled down. I had bought some supplies in case we did not get any supper. No one knew where the train was going: the general idea seemed to be somewhere in the Toulouse district. I planned to go with the children; see them settled somewhere and then get back to Perpignan to work with the Commission. After waiting an hour in the train, I got out to see if anyone had learned its destination in the meantime. A porter said casually: 'I think it is going straight through to Geneva.'

I ran along to the station-master's office. On the way I asked another porter. He thought, but was not at all sure, that the train was going to Belgium. The station-master had no idea. 'It goes to Narbonne,' he said firmly. 'What they do with it I do not know.' There was no engine so one could not ask the engine-driver.

I went back to the children. I hated leaving them, but there was nothing for it. I could not go tearing all over Europe without any money, and I was needed in Perpignan. The children had the Casanovas and Leonor. I broke the news. I do not know who was the most miserable of us all. The Casanovas promised to wire us the moment they arrived somewhere. I gave them and Leonor all the money I had, several hundred francs, and promised to send more. I swore I would never abandon them. At last it was so painful that I tore myself away and rushed out of the station. I went straight to the Hotel de France and ran into Dashiell Whidden in the hall.

'Hello!' he said.

'For God's sake take me out somewhere, give me a drink and a huge dinner. Talk to me about newspapers or anything, and don't mention children.'

That night I took advantage of an offer made me in Le Perthus, just after we had crossed in France. I had been sitting with the children waiting for the bus to take us away when a tall, aristocratic-looking English woman came up and started talking to the Casanovas in French. She turned to me and said how she sympathized with the frightful tragedy that had overtaken my country; how she wished she could do something for us; that she had come to Perpignan to help in any way she could. I finally grasped that she thought I was a Spanish refugee, and for a moment she was being so charming I did not like to interrupt her odd French. At last I said gently, 'Aren't you English? So am I.' She was overcome. She apologized profusely and finally said, 'You see, I thought you were a refugee.'

'I *am* a refugee,' I explained. She was most interested and helpful, and when we met her again in Perpignan she offered me that most precious thing in the whole town, a bed. She had a double room and one bed was spare.

When Dashiell, nobly ignoring my unkempt appearance and the straw in my hair, had fed me, I retired to Margaret Travers' room and took off my clothes. I took off my clothes—it was incredible. I took off my clothes for the first time for twelve days and got into a bed.

I was nearly asleep when Dashiell looked in to tell me that he had been to the station and that the train had gone. No one knew its destination. I thanked him sleepily and turned round. I hated parting from the children; I loved them dearly, but there was something about sleeping in a bed and knowing that one would wake up free of the responsibility of sixty children.

During our work for the International Commission, Archie and I seldom met. We occasionally found ourselves in the same lorry; we sometimes met at the same restaurant; once or twice we even found ourselves in the same bed; but we deliberately avoided any opportunity for talking to one another. We had nothing whatever to say. We both realized that some time we would have to get down to facts and make plans, but in the face of the overwhelming catastrophe going on around us our own affairs were of small importance. We only knew that we could not face going back to England and be asked what had happened to the Casa Johnstone. We did not know the answer and we did not care. We plunged into relief work at Perpignan not because we had any hope of achieving anything—there was no future for the hundreds of thousands of refugees, there was no future for Europe—but because we needed the relief of doing relief work.

Archie and I met in a car going back into Spain. We were clearing out the last of the food supplies in the Quakers' canteen at Pont de Molins. Figueras was deserted. Archie had gone back there while I was still with the children, and he met a small dark figure striding energetically up the road out of the town. It was Rosita. She had a rucksack in one hand and my typewriter in the other. She told Archie she was getting out. Her temporary office had been hit in the raids; she managed to crawl out of the debris; she was unable to find Sanidad; she was through until further orders. We heard from her that the theatre had been struck, but that Richard Rees had got the last child out in time.

We set up a canteen on the Figueras road and handed out everything in the store. Archie tried to keep some kind of order; he bullied the people into queuing up, standing just below the notice saying it was a Quakers' canteen, using surprisingly un-Quakerlike Catalan oaths. Just when he got some semblance of order, some one would come out of the store with a bag and say in dulcet tones, 'Anyone like some sweeties?' resulting in utter chaos.

The International Commission had three lorries which they put in charge of teams for distributing food to the refugees and camps. I was in charge of one lorry, and my team consisted of a tough Lithuanian-American lorry driver called Charlie, and a languid lady called Poppy. Audrey Russell seemed overwhelmed when I especially asked for these two, as they were both rather a problem for the more orthodox side of the Commission, but I knew what I was doing. Charlie worked like a slave and was always good-humoured on the toughest job; Poppy's eyelashes were worth a fortune when it came to haranguing French officials; she got us through cordons of Mobile Guards; she procured permits from *sous-prefets*; she left gendarmes sweating in a rich glow. And when it came to cutting up hundreds of loaves and cast-iron cheese, Poppy's languor disappeared completely.

Charlie was an angel, but he had his faults. He had no use for this trifling with French officials; his method was to pull up with a jerk every time a patrol stopped us on the road, flick down the window and bawl, 'Wal, frawgs!' at them. He was also a too enthusiastic photographer. On one trip, when we tried to take a load of bread into St. Cyprien camp, we had to drive the truck through the sand to reach the barbed-wire enclosure we wanted. We also had to pass through columns of starving Spanish troops just entering the camp. Dashiell and I were perched on the bread in the back of the truck, trying to explain to the frantic men that it was for delivery in the camp. As long as the truck kept moving it was all right—there is nothing more reasonable than a Spanish soldier, even if he is starving, but we kept stopping and the soldiers closed in and started helping themselves. I was afraid the French authorities would send up their black troops who were all wandering about with rubber thongs, longing to use them, and I said to Dashiell that we could just heave out some loaves to keep the crowd back. It was successful, except that some of the French guards mistook Dashiell and me for refugees looting the lorry. A husky mobile guard clutched Dashiell by the hair and tried to pull him out of the truck. Dashiell gripped the guard round the collar and pulled him slowly up until their faces were level. 'Je suis Américain,' said Dashiell grimly, and lowered the guard again. He had to repeat this several times before the guard grasped the fact that we were merely relief workers. Meanwhile a gendarme had clutched me by the coat collar which he promptly pulled up over my head in his efforts to drag me off the lorry. There were ominous murmurs from the Spanish soldiers who did not care to see a woman molested, but fortunately the French guards realized their error and allowed us to proceed on condition that we gave out no bread on the way. I found that the delays were being caused by Charlie taking photographs of the Spahis, galloping about on hysterical horses.

Poppy also had one disconcerting fault. She was free with other people's beds. Beds were at a premium in Perpignan, and Poppy, ever ready to give up her own to refugees, was inclined to give away every one else's as well. She nobly allowed Archie and me to share the second bed in her room when we were unable to find hospitality elsewhere, but we never knew who else might be there. Even this generosity about beds had advantages. It supplied much needed comic relief when Poppy strolled into a café in Perpignan and leaned confidentially over a table of weary relief workers. 'I do hope you don't mind, but I know you won't really. I have had to put a sanitary inspector in Barbara's bed.' Sometimes it was a Madrid dancer, a member of the Government, or a Spanish lorry driver.

There were many difficulties about doing relief work

in Perpignan. The chief trouble was the attitude of the French, who refused to admit that any help was needed. 'Thank you, we have the matter well in hand,' was the death knell of relief work. The French were torn between a feeling of hopeless inadequacy and pride in La Belle France. La Belle France would provide for refugees. She provided a sandy waste at Argelès; another at St. Cyprien. She provided several miles of barbed wire; two pounds of bread between twenty-five men *after* they had been behind the barbed wire for three days; a trickle of brackish water; several thousand Senegalese with rubber batons; a number of machine-gun nests directed at the barbed wire; several thousand uncontrollable Spahis, who galloped about in circles with drawn swords, and a number of harassed mobile guards and army officers. La Belle France also provided some smaller camps in the Pyrenees, including one where four thousand men were huddled on a football pitch. La Belle France omitted to provide latrines or the spades to dig them with; she omitted to provide firewood; she ignored such necessities as the most primitive hospital arrangements, leaving wounded and sick to take their chance with the soldiers and the mules on the bare ground. Admittedly it was a situation without precedent, the exodus of a people, and it was impossible to say whether it was criminal carelessness, deliberate sadism, or just incapacity that was to blame. It seemed a mixture of all three.

There were roads where the refugee soldiers were stopped and asked if they wished to go to the Negrin or the Franco camps. The ones plumping for Franco were given immediately a loaf of bread and a tin of sardines; the others were sent hungry down the road, where they waited three days behind the wire without food. There were situations where wounded soldiers sat in the sand while their wounds rotted for lack of dressings, and the sick lay down and died. The Senegalese and Spahis were either out of control or they were given a free hand to knock about Spanish soldiers with their rubber truncheons and the flat of their swords.

We had almost to crawl on our knees to French officials to be allowed to bring dressings and bread to the camps; it was the work of a whole afternoon, with Poppy using all her wiles, to be allowed to put up a hospital tent. There were bright moments, such as when a charming mobile guard wept when we came to his section in a camp with a load of bread. The men were crowded behind the wire like wolves, gaunt with hunger and misery. The guard said we had saved a desperate situation, but he was afraid that there would be a massacre if we tried to distribute the loaves. I asked to be allowed to go into the camp. The guard was horrified, but I had not lived through the Spanish War without getting to know Spanish soldiers.

I asked for the Spanish commandant of the camp. Immediately a distinguished-looking officer came up and saluted. I explained the difficulty about distributing the bread. He shrugged his shoulders. 'I think I can still control my men,' he said. He ordered them to stand back against the wire at the far end of the camp while we brought in the lorry. A number of them came forward to help unload. There were one or two incidents of crowding and snatching, but I stood by the lorry, and they could not rush it without upsetting me. They had one or two noisy arguments among themselves about the best place to store the bread, and I slapped a Spanish colonel on the face for pushing. I apologized to him immediately. The French guard thought my last hour had come, but the colonel protested that I was quite right. He said ruefully that he deserved to be shot for not being a better example to his men, but that perhaps there were mitigating circumstances. We left enough bread to feed the whole camp for one day. The guard told us that he expected the usual ration of two pounds of bread between twenty-five men to arrive the next day.

There is no doubt that France will go down in history as the one country that, during the years of the Nazi annexations, attempted to do something for refugees. France's reputation as a haven for the homeless stands well above that of any other European country. England's record is pathetic. When people say complacently that England gave hospitality to 4,000 Basque children, they should remember that France sheltered over 50,000. One of the reasons that the British Relief Commission in Perpignan was hampered by French officials was the fact that these Spanish refugees were to cost France £17,000 a day, and the British Government gave a grant, to be distributed through the Red Cross, of £12,000 in all. British parsimony should have been no excuse for the revolting conditions in the camps, where much of the misery was caused by lack of the simplest necessities costing comparatively little, but the British attitude was undoubtedly partly responsible for the French hysteria as the hordes of refugees poured into the country.

If official support was meagre, there was the small band of the faithful who dug yet deeper into their depleted pockets. Voluntary organizations still sent contributions. And there were still people like Miss Jones.

I met Miss Jones as I was coming out of a camp at Amélie-les-Bains. A fury in purple silk attacked me as I was about to get on the lorry with Servicio Ingles written on it.

'It is a scandal the way these men have to live! Why don't you do something about it? It is a disgrace to civilization that men have to be treated like this. Call yourselves a relief organization! What are you doing about these men, may I ask? It is time you did something. I and my friend cannot feed all the camps alone!'

Miss Jones was a wonder. She calmed down when she heard that I really was trying to feed the camps, and she introduced me to her collaborator, a charming English gentleman with a white moustache and a white bull-terrier. They were both staying at Amélie and both were overcome by the conditions in the camps. Their horror took a practical form. Miss Jones introduced me and said:

'Have you brought the meat?'

The Englishman produced an enormous newspaper parcel. Miss Jones swept past the dazed guards into the nearest camp. Several soldiers sprang to meet her; they all knew Miss Jones. Some of them started to grill the delicious lamb chops over a sheet of iron balanced on a burning log. Miss Jones shook her head and the earrings and gold brooches rattled.

'There is nothing to cook on,' she said. 'It is absurd. Ruining the chops—no, no, no,' she pushed the grinning soldiers aside and snatched the piece of stick used for turning the chops. 'That isn't the way. I've told you all before. *Sear* both sides thoroughly *first*, like this.'

For this Relief

Later I met the Englishman going into one of the camps with a bundle of copies of *The Times* under his arm. He said Miss Jones was resting—the men had quite worn her out. He also mentioned that Miss Jones had spent over a hundred pounds on food and supplies. 'She is so energetic, you know,' he said wistfully. He showed me *The Times*. 'I am just going in to give English lessons,' he said. 'It helps the men pass the time and it helps me pass the time as well.'

We met our friends one by one. Marcelino and Juan were in Argelès camp. We brought them food and clothing; they asked for a spade and something to make a shelter against the icy mountain winds and the blowing sand. Stray mules huddled together, their backs to the sandy blasts, heads lowered, tails tucked in. Men huddled together behind the shelter of the barbed wire. They stood with their backs hunched against the wind; the wounded lay in little depressions, the sand gradually seeping over them. We met the carabinero who had escorted Dr. Collier as a prisoner to our house. He burst into tears and begged us to take him out of the camp. We found Massana, chief of the Tossa police, in St. Cyprien. He shook us warmly by the hand and asked us if we could get him out. With him were the two other Tossa policemen. We gave them food. We could do nothing else for them. We could have risked getting our friends out of the camp, but where could they go? They had no friends in France. We could only promise to put their names down for Mexico; there were 200,000 names down for Mexico. We came across Ribas of the International Solidarity Fund in Argelès. He smiled sadly and asked about the children.

'How lucky we made those capes,' he murmured. 'So useful for travelling.'

It was depressing work. We could feed three or four thousand every day, out of three or four hundred thousand. We could get a few hundred wounded under cover. Each day was a battle against the French authorities. The little hospital in the Pyrenees at Prats de Mollo was drained of supplies. It was being run by a French voluntary medical unit that had not been in time to get to Spain. Rosita re-equipped it. The day we took up the supplies the doctor in charge asked us to take some stretcher cases to a hospital in Le Boulou. We packed ten men and two small children with machine-gun wounds on to the floor of the lorry. One of the children was clutching a book of geometry problems. We went to Le Boulou; the hospital was full. We tried Perpignan; no room. We drove round with those wounded men for four hours before we forced Le Boulou hospital to take them. They were dumped on a floor packed with other stretcher cases.

I went out with the lorry in the daytime as a relief worker; in the evenings and at night I became a journalist. I went out with Dashiell on his night assignments. It was a rest being with competent journalists, with their fixed press times, after the haphazard hanging about of the relief work. The French authorities could not sabotage us as journalists although they did try to stop journalists from going into the camps. Dashiell's chief work was dashing up to Le Perthus frontier to see which troops were coming in. The straggling refugees and the suit-case soldiers had all passed through, the real army was marching through in units.

We saw the Garibaldi battalion of the International

Brigade. They had shaved and they stood at attention waiting to cross the chain, looking like statues. They had to wait while the Mobile Guard squads changed over. The new contingent were clumsy, a man stumbled and his officer struck him. The guard struck the officer. There was a tussle. The Garibaldis started chanting gently, still staring straight before them, '*Disciplina, disciplina, disciplina*'.

We saw them all come through, the International Brigade, the Lister Brigade, carabinero units, *asalto* guards. They were tired, but they carried their rifles. They knew they would have to give them up at the frontier, but something compelled them to bring them out of Spain. They swung in to France shouting, '*Viva Francia!*' The ones I spoke to all asked the same thing, 'Where are we going? When do we go to Central Spain?'

Up in the little mountain passes troops were pouring in. They were the units who had held the line to allow the refugees to get over. They were well fed and had their provisions with them. They waited patiently while one or two guards searched them for arms. I saw one soldier walking on after his search, and suddenly realizing, as he passed a pile of revolvers, why the guard had been patting him all over. He gently shook two more revolvers out of his sleeves on to the pile. These were the crack anarchist and communist units, these were the real 'reds'. The French had not expected so many troops over the mountains; they had posted a few of the mobile guard at the outposts and the Spanish troops had to march many miles down the winding roads entirely unescorted. They marched singing and waving flags. They called greeting to the startled French peasants;

they stopped off when they felt like it and rested. I talked to some who had made a little camp by the wayside. They had meat and were roasting it.

'What are these camps like?' they asked. 'How do they treat us?'

I thought of a frantic group of sand-blown figures I had seen wolfing a dead mule. They had hacked bits off with a penknife and stuffed them raw and bleeding into their mouths.

'I shouldn't hurry to get to Argelès,' I said.

It was thanks to Dashiell that we got Nikolaus and Ulrich out of the camps. I did not like to use the Quakers' lorries for smuggling refugees out of camps. As it was, the French authorities had no excuse for trying to keep the lorries away. I located Nikolaus in the International Brigade camp. It was ironic that he should have at last been thrust into the International Brigade. He had relations in Paris if he could only get out and get the money to get there. I did Dashiell a favour by letting him into the camps in the lorry disguised as a relief worker; he always kept his car outside to enable him to rush back to Perpignan with a story. We sneaked Nikolaus out of the camp and Dashiell took him to Perpignan. We paid his fare to Paris and put him on the train.

It was Ludwig Renn, the famous German writer, tall, charming, radiating dignified personality, who told me that Ulrich was in the camp. I found him after a search. He looked ill and wretched. I told him I would get him out and send him to join Marianne in Paris.

Donald Darling was doing marvellous work getting intellectuals out of the camps and arranging for them to get hospitality in England and France. It was shortly after we smuggled out Ulrich that Ludwig Renn was allowed to leave. Dashiell lent us his car for Ulrich and we took him back to the hotel. He was ill with colitis; he told us every one in Argelès camp had colitis because of the brackish water. We nursed him for a few days. Poppy rose to the occasion and we put him in the communal bed. Sometimes Archie slept in it as well; sometimes I did; sometimes all three. Poppy had a Spanish girl in her bed. At last we got him away safely to Paris where Marianne was earning a precarious living by odd jobs of typing and showing round tourists.

It was terrible to have to abandon Marcelino and the others, but when we found Captain Arjona and Serjeant Bueno in St. Cyprien we felt we must do something. There was nothing to be done. They had no friends in France; we had no money anywhere. If we smuggled them out they would only be arrested, sent back to the camp. We did all we could for them. Donald said he would do his best to get them put well up on the Mexico list. We knew that if anything could be done, Donald would do it. We wrote to Azaña, the ex-President of Spain, telling him what two members of his bodyguard had done for us, and asking him to help them. He replied that he would do everything in his power, but that he had not much power. In the meantime Captain Arjona and Serjeant Bueno rotted in the sand.

Perpignan had a peculiar atmosphere of its own. It was not unlike being in Barcelona again. The French were scared of everything. It was impossible to go out after dark without being arrested. The town swarmed with Spanish refugees, some legitimately in France, others escaped from camps. Sixty Catalan intellectuals had a collective passport. Only those with the passport were safe. Either the whole sixty had to go about in a body or those without were liable to arrest. Donald spent most of his time getting intellectuals out of prison when he was not getting them out of camps. Audrey Russell was battling with French and British governments, always good tempered, gravely staring through her glasses at the unruly mob of relief workers. Richard Rees, known as the best truck driver in Spain, was at last out of Spain and working in Perpignan in between sneezes. Poppy went her benign way, curling her eyelashes with a wet finger and getting on with the job.

The old Barcelona newspaper crowd was there. I met Swire of Reuter's in the street, and we talked eagerly about our adventures. A factory siren sounded while we were talking, but it was not until we were going our ways that we realized that we had instinctively stepped into a doorway.

Miguel suddenly turned up. He was worried because he had no news of Concha. He was going to America. He told us that he had left the Casa Johnstone just before the fighting reached Tossa. Every one was calm and Francisca seemed happy because Pepito, her husband, had returned. They were living in the Casa Johnstone. Beetle seemed to have settled down.

Miguel jerked Archie and me back to realities. We were in France with two small suitcases and a typewriter. We were lucky to have the typewriter. We made enough money by journalism in Perpignan to keep us for a time when our work there was over. The relief work depended on what help the British Government

For this Relief

cared to give. Voluntary organizations were drained. But one organization was still going strong. A contingent of plus-four clad gentlemen arrived from England to shoot painlessly the wandering, starving Spanish mules. It seemed a pity that they did not first shoot painlessly the cooped-up, starving Spanish refugees.